Southwestern Women Writers
and the Vision of Goodness

Southwestern Women Writers and the Vision of Goodness

Mary Austin, Willa Cather, Laura Adams Armer, Peggy Pond Church and Alice Marriott

CATHARINE SAVAGE BROSMAN

McFarland & Company, Inc., Publishers
Jefferson, North Carolina

LIBRARY OF CONGRESS CATALOGUING-IN-PUBLICATION DATA

Names: Brosman, Catharine Savage, 1934– author.
Title: Southwestern women writers and the vision of goodness :
   Mary Austin, Willa Cather, Laura Adams Armer, Peggy Pond
   Church and Alice Marriott / Catharine Savage Brosman.
Description: Jefferson, North Carolina : McFarland & Company,
   Inc., Publishers, 2016. | Includes bibliographical references
   and index.
Identifiers: LCCN 2016027897 | ISBN 9781476666471 (softcover :
   acid free paper) ∞
Subjects: LCSH: American literature—Women authors—History
   and criticism. | American literature—20th century—History
   and criticism. | Good in literature. | Women and literature—
   Southwestern States. | Southwestern States—In literature.
Classification: LCC PS152 .B76 2016 | DDC 810.9/92870904—
   dc23
LC record available at https://lccn.loc.gov/2016027897

BRITISH LIBRARY CATALOGUING DATA ARE AVAILABLE

ISBN (print) 978-1-4766-6647-1
ISBN (ebook) 978-1-4766-2595-9

© 2016 Catharine Savage Brosman. All rights reserved

No part of this book may be reproduced or transmitted in any form or by any means, electronic or mechanical, including photocopying or recording, or by any information storage and retrieval system, without permission in writing from the publisher.

Front cover photograph of Canyon De Chelly's White House © 2016 David Hughes / iStock

Printed in the United States of America

McFarland & Company, Inc., Publishers
  Box 611, Jefferson, North Carolina 28640
    www.mcfarlandpub.com

Table of Contents

Acknowledgments   vi
Preface   1

One. The American Southwest and Women Writers   7
Two. Mary Austin   31
Three. Willa Cather   65
Four. Laura Adams Armer   92
Five. Peggy Pond Church   120
Six. Alice Marriott   146
Seven. Lands of Enchantment   174

Chapter Notes   183
Bibliography   207
Index   215

Acknowledgments

The following libraries and archives granted permission to include in this book illustrations from their collections: Archives and Special Collections, University of Nebraska–Lincoln Libraries; Oakland Museum of California; Oklahoma Historical Society; San Francisco Public Library; and Western History Collections at the University of Oklahoma. The author wishes to express appreciation to the courteous staff members who assisted her in identifying images and acquiring permissions for use. Thanks are due likewise to Kathleen D. Church, who graciously gave permission to use two photographs from her collection. To Tim B. Gannon and Caitlin L. Gannon, heirs of the late publisher William Gannon, for permission to include lines from *Birds of Daybreak: Landscapes and Elegies*, by Peggy Pond Church, and to the Ahsahta Press (Boise State University), which granted permission to quote liberally from Church's *New and Selected Poems*, the author is particularly grateful.

Preface

This book, a project in literary history and criticism, examines five women authors of the American Southwest, two well known, three much less so: Mary Austin, 1868–1934, Willa Cather, 1873–1947, Laura Adams Armer, 1874–1963, Peggy Pond Church, 1903–86, and Alice Marriott, 1910–92. They stand out for their striving to give a woman's voice to aspects of the Southwest as it was during their lifetimes. As readers will see, they have many "firsts" to their credit. None was, however, a radical for her age, a George Sand or a Margaret Fuller. Their pertinent publications appeared over a period of roughly eighty-five years, starting near the beginning of the twentieth century—a period that, except for the final decades, is now significantly removed from the present. While they do not constitute a school or a generational grouping, their work illustrates certain shared aesthetic, moral, and cultural understandings, which undergirded and were promoted by their writing.

All five authors displayed sensitivity to and concern for southwestern landscapes, arts, and peoples; they valued harmony in human relationships and endeavors; they were interested in the past and sought to preserve it. Marked differences in experience, temperaments, talents, and perspectives exist among them, however, although their common feminine condition supposes some similarity of approach, including limitations (biological and, to some degree, social). Armer, Austin, and Church were married (Austin later was divorced) and had children; the other two were single. Armer was a Californian but spent long months in Arizona. Austin, from Illinois, moved to California as a young woman and is associated with that state and New Mexico, where she settled ultimately. She is the only one who attempted to make a living from desert soil; her connection with it is thus more intimate in a way but, until her income came from publishing, she was also involved in direct exploitation of the land, whereas the others, with different resources, could approach it impartially or aesthetically only. Church was a native New Mexican. Both Cather and Marriott were from Plains states but wrote about New Mexico also. Cather's Plains novels are not part of the present corpus, although similarities exist between the skies and spaces described there and southwestern panoramas, and the pioneer, homesteading experience she depicts has something in common with Austin's homesteading in California. Marriott's writings set in southwest Oklahoma will be considered below, however, because they deal with Indian tribes.[1]

A distinction among these women is their different standing, a function of their respective achievements and of cultural trends. Austin and Cather, classed among important American authors of their period and the subject of numerous scholarly investigations, must be examined as "major voices in defining the meaning of the West" as now perceived, involving ecological and feminist vantage points. Marriott is known as an ethnologist, especially a sympathetic student of the Kiowa tribe, but she is rarely studied as a creative writer. Church has a solid reputation in New Mexico but not elsewhere. Armer is an obscure figure, and her literary achievement is underrated. Almost no literary studies dating from the twenty-first century mention any of these three women. Such neglect does not correlate, however, with their literary worth. It is time to enlarge the corpus of American women's writing by drawing attention to authors previously overlooked and thus broaden the experience of readers and critics.[2]

This investigation is not founded on popular social pieties nor postmodern orthodoxy, although reference is made to postcolonial critics and to the body of feminist criticism that has developed in connection with the American west. I do not wish, in R. V. Young's words, to adopt theoretical perspectives that "conscript past writings for favored political projects." In the first chapter, I consider the background—historical, social, ethnological, literary—against which these women developed their oeuvre. This introduction is directed partly to non-specialists and to readers in other fields and those abroad who can profit from such an overview. The succeeding chapters take up the principal figures—their lives and careers—and their writings, usually treated chronologically, despite present challenges to the linear model. While the biographical sketches of Austin and Cather, based on the work of several biographers and, in Cather's case, her voluminous and important *Selected Letters* (2013) (the first publication of her correspondence), will prove unnecessary for readers well acquainted with those authors, other users may find them useful. The thorny theoretical challenge of connecting life and work is not confronted directly; this is a study *in* literary biography, not *on* it, and much must be taken for granted. Examination of the writings includes descriptions, commentaries, and assessments. Style, technique, and questions of genre are emphasized, and basic narratological analysis is used on occasion. Eschewing the position of Hayden White, who views all written history as myth because objective truth cannot be determined, I hold that the ideal of objectivity remains proper in literary history as an aim and a regulative standard; interpretation is necessarily founded in fact.[3]

Following the authors' own terminology and widespread regional usage still, indigenous peoples are generally called Indians. Certain older terms are retained in quoted material; current terms appear likewise. Older spellings such as *Navaho*, *Zuñi*, and *cañon* are modernized except in quotations. There is no presumption that writings germane to Indians present thoroughly authentic native voices, even when the texts concerned are based on long observation and acquaintance, as with Armer's *Waterless Mountain*. While some texts have been viewed as legitimate sources and may be used by native researchers, only those of Marriott, an ethnologist, have a claim to authority (superseded perhaps subsequently); in any case, only indigenous specialists can judge, ultimately, the affective value of outsiders' writings to their community.[4]

That conviction does not exclude sympathetic comprehension of any particular group on the part of others, nor, of course, scientifically-grounded studies. The present work, while making a contribution to women's literary history and thus women's studies, does not imply, consequently, ipso facto belief in a strict sexual essentialism, implying that only women can write truly about the feminine experience or that only members of a "striving community" or a people who have suffered have the right to talk about their heritage. Toni Morrison is one who rejected this narrow view, asserting that what Jane Austen and Emily Dickinson wrote was of wide application, having "something to do with life and being human in the world." As Shirley Ann Grau observed, the supposition that only those who have had the direct experience of being a woman, a cripple, an Indian, and so forth can write about it "would turn fiction into nothing more than autobiography. And it would completely remove from fiction its basic, essential element: imagination." A younger figure, Mónica de la Torre, objected similarly to the supposition, which she called "dangerous," that "if I am Mexican-American I can express only that particular community." Women share with their male counterparts the fundamental human condition. Women's situation is, however, often different from men's, as Marriott's title *Hell on Horses and Women* suggests. Women writers tend to favor small, quotidian topics over expansive ones, linger over the domestic, eschew aggression (in characters and themes), and approach their topics patiently. (These leanings are explored further in chapter one.) The fact that four authors here published books on the Southwest for children underlines their feminine sensibility as well as a pedagogical concern.[5]

The psychological origins of art, as viewed through screens furnished by Sigmund Freud, Carl Jung, Jacques Lacan, or various other systematic interpreters of the mind, are not the focus of this study, despite the fact that three authors were sometime enthusiasts of Jung. Nevertheless, biography is considered, and evidence of personal traits, bent, or convictions may be cited to illuminate works. Nor is the purpose here to identify interiorized patriarchal assumptions. It is not a question, either, of deconstructing texts. Those who assume that authors do not mean what they say, supposing coded language or unconscious intentions, overlook the obvious corollary: that what they claim to discover as subtext may be a function of their own agendas. Those who reject the authority of the author, text, and history simply impose another authority. These women were creators, and their working personalities and achievements are at stake here, not their perceived dysfunctions or unpleasant traits. To paraphrase André Malraux, a woman is what she does, not the secrets concealed in her heart. A "complex," if it is pertinent, is not the same thing as a poem, a painting. Moreover, wise is the critic who can identify origins, or cause and effect, in art. As Katherine Anne Porter noted, "All my past is 'usable,' in the sense that my material consists of memory, legend, personal experience, and acquired knowledge."[6]

Yet woman, project, and product are not totally separate. Neither context—biographic or historical—nor authorial intention is a uniquely valid point of view, nor is textual immanence (independent of the creator) nor subsequent interpretation, though all are germane. As Hans Robert Jauss correctly saw, the work always exists in a triangular relationship that includes, besides the text, the author (in the original context of production) and the reading public; as the public changes, so does the work, in a pragmatic sense. But, as was remarked, these writers should not be viewed through a contemporary grid that would exclude author and context. Their sensibility is of their own time, not the present, and it is not a question of finding in their writing what we would like to see there, according to what today are called "priorities," but rather seeing what they saw. (To speak of "their own time" is not to suggest they were socially obtuse, still less bigots; these authors were properly sensitive to various social issues, and sometimes well ahead of their time in their response.)[7]

To the personnel of archives, museums, and libraries where I consulted materials or which lent books directly or by Interlibrary Loan, or offered information, I wish to express my appreciation. They include the Southeastern Architecture Archive and Latin American Studies Collection, both at the Howard-Tilton Library of Tulane University; the Penrose Branch of Pike's Peak Regional Library and its Southwestern Collection; the Fondren Library of Rice University and its Woodson Research Center; the library of Colorado State University; and the library of the University of Colorado, Colorado Springs. I am grateful to Alex Pepple, the editor and publisher of *Able Muse: A Review of Poetry, Prose & Art*, for permission to use here phrasing and interpretations from my essay (summer 2015) on Armer. Acknowledgment is due likewise to the Bonnie Bourg Lecture Committee of Nicholls State University for inviting me to lecture there in March 2015 on three women writers, including Armer and Church. I treated them and Alice Marriott in a similar talk (October 2015) at the Newcomb College Institute of Tulane University. For the financial support of these institutions I am grateful. I should like to thank also Kathleen D. Church, Nell Norris, and Corina A. Santistevan for their willingness to speak with me in person. Likewise I am grateful for assistance and encouragement from my friends Anne Schnoebelen and Patricia Teed, as well as from my wonderful husband, Patric Savage, a fine amateur tennis player for decades, who taught me about "shot selection," by which one stays in the game.

Chapter One

The American Southwest and Women Writers

Five Women and the Southwestern Scene

To many, the vast American Southwest is an ideal, an *imago*. Does the ideal choose its voices among men and women? Prophets and seers, and some poets, prose writers, and graphic artists have believed so. Art is a means and a form of knowing. Writers and other artists (including pre–Columbian petroglyph carvers and more recent indigenous craftsmen) have created a rich body of images connected to the region, screened through their particular sensibility. The region is also, obviously, a topographical and historical reality, with its climate and geology, its pre-history, history, peoples, cultures, and governments—all of which entail large bodies of factual information. Art draws on this, the real, but goes beyond it. While landscape may be defined simply as natural features and conditions, its significance is never independent of meanings introduced by observers—their aims and judgments—as Joseph Wood Krutch saw by posing the question, "What does this canyon mean?" That is, beauty or ugliness, as well as utility, is in the eye of the beholder. Wallace Stegner said, "The art of the west is founded on fact and just as firmly on myth"— a "perpetual mirage" of words and vistas.[1]

The five authors examined here, born within a forty-two-year period—Mary Austin, Willa Cather, Laura Adams Armer, Peggy Pond Church, Alice Marriott—were connected principally to western Oklahoma (Marriott), New Mexico (everyone but Armer), Arizona (Armer), and the arid valleys of California (Austin). Grouping these women together is not merely a convenience. Although they were not by any means a school, they do not constitute just a random gathering either, having many common concerns and shared interests and assumptions (often unstated).

Their views, some of which now seem dated, have appeal for that very reason, offering what were for the time fresh insights into aspects of the Southwest observed through keen eyes and providing thus a measure of what has changed in cultural history. Shedding light on how the Southwest appeared to those writing from as early as one hundred years ago and more, up to the mid-twentieth century and later, their pages can provide a context for future investigation of other authors concerned with the environment and conservation, marginalized groups, aesthetic values (especially in nature), community life and women's particular connections to it, and other pertinent topics, to which they took moral approaches (and invited readers to do likewise).[2]

Their common points include honoring connections to the past—personal, pre-historical and historical, and geological. They had a strong interest in American desert and canyon lands, admiring what photographer Barbara Morgan described as "those primordially eroded strata of red sandstone, sculptured by grinding earth pressures, wind and water." That some among them came to know the Southwest well only as adults is significant; the topographic and cultural novelty was an impetus to writing. "Perception begins with the change of sensation," wrote André Gide; "hence the necessity of travel." They were likewise all concerned with conservation and American Indians.[3]

As the preface indicated, the initiatives taken by these writers included a number of original steps—"firsts" or nearly so—which demonstrate how fresh their vision was. These steps were both personal and cultural. They were among the first American authors to valorize strongly the desert, viewed broadly until then as hopelessly inhospitable (when even some of the Great Plains area, such as eastern Colorado, was considered desert, how much more so the sands and rocks to the west). Austin seems to be the first non–Native woman to give literary voice to the Paiute tribe. She was also among the first writers to propose for America (in *The Trail Book*, 1918) a historical narrative inspired by Native American lore and reference points, as an alternative to the Eurocentric one. Additionally, she was an early writer on aboriginal poetry. Marriott was the first woman anthropologist to work with the Kiowas; she was also the first biographer to give voice to New Mexican potters and, through them, other local women. Armer was the first white woman for whom a sand-painting was prepared, and was among the earliest and most important non–Native authorities on that art; she also set an early example of writing for juveniles elsewhere about native children. In addition, she is credited with making the first all-Native American film (setting, actors, oral commentary). Cather was a pioneer in drawing inspiration for major fictional works from the Anasazi ruins and Spanish heritage of the Southwest. Church was the first poet to write about the cultural and military importance of Los Alamos and thus was a pioneer in expressing the fears of the new atomic age.

For readers' convenience, the term "American Southwest" may be defined as stretching from a longitudinal line west of Fort Worth, Texas (near the hundredth meridian) westward through the Mojave desert and other desert lands of California, comprising all of New Mexico and Arizona. Southward, the region reaches to the Rio Grande and the land border with Mexico, and northward, into western Oklahoma, the lower tiers of Colorado and Utah, much of Nevada, and certain central areas of California. This circumscription, large and varied, embraces high mountains as well as desert and contrasting climates; aridity is a general marker.[4]

In the first half of the twentieth century, the artistic appeal of the Southwest was enormous. Taos poet Phillips Kloss felt in the Four Corners region "a definite intimation of great things past, great things to come. There is a spirit to the land that arouses and awakes, stimulates and inspires." "The conditions that bring forth great art are inherent in the soil, skies, wind, clouds, spaces of the great southwest," wrote enthusiastically the anthropologist Edgar Lee Hewett. Men and women alike were inspired by the harshness of the mountains, the "quintessential air of privacy" in its "bleak, gray parts," as Oliver La Farge wrote, and by what poet Alice Corbin called "the desert of silence / blinking and blind in the sun." Northern New Mexico in particular was a magnet, offering beautiful natural features, exotic cultures, and a congenial atmosphere for writers and painters. Church, the granddaughter of a pioneer rancher, was born and reared there; Austin and Marriott settled there; Cather paid visits. "Pretentious as it sounds," wrote Tony Hillerman, "and tough as it is to prove, there does seem to be something about New Mexico which not only attracts creative people but stimulates their creativity." Austin thought the area would be the site of the next American Renaissance. D. H. Lawrence and Frieda, Mabel Dodge Luhan, La Farge (all four of whom Armer met in Arizona), Witter Bynner, Willard "Spud" Johnson, John Gould Fletcher, Corbin and William Penhallow Henderson (her husband, an accomplished painter and architect), Nathalie Curtis (Burlin), and many other figures were part of the artists' colonies in Santa Fe and Taos. Starting in 1925, Corbin and Henderson were among the most important figures and hosts to a circle of literati at their Poets' Round-ups, held at their house on Camino del Monte Sol in Santa Fe.[5]

Since 1950 and particularly after 2000, many parts of the Southwest have become radically different from the earlier region as conventionally understood—as these five authors viewed it; the region has been, in Krista Comer's word, reified. What is called *development* (agricultural, industrial, and urban) and the huge population increase in the region, insufficiently acknowledged and discussed because of its unavoidable connection with the controversial issue of immigration, have wrought tremendous transformations. Except for the shared concern for water, southwestern cities and huge irrigated valleys have little in common, to many observers, with the "other" West, vast territories of low populations.[6]

The term *culture* is used in this study primarily in its ordinary anthropological sense: the ensemble of arts, skills, attitudes, customs, language, beliefs, and rituals, of a people or sub-group, as transmitted normally from one generation to another. It is "part of how human beings interact with the environment." The adjective *cultural* refers to what is associated with these products and mores. Anthropologists argue that in this sense cultures are of equal value. The authors studied here acknowledged, explicitly or implicitly, much truth in this viewpoint. Marriott wrote: "To know is to understand; to understand is to accept. And to accept is to perceive that racial and cultural differences are quite literally only skin deep." Secondarily, since aesthetic objects, including poems, literary prose, paintings, pottery, textiles, and photographs are considered in the chapters to follow, the term *culture* is used also with reference to aesthetic works and values: arts that do not have solely a practical intent, and which aim at style and an ideal going beyond the immediate. A poem, for instance, is chiefly itself, autonomous; it is not primarily a vehicle for conveying information. Decorative utilitarian objects and lesser arts, as well as high culture—between which distinctions are often blurred—belong to this category.[7]

The authors under examination can be connected generally neither to literary Modernism (despite some Modernist tendencies in the work of Austin and Church) nor postmodernism. Rather, they can be situated in the line of American romanticism, which dominated their cultural context and which, after flourishing in work by Henry David Thoreau and James Fenimore Cooper, remained, at least through the twentieth century and despite challenges, the default mode of American literature and culture. Mixed with exoticism, it had became firmly identified with the American frontier, its scenery and life. The Southwest was a pole of attraction, or desire. Though Arcadia existed chiefly in the imagination, that imagination of the ideal was powerful; unpleasant details could be blurred or obliterated as by an airbrush. The ethnologist and novelist Adolph Bandelier spoke of "clothing sober facts in the garb of romance" to make the truth of the Southwest more accessible and more acceptable. Among some writers there were also nationalist aspirations, associated with European Romanticism from its beginnings, with added biblical overtones: "The desert shall blossom like a rose."[8]

Though only Marriott was a professional ethnologist, Austin considered herself a specialist in the field despite having no formal training, and all five women shared a strong interest in indigenous peoples, a particular sort of common man, which they connected, rightly, to nature, as their Romantic predecessors had — and, like these predecessors, without condescension. Accustomed to being viewed as "the other," "the second sex," women detected quickly and resented the patronizing dichotomy Europeans / natives, by which the latter were considered as different and inferior — human but not quite so. They saw that a large body of human resources and achievement had been nearly overlooked in social and cultural history. The examples of southwestern tribes, among the most settled, presenting "integrative tribal ways, nurturant communitarian values, rich interplay with nature," appealed to their moral vision, which included concern for the Other, tinged with wishfulness and suspicion of Occidental civilization. They understood what Kenneth Lincoln described as "a common, organic aesthetics — a poetic kinship that unites the people, other earthly creatures, the gods, and nature in one great tribe." They searched for authentic native voices (literal and metaphorical), believing that such voices, including prehistoric ones, were available to them. Austin wrote about California tribes and worked to help preserve Pueblo arts. Armer, with permission, copied Navajo sand-paintings. Marriott devoted most of her career to Indian matters.[9]

Thus what early Romantics fancied as "primitive" (the noble savage), genuine and child-like was a recurring ideal for these writers. That such understanding of indigenous peoples has been discarded and that the term *primitive* is no longer popular does not change the ideal. Armer frequently used the term, not considered judgmental, since it came from the prevailing anthropological vocabulary. Other commentators preferred the term *primal*. "The Navajo and Pueblo Indian tribes who danced their rituals ... as partners in the cosmic process attuned me to the universally primal—rather than to either the 'primitive' or the 'civilized,'" wrote Morgan.[10]

Like romantics in general, these authors were self-identified lovers of nature, onto which they projected their personal sense of beauty, timelessness, and simplicity. They were drawn, certainly, to both the fact and the idea of the wilderness, appealing to the imagination and offering a sense of liberty (another romantic motif)—"sensations of open space, light, altitude, and immense vistas ... a sense of wonder." (This ideal contrasts with the wilderness of the early settlers in New England, for whom everything beyond their small circumscriptions constituted threat—not only genuine potential danger but also the realm of evil spirits, sometimes identified with the Natives.) The authors presented here did not, however, generally emulate poets and painters who favored dramatic panoramas: chasms, waterfalls, majestic forests for solitary reflection, vast prospects—the "Nature untamed" of Matthew Arnold, described at Niagara Falls by François-René de Chateaubriand, painted in Yosemite by Albert Bierstadt, in Colorado by Thomas Hill, photographed by Edward S. Curtis. Rather, they leaned toward viewing this rough environment as one to be respected, yet circumscribed and tamed according to human need, leading to enclosed gardens, sheep pastures, and tilled fields. Armer photographed and described striking canyon topography, emphasizing its separateness from human life, and yet put human figures in the picture and, in particular, showed her Navajo characters in their domestic settings. (This topic is taken up again below.)[11]

An additional romantic marker here is these authors' enthusiasm for dead civilizations—the "Ancient Ones"—and ruins. The echoing questions, "How long ago did the last native set foot in this cliff-house? Where did he go, and why?" connected them to ancient inhabitants as canyon strata did to geologic time. The pathetic, or sentimental, fallacy (identification of human emotions in nature—that is, nature *feeling*), similarly a romantic feature, looms large in their writing, along with innumerable anthropomorphic attributions.

In addition, a deep spiritual dimension, with sympathy for native cosmology, characterizes much of this corpus—intimations of another reality, a mysterious presence, expressed in standard religious terms or, more frequently, time-honored myths, and to which point totem animals, trees, clouds, and sun. Thus natural religion, whether organized (as in the kivas—underground ceremonial structures) or simply practiced out-of-doors in a Rousseauistic manner, is honored. With the exception of Marriott, trained in scholarly objectivity, these writers tend even toward what they or others call mysticism (defined for current purposes as a direct relationship with God or some other Absolute), with veins of pantheism, Platonism, and Christian belief. Such spiritual experience was not confined to women; the nature writer John Muir showed otherwise. But mysticism suits the feminine vision of those who embrace the earth. Even Marriott, in "The Top of the Mesa," describing a rarely-visited scene to which an indigenous friend has led her, asks, "How should we question what she so surely knew? Earth spirits, magic, power—those things must in some way have been."[12]

Foreshadowing environmentalism and the sustainability movement, all five authors were concerned about preservation of sites and traditions, and stewardship of natural and human resources. Thus, their shared romantic outlook involves a vein of what Austin called *naturism*. Most expressed dismay at always-expanding industrialization ("the machine in the garden") and the power of big business. In one work or another, each illustrated what has been described as Cather's fictional method: "Center on a character whose commitment to life-affirming past values makes him or her a source of strength in the midst of decay of belief in the modern world." Austin in particular emphasized how the pastoral dream of earlier America, having slipped away in the East, had moved west and was threatened even there; *The Ford* (1917) denounced monopolies and exploitation. Church and others adopted pacifist views, in revulsion against twentieth-century industrial warfare. This stance doubtless reflects the Protestant background these authors shared and its moral imperatives.[13]

These women responded powerfully and continually to beauty, both man-made and natural, and entered easily into communities of the like-minded. For them, the Southwest itself was the supreme source of beauty, and "Finished in beauty" could have been a mantra for all five. Their canons of beautiful features and artifacts, though having much in common, were nonetheless individual more than collective, that is, personal and without dogmatic origin. These canons were neither classical in the European sense nor composed simply of romantic commonplaces, though a strong exotic (or unusual) element is visible in the women's general understanding of beauty, including Native American criteria, present and past (for materials, design, finishing, and spiritual meanings). Details, whether in nature or artifact or art, were important: a cowslip in a bog, a yucca plant in bloom, the shape or finish of a pot, and ultimately the fine points of literary style.[14]

Thus it is not surprising that all five authors were interested in other arts, whether as practitioners themselves, friends of artists, or when choosing illustrations for their books. Armer was an accomplished, indeed famous, photographer, as well as a painter. Austin likewise painted. A subtle connection between aesthetic values and authenticity (personal, cultural) can be traced in their thinking; truth is implied. None should be accused of a decadent aestheticism, however, since, to them, beauty existed for human beings—that is, welfare and happiness—not the reverse. Nor was theirs a Kierkegaardian idolatry; beauty was part of, not rival to, the sacred, connected ultimately to goodness and to truth, or what David R. Slavitt calls "the morality of vision."[15]

To add, then, that all these women were considered somewhat physically unattractive or at least sometimes viewed themselves so (based on comparisons or others' evaluations, as cited later for each) is not to injure their reputation but to consider what such a condition may have meant for them. That self-image shaped, perhaps, their drive toward careers, though no causal connection can be established between it and their aesthetic sense, doubtless innate (as well as cultivated). Marriott was told not to expect marriage; she would have to work.

Historical Markers and Cultural Conditions

A sampling of historical markers in New Spain particularly significant for this study, some mentioned by these authors, deserves inclusion, along with notes on cultural conditions. Álvar Núñez Cabeza de Vaca (c. 1490-c. 1560) provided accounts of the legendary Seven Cities of Cíbola and thus inspired probably the expedition of Francisco Vázquez de Coronado (1510–54), who fought against certain Tiwa pueblos and reached the Zunis. Successive waves of military occupation, called *entradas*, followed, bringing settlers and Franciscan friars, who tried, by force and persuasion, to extirpate native beliefs and customs and impose Christianity. An important undertaking was that of Juan de Oñate, begun in 1596. He was known for his severity and his extraordinary cruelty to the Ácoma people. In 1610 Gaspar Pérez de Villagrá (1555–1620), whom Marriott calls "the first southwestern anthropologist," related the conquest as he saw it and described the peoples. Explorations and colonization multiplied, creating what Jonathan Swift (writing about English settlement) called "a new dominion, acquired with a title by divine right." "The natives [are] driven out or destroyed; their princes tortured to discover their gold; a free license given to all acts of inhumanity and lust; the earth reeking with the blood of its inhabitants: and this execrable crew of butchers ... is a modern colony sent to convert and civilize an idolatrous and barbarous people."[16]

In the mid-seventeenth century, the Franciscan Alonso de Posada proved to be an especially vigorous enemy—the first among many—of indigenous culture in the form of dancing and its accessories, such as prayer sticks. The 1670s, difficult years because of drought, witnessed arrests of natives, who doubtless multiplied their rain dances, for "sorcery." In August 1680, a well-planned, though not flawless, uprising took place (the "Pueblo Revolt" or "Popé's Rebellion"), which involved numerous tribes, among them Zunis and Hopis. Four hundred Spanish (including some mestizos) were killed, Santa Fe was attacked, and most remaining foreigners were driven out. Churches, crops, trees, and livestock connected to the Spanish were destroyed. The aftermath was not favorable; conditions remained difficult and the separate pueblos could not create a general civil authority. The Spanish re-established their presence in 1692. Adjustments were made, however, including the issuing by the crown of large land grants.

By the Mexican-American War (1846–48) and the Gadsden Purchase (1853), territory that had been Spanish, then (after 1821) Mexican was transferred to the United States, an enormous cultural and political change. Anglo settlers, historians, geologists, archaeologists, and others began to amass extensive information on the region, some concerning pre–Columbian periods. Certain dates are of particular interest for the present study. In 1869, John Wesley Powell descended the Green River and the Colorado, the first non-aboriginal, it is believed, to do so. His *Report on the Lands of the Arid Region* (1878) stressed the scarcity of water, urged the adoption of watersheds as boundaries, and proposed low-density grazing and other measures. In 1890, C. Hart Merriam made for the Department of Agriculture the first "biological survey" of the Little Colorado River in Arizona. In 1888 Richard Wetherill and his brother-in-law Charles Mason, who had been chasing wayward cattle in a canyon complex, reported their discovery of Cliff Palace at Mesa Verde, in Colorado, the grandest of the Anasazi ruins. Kiet Seel in Arizona (part of the Navajo National Monument) was discovered a few years later. It was Wetherill who bestowed the name *Anasazi*—Navajo, as he knew, for "Ancient Ones" or "Ancient Enemies." It is a misleading term, viewed now as offensive, since later natives have enormous respect for their predecessors. The first published examination of Mesa Verde was a 1890 article by Frederick Chapin, illustrated by his photographs. In 1893 Gustaf E. A. Nordenskiöld produced *The Cliff Dwellers of the Mesa Verde, Their Pottery and Implements*, based on his explorations and studies. Chaco Canyon, now a National Historical Park and UNESCO World Heritage Site, was partly known to explorers well before 1850, but only in 1896 was excavation work begun on its ruins. At some locations, digs continued throughout the twentieth century and later.[17]

While the history of pertinent Indian displacements and assignment to reservations cannot be traced here, the status of native tribes at the turn of the twentieth century and beyond warrants a word. As late as the 1920s there were still tribes considered unruly and hostile, mostly Apaches. Borders of tribal lands had generally been agreed upon, but controversies over them and cultural rights continued, and the prevailing view among whites of Native Americans was unfavorable. Native languages were under attack, officially. The Bureau of Indian Affairs and other government officials perceived the native peoples in terms of crude "stereotypes—savages, children, wards—inferior to civilized peoples" and "utterly devoid of the wisdom or ability to plan and manage their own affairs." In 1923, the federal commissioner of Indian Affairs, Charles H. Burke (called by Nina Otero-Warren, then superintendent of schools in Santa Fe County, "a small politician with an abysmal outlook"), issued a proclamation "To All Indians" demanding that they discontinue their "pagan" ceremonial dances, which he qualified as "useless and harmful performances." It was not until 1924 that Indian tribes had the franchise in federal elections. Only in 1948 could they vote in local (non-tribal) contests in Arizona and New Mexico.[18]

Beyond 1900 there was prejudice likewise, on the part of Anglo-Americans, against the Spanish influence in the Southwest—the customs, language, architecture, religion (Catholicism as practiced by Indians and Spanish—viewed as superstitious). Adobe structures were called by Anglo observers "a miserable collection of mud hovels," a "degenerate Spanish (Mexican) style of architecture." This judgment is in striking contrast to the appreciation, displayed by many visitors and the authors studied here, for Hispanic styles and materials. The Hispanic concentrations were viewed as primitive and foreign as well as obscurantist. In 1919 a New Mexico resident, writing of the differences between her state and others, noted that travel was still "by narrow-gauge railway, stagecoach, bronco, or burro, over ... rugged and sandy landscapes ... where the distances between houses are measured not by blocks but by arroyos, mountains, or mesas," adding that there was not another state where one half of the population could not understand the other without an interpreter.[19]

While nineteenth-century ethnologists and art critics—Henry Rowe Schoolcraft, James Stevenson, Matilda Coxe Stevenson, Washington Matthews, James Mooney—had examined artifacts such as painted hides, pottery, and basketry and studied ceremonies and songs of the indigenous peoples, immense cultural areas were still unexamined well into the twentieth century, and preservation as now understood was not necessarily the goal. The federal Indian Arts and Crafts Board was not established until 1934; Marriott was appointed in 1936 to head it. Even among Hispanics crafts were suppressed rather than encouraged.[20]

The Manitou Cliff Dwellings outside Colorado Springs offer an example of attitudes shortly after 1900. With the approval and participation of Hewett, Anasazi structures were removed from near Cortez, Colorado, shipped by rail, then re-assembled and fortified to create a visitor site, which opened in 1907. Well in the future still—toward the end of the twentieth century—was the time when indigenous peoples, supported by changing public views, would question the investigations of white specialists, protest against their previous methods and policies, and, on religious or other cultural grounds, demand restoration of certain sites and de-accessioning of artifacts in museums and other collections.[21]

American Regional Writing and Writing About the Past

The term *regional*, used in this study, requires comment. Since what is general, appealing widely or having the highest truth-value, arises from the particular, terms such as "local" or "regional" need not mean "narrow"; the regional is the crucible of human verities. Someone defined it as "our concrete, not abstract, level of existence, our richest sense of life." "The classic is the local fully realized, words marked by a place," asserted William Carlos Williams. "The history of the United States in written in hundreds of regional histories and literary works," observed a publisher. After the Civil War, however, the strong prejudice against the South and authors such as William Gilmore Simms, a secessionist who supported slavery, colored judgments; regional identification and pride were viewed as "sectionalism." By the twentieth century, and especially the third decade and thereafter, thanks in part to William Faulkner (though his racial attitudes remained tainted, according to some), efforts to promote truly regional voices had made headway. A defender of southern and Midwestern poets in the magazine *Poetry* was Corbin, who found New York City "forever the same: / There is no *life* there," adding, "Nothing but life on the desert, / Intense life." No one can dismiss Faulkner and Stegner today, nor Robert Penn Warren nor Eudora Welty, but western and southern writers remain suspect. What Van Wyck Brooks titled "the flowering of New England" remains the literary standard, its chronological priority reinforced by its homogeneous origins and monolithic density. That it gives little place to humor, so frequent in western writing, is simply another reason for ignoring or disparaging the latter, despite the honorable place of humor in British and French literature. The body of twentieth-century writing produced in New York and other Atlantic states similarly reinforces cultural monism. Scholars characteristically assign more value to studies connected to the Northeast than to works on the Southwest. This tendency is still acknowledged (with regret by some): writing in 2000, Anne E. Goldman argued that the American "national literature remains centered within the culture of New England ... so that other points west and south ... remain vanishing points on the horizon line." In the twenty-first century, studies that can be thought of as particularist have increasingly lost value, disparaged by globalists and others who deny the importance of the local.[22]

Austin addressed this topic in a 1932 essay, "Regionalism in American Fiction." Literature, she argued, is as a rule generated from the region where an artist lives and works. To insist upon material common to all regions or centered in the Northeast is restrictive and weakening in the long run. Suspicious of East Coast intellectualism, she attacked explicitly the New York literary establishment for its dictatorial ways and general dismissal of work produced elsewhere. For a western writer to be successful and recognized in eastern capitals, it was necessary, in the words of Ambrose Bierce, "to hammer and hammer again and again before the world will hear and heed." Unsurprisingly, writers often suffered from the label *regionalist*. Cather told a New York *World* interviewer that she did not want to become too much identified with the west, adding (erroneously) that there was little of it in *The Professor's House*.[23]

Austin did note, however, that the story should be *of*, not *about*, the region, and those who live there should recognize the truth of the land among the incidents and particulars. "A regional culture is the sum, expressed in ways of living and thinking, of the mutual adaptations of a land and its *people*" (Austin's italics). The area must be integral to the story and its structure; it must enter into the story constructively, and may act even as a character, an instigator to the plot. She cited work of Cather, Nathaniel Hawthorne, Sarah Orne Jewett, Mark Twain, James Branch Cabell, and Hamlin Garland as prototypes of genuine regional writing, while noting that, despite Cather (and others), the Southwest had yet to receive full literary expression.[24]

Acknowledgment must be made of various feminist critics, including Comer, who have approached the question of regionalism ideologically, writing of "the new female regionalism" and connecting western space to the production of power, that is, the dominance of men in and through western spaces. (For general purposes, feminism will be defined here, briefly and roughly, as the belief that women are an oppressed caste.) While Austin's writings on the California desert may be read as adumbrating this connection—and she did adopt elements of a feminist platform—she did not discourse on the desert in today's feminist terms. In any case feminine regionalism has developed beyond that (and beyond the concerns of the present book) into what Comer terms an "alternative, geocultural imaginary, one that puts female-centered ... western space at the heart of the western drama"—including female sexuality. Similarly, in *Writing Out of Place*, Judith Fetterley and Marjorie Pryce, influenced by Michel Foucault, among others, tie regionalism, "the site of a dialogical critical conversation," to gender, "feminist epistemology," and power structures. Citing as examples Austin and Cather (as well as Jewett, Grace King, and Kate Chopin), they note that "regionalist texts call into question numerous cultural assumptions about literary history, poetics, thematics, genres, and reading strategies"—assumptions their authors might or might not recognize as having made or rejected. Race, class, and sexual theories as well as geography are involved. Ultimately, these critics deny that regionalization is connected to geographic reality; it involves a discourse, not a place.[25]

Another matter deserving attention is writing about the past—recent, more distant, or geological. In "The Top of the Mesa," Marriott provides a synthetic understanding, human and scientific, of past and present, individual and species, as she and others discover on a mesa-top ancient shards of pottery, resembling nothing known presently, along with shells from aeons before, when the entire Southwest was covered by ocean. Similarly, Armer focuses on arrowheads, fetishes from earlier peoples, fossil oyster shells on a mesa-top, and dinosaur bones in a dig, and Cather and Church reflect on the import of petroglyphs and ruins.[26]

The challenge of re-creating the past is well known. From evidence that may be limited, the author must reconstruct a persuasive segment of time or panorama, using narrative conventions. For an historian, the truth factor is crucial. In contrast, older creative writers (from the ancients and Shakespeare onward) were granted wide latitude to embroider on what was known. Now, when facts are frequently abundant and others have examined them already, the standards for fidelity are higher, except in cinematography and television, held to low levels of verisimilitude and accuracy. Today's well-informed readers would generally feel misled if they recognized distorted pictures and erroneous accounts. All five authors treated here published narratives requiring use and assessment of facts. They were clearly aware of the obligation to work within limits set by present or historical knowledge or recognized tradition.

Yet they put much of themselves into these narratives. In any case, the distinction between "subjective" and "objective" (or "scientific") history, as John Lukacs uses the term, must be qualified; to some degree, all writing of the past is subjective (though not "myth," as Hayden White claimed). That historical re-creations by novelists and poets are clearly shaped, often altered, indicates public taste for personal treatment. At best, such subjective narration has not only appeal but more intimate, even greater truth. The point was made in Aristotle's *Poetics* that (simply put), history being the account of what was, tragedy (or poetry), the account of what might have been, the latter is superior, as it calls on the imagination for understanding. "Our historical knowledge, like nearly every other kind of human knowledge, is personal and participatory, since the knower and the known, while not identical, are not and cannot be entirely separate," writes Lukacs, with approbation.[27]

A Different West: Men's and Women's Perspectives

Words are required here on the broad question of sex and authorship. Is there a woman's art? A woman feels her body from the inside and knows it from the outside, as a man feels and knows his, but what she feels is not identical. Yet strict sexual essentialism is ruled out by the common human condition. To deny all operative differences between the sexes—or, particularly, to ascribe them only to cultural conditioning or "construction" resulting from sexual subjugation—is similarly erroneous, as when Catharine MacKinnon asserts that "male is a social and political concept, not a biological attribute. It has nothing whatever to do with inherency ... or the body as such." This postmodern view of gender as socially constructed—women being a caste, not a sex—makes it difficult to discern or argue for sex-specific responses. Is role identical to being, or merely its shaper? Does being follow function, or the reverse? Genetically-encoded behaviors cannot be ruled out. In anthropological and biological disciplines there is currently a growing recognition of the complex relationship between genes and culture, or environment. "Culture is not separate from evolutionary biology at all, but bound up with it." "Each one of us is a product of our genes and our environment." Modifications to DNA can be passed on to offspring, and one may speak of a "co-evolution" of culture and biology. A reasonable evaluation taking into account these truths will serve in the present case.[28]

Certainly, women may bring a feminine vision to their writing. Janis P. Stout, mentioning, among others, Austin and Cather, identifies "a different west," contrasted to men's. Even Armer, Church, and Marriott had their own vision, not just individual but proceeding from their woman's condition. The west had been, Stout argues, "gendered" (*masculinized* would be a better term) by fact and convention—white men being the mappers, developers, and principal figures in historically measurable achievements; and this pragmatic gendering brought about a hundred years and more of writing and iconography (in painting and motion pictures) by "Triumphalists," based on their masculine vision. Yet Frederick Jackson Turner argued that the west was a woman, holding the hope of regeneration.[29]

The Triumphalists "often depicted inanimate landscapes rendered in a sublime way.... Nature was seen as a model of grand order and serenity, redemptive and divine. With few exceptions, these landscapes were awesome and unpeopled, the angle of vision and manipulations ... a grand comment on the fruits of Manifest Destiny." Speaking of the California desert, Austin wrote, "'Tis a hard country for women.... Men love it, just, but women—they want different things." In *I'll Take My Stand* (1930), John Crowe Ransom noted regretfully that "the masculine" had become "hallowed by Americans ... under the name of Progress," that is, "man's increasing command ... over the forces of nature." Church spoke of her own forebears as "aggressive masculine spirits, buying and selling land, dealing in cattle, dreaming of profit, of riches, as the Spanish conquistadors dreamt of gold, of power." In much popular art, the Southwest remains a male world.[30]

It has been argued that the male myth "narrates a confrontation of the American individual, the pure American self divorced from circumstances, with the promise offered by the idea of America." This myth, antisocial when taken to the extreme, is expressed by situating an exemplary romantic figure in the wilderness, "on which he may inscribe, unhindered, his own destiny and his own nature." (This "nature" is, of course, an individual creation, neither human nature as understood by Aristotle and his followers nor the elemental natural givens.) Examining western history, present revisionists deem the winning of the west a "mosaic of failure ... an irresponsible white male's adventure, hugely destructive of the land itself, of the native peoples, and even the white males' own women and children." The male attitude, frequently characterized by an obsession with what Austin calls "ascendancy," was, in the words of Kirkpatrick Sale, one of rape, part of "the masculine attitude toward the feminine, the acquisitive toward the desired, the dominant toward the weak, the civilized toward the natural"—all "bounty due the conquering Europeans." It is, however, erroneous to suppose that feminine vision was always in opposition to masculine Triumphalism. Studying western women's writings from two centuries, literary historian Brigitte Georgi-Findlay found that their narratives were not necessarily more "detached and critical" than men's; "white women emerge as authors and agents of territorial expansion, positioned ambiguously within systems of power and authority."[31]

Whatever the dominant vision, it is certain that introducing a feminine perspective to the masculine always creates a qualitative difference, occasionally tension and discord, but usually a softening of approach; woman's presence is not the same as her absence. The camerawoman Gertrude Käsebier photographed Auguste Rodin. When someone said that he had never seen such tenderness and gentility in any other portrait of the sculptor, she replied, "That is Rodin in the presence of a woman." Stout sees the southwestern "difference" not, however, in a resultant feminizing of the material but a kind of cultural androgyny, characterized by *absence* of male features such as the urge to dominate and exploit territory, animals, and human beings. Of course, since such absence characterizes the *feminine*, not the androgynous, Stout must mean that it is joined to other traits not viewed normally as feminine.[32]

Comments on Stout's position, as it applies to women observers and interpreters of the Southwest, seem warranted. Indeed, androgyny must include the male element. As Simone de Beauvoir stressed in *Le Deuxième Sexe*, women who use the written word to denounce (even implicitly) aggression and domination by men assume a masculine role. The very act of writing is an act of *production*, by which subjects go beyond their condition, opposed to *reproduction*, the creation of identical biological life. Julia Kristeva similarly saw how in a male-dominated system women given access to power or any other structure of importance, including language, may be neutralized or even incorporated by it. All those who write, but especially women, take risks—artistic, emotional, professional. These tendencies (reaching beyond one's condition and risk) may be viewed as part of the androgyny that Stout identifies. Austin, Cather, and Marriott illustrate especially well the ambitious drive toward literary accomplishment and recognition that characterizes many male authors, joined, in Austin's case, to a feminist outlook. Church remained less aggressive (though she took emotional risks); Armer was self-directed more than outer-directed. Certain southwestern women of accomplishment—Cather, Laura Gilpin, Luhan, Marriott, her friend Margaret Lefranc, and the painter Georgia O'Keeffe—showed their androgyny in bisexuality or lesbianism, overt or not. That there is a causal connection between their sexual preferences and their adoption of the Southwest as their home—even their achievements—is uncertain, however.

To the degree that the "culturally androgynous" label suits women writers of the west, it fits also countless other American women who displayed independence, vigor, strength, often in a partnership that amounted to a kind of cooperative androgyny. Such figures appear in writing by all five authors under examination here. Though panoramic painting as evoked above and certain earlier American writings do not emphasize feminine strength, it comes through, despite sartorial conventions, in family portraits and photographs of the nineteenth century as well as much writing and oral history. A cursory glance at ante- and post-bellum writing from the South, where women were ostensibly passive, illustrates the point. The fiction of Constance Fenimore Woolson and that of King, for instance, shows how women's energies and initiatives, their assumption of responsibility, were key to survival. Armer, emphasizing feminine toughness, reports how, in the mid–1850s, the men among a small party of emigrants returning from California over the desert "had given up from pure exhaustion and lain down to die"; but the women had continued, climbed higher, found water, and returned to resuscitate them. Marriott's *Hell on Horses and Women* gives evidence from the early 1900s to the 1950s. Photographic portraits of the authors examined here suggest determination and hardiness, even ruggedness; they have character and will, their strong features conveying the firmness and insight that feed literary success. Yet their vision remained feminine in many ways.[33]

While women are sometimes considered closer to culture than to nature, the more widespread view (whether condescending or not) is that they are closer to nature, the realm of natural accident, needs, and frailty, and removed generally from pure reason. The conviction that women are close to earth is part of the Earth Mother tradition, highly ambivalent, as Beauvoir saw.

Certainly, mothering is necessary to sustain life; earth is necessary. But the transcendence represented by men's rearranging of nature, partly a denial of the latter, constitutes the default understanding of civilization. Hunters and gatherers were passive users of their surroundings; organized societies began to redesign them. So the maternal is valorized in its earthiness (moist, dark), but it constitutes also an earthy limitation, again, reproduction as opposed to (original) production.

Thus women are "closer always to the moulding realities of earth," reflects one of Austin's male characters. Nature is "a female domain," in Camille Paglia's term. As Monsieur Thibault observes disparagingly, speaking of women's bodies, in Roger Martin du Gard's series novel *Les Thibault*, "There's always something out of order with those mechanisms." Whereas men tend toward autonomy, women tend toward connectedness and holistic views. Aggression and expansion attract them less than the proximate, the domestic; they are more at home in small-scale economies than vast enterprises. It is a sign of their times that the authors under examination did not attribute these tendencies to patriarchal oppression; rather, they were considered innate. Austin associated homemaking activities, or "givingness to others," with "the intellectual, prophetic, and intuitive qualities in women that make their acts or arts contributory." When she describes the Long Trail by which sheep are driven hundreds of miles, what interests her most are not the great action scenes but the discrete moments under a lone tree or around a small fire. Though unconventional, May Sarton believed that women were "primarily nurturers"—more elemental, or, as Church believed, attached to primal sources and possessing a unique wisdom. Woman's role in giving and sustaining life was woman's meaning; meaning was not imposed from the outside. Culture may transcend nature, of course, but culture begins with nature—the body, the earth, the given. Women's culture uses the physical to improve the physical. Thus their closeness to hearth, land, and water.[34]

Many southwestern tribes were matrilineal; women had inheritance rights among them and in New Mexican Hispanic villages. (Anthropologists observe that matrilineal societies subsisted usually on gardening and caring for small animals; herding of large animals was associated with patrilineal cultures.) The cult of the Virgin Mary contributed likewise to women's importance. Among the Navajos and Pueblo dwellers, women tended the sheep; among Hispanics, though men were herders, women did much of the wool processing. Church wrote of "women's vegetative nature, the powerful earth tie which arises with the development of gardening and agriculture by women." Canyon bottoms such as Canyon de Chelly and Chaco, which the Indian women help cultivate, and fields watered by small rivers and *acequias* in the Rio Grande Valley are closer to domestic gardens than to vast stretches of tilled land.[35]

The Earth, Landscape and Women's Work

Not surprisingly, thus, writers examined here favored the proximate, the everyday—the "worm's-eye view" of history, not its great lines. They learned from Indian and Hispanic women that long-term survival depended greatly on domestic skills. They knelt in the sand (literally or figuratively), learned local ways of cooking, worked side-by-side with native women, helped with the children, and displayed concern for the sick. (In Navajo society, though healing dances are men's work, women share the emotional strain; and healers among the Pueblos and Hispanics were women.) Austin stressed the "intuitional" approach of the Anglo pioneer women confronting the wilderness—the work of their hands, their "intention"—as opposed to male "ritual of rationalization." Marriott showed how even in the mid-twentieth century women's functions in a man's world were both essential and particular.[36]

The traditional personification of earth, often capitalized, as womanly or maternal recurs over and over. Austin's novel *Cactus Thorn* and the conclusion of her essay "The Land" illustrate her conviction that "the desert is always a woman." The people themselves, blanket-wrapped, look like their landscape: brown, rounded by age like wind-eroded rocks, the faces of the old rutted but thereby striking. She remarked that in the desert "even the human inhabitants took on the tawny colors of the soil." She uses the phrase "earth mother," and her title *Earth Horizon* ties her autobiography to the life-giving planet (although actually she found her portion generally infertile). Armer likewise spoke of "earth mother," having in mind the Navajos and their connection with the ground, and noted that "earth, a house, a square and a woman are four sisters the world over." "[The] very nudity [of the desert] makes it intimate." Church attempted to understand herself in relation to her "feminine landscape" (but also to her father and husband). According to one critic, the Southwest is "the most thoroughly elaborated female landscape in literature."[37]

Women's vital power radiates perceptibly there within a circle of delicate equilibrium, not the rich, loamy soil of agricultural America, nourished, before water control, by periodic inundations of great rivers and now irrigated—the sort of fecundity associated with women from early millennia—but stony, chary soil, with little rain, sparse vegetation, small aspirations. Thus the interest in conservation—not limited to women, obviously (Muir was an early, energetic apostle, as were Theodore Roosevelt, Ernest Thompson Seton), but characteristic of those who husband resources. In New Mexico, as Sale put it, "the glory of conquest" gave way in public imagery of the early twentieth century to "pride of perseverance" and "feminine imagery." Nature may be utilized, but discreetly, within the bounds of need, and a quiet stewardship is taken for granted, dictated by the almost-sacred closeness between self and environment.[38]

The masculine is not absent. Rain is viewed as virile, fertilizing the soil, as in Gilpin's photograph "The 'He'-Rain." Austin described rain as a "great male divinity ... that tore against the hard dryness of the rainless season." But in Gilpin's companion shot, rain is, alternatively, feminine. As Armer noted, it is so fundamental that it is connected to both sexes. The difference illustrates a common distinction, by which the softer of two things is the feminine (in Gilpin's photograph, a shower), whereas the harsher is the masculine (a rainstorm with thunder and lightning). Similarly, though the sun is traditionally viewed as masculine, woman likewise is associated with the sky because of its fertilizing power. Church reported how the night after her friend Edith Warner, newly arrived from the East, was taken to the stone ranch house where her new life was to begin, "she slept in the greatest quietness she had ever known.... She waked feeling as though the strength of the earth and sky had filled her." Stones themselves and the shape of the landscape are feminized, occasionally eroticized. The New Mexico landscape is "phallic" but has "the noble curves, the brooding quiet of maternity," wrote Austin. Canyons, rocks, mountain flanks are as extensions of being, correlatives of the self.[39]

Yet, as Church emphasized, the earth is "not to us an entirely benign mother, but a place of uncertainty and strangeness." The volcano at the base of which her family lived "had so recently grown cold that some of the ash was barely solidified into stone." Dark, unknown forces had once broken through the earth's crust and might do so again. It is, however, on such a crust that life, in its vulnerability, must flourish, if it is to flourish. Church's own approach to the land was ambivalent, "the woman hating it because ... in a way it is her rival." Armer emphasized how the Navajos dealt every year with the caprices of nature, even its cruelty; hence the role in her stories of propitiatory acts.[40]

Dwellings are earth-bound. As described by Cather and Armer (who built one), Navajo hogans resemble the land and are made of local products; the Hispanics' and Pueblos adobe—including the *horno* (outdoor oven)—is earth itself; the cliff-dwellers lived within stone walls. In Cather's *The Lark*, Thea creates for herself a womb-like refuge in which self, artifact, shelter, and stony cliff side are nearly one, providing "the strange mothering of stones." Armer's Na Nai, known as The Crawler—a famed Medicine Man, born without feet—spent his life on the soil, from which he also drew the materials for his sand-paintings. Armer, Cather, and Church all camped out right on the ground. Armer and Church lived on earthen floors. In a poem entitled "She Will Want Nothing But Stones," Church, for whom stones were, with birds and bread, a major motif, wrote, "Perhaps I will take root here like the pines." Even houses of European design in the Southwest are often made of local stone or plain wood; many Europeans preferred adobe. The material was dictated by practical considerations, but its use illustrates how—as in many other cross-cultural contacts—Anglos borrowed from those they often despised. "Because the towns [pueblos] came out of the earth and were part of it, they hardly showed against the countryside," noted Marriott. Erna Fergusson, the author of *Dancing Gods*, wrote that the river bank below the Zuni pueblo was "the same color as the stone and adobe houses"; all the colors, "terra-cotta, gray, dull green and smoke blue"—from fires, were repeated some miles away in Corn Mountain and its "sculpted buttes."[41]

The practical and decorative arts that attracted these writers were native: pottery, basketry, weaving, jewelry (the handiwork of men but worn by both sexes), sand-painting (practiced by Medicine Men but directed at all the ailing), domestic architecture. They draw on natural materials with relatively little processing and few intermediaries. "Every Indian woman is an artist,—sees, feels, creates, but does not philosophize about her processes," wrote Austin, stressing that "the weaver and the warp lived next to the earth and were saturated with the same elements." Established forms are enriched by innovation and aesthetic aims. Cather stressed how potters experimented with form and color "to gratify something that had no concern with food and shelter." When Church went picnicking with her husband in "slits of cave dwellings," she noted decorated pottery fragments and coated floors—the use of nature to improve upon nature. She thought of the women who had lived there and, "in the midst of their hard, uncomfortable lives, made their pots and decorated them." She compared implicitly her work ("texts") to textiles: "A woman's work is not heroic but a weaving. The power to spin and weave, this is her alchemy." Armer, admiring a pre-Columbian basket, wrote that "she could feel the power of her weaving sisters who lived long ago."[42]

In short, numerous centers and motifs of southwestern life as depicted by the writers here—oven, chapel, loom, pot, water jar, *acequia*, child at the breast—were and remain feminine points, intimate, drawing to themselves the essential qualities of life there, past and present. Even when whole tribes or peoples are concerned, their history is individualized by discrete, sometimes personal stories. An ethnologist reaches broad conclusions only by studying detail. As Cather asserted when, in connection with *Shadows on the Rock*, set in Quebec, she dismissed any epic ambitions, "An ordinary little French household that went on trying to live decently ... interests me more than the Indian raids or the wild life in the forests." For Church, as a poet, detail was particularly important; even verse with a narrative cast can be intimate.[43]

The fact that these women authors also wrote about men—warriors, Medicine Men, farmers, builders, sheepmen—does not exclude a feminine viewpoint. Their male characters, historical or invented—from Austin's Arrowmaker to Cather's Tom Outland and Bishop Latour to Armer's footless Medicine Man to Tilano, Church's Indian friend—are strong and convincing portraits. Yet Cather, for one, acknowledged her limitations in depicting the other sex. "The trouble about this story is that the central figure must be a man, and that is where all women writers fall down." Her friend Jewett advised her against the pitfall of writing in a man's character, and critics generally take her women to be finer creations. Austin, for her part, seems to have been torn (perhaps a false dichotomy, however) between writing in a man's character, at the risk of betraying her authentic voice, and writing like a woman and thus producing what one critic calls "constricted fictions."[44]

Additional Features of Writing Examined Here

Four authors examined here published literature for young readers that is closely connected to the Southwest. (Cather is the exception.) In every case such writing is an integral part of their oeuvre. Their commitment to such work bespeaks a pedagogical drive that may be viewed as feminine, although male writers may display it likewise. Whether in fictionalized form, as legend, or in the form of straight history, important insights into the southwestern past and its peoples are central to numerous writings by them, all reminiscent of the didactic tradition in juvenile literature. Some can be placed also in the line established in the "first golden age" of juvenile books, dating from the 1860s and onward into the 1900s, which moved toward fantasy. While these authors were well removed from the social concerns of Victorian England, they were sensitive to broad questions concerning the relationships between children and society and what was suitable for young people, and they had an enormous mine of exotic materials on which to draw, not strictly foreign but with appealing strangeness.[45]

One additional trait noticeable in these women's careers is their willingness to draw others into their work. Armer and her husband, a graphic artist, produced several works together; Marriott and her friend Lefranc similarly created work together as author and illustrator, and Marriott also collaborated with Carol Rachlin; in her book *The House at Otowi Bridge* Church wove part of her own story into that of her friend Warner; Austin worked with Ansel Adams and wrote various prefaces and introductions. There are also, of course, collaborations of the mind and heart, as these authors' biographies suggest.[46]

All five writers here adjusted forms to fit their material and showed flexibility in handling narrative and exposition. Their approaches are consistent with the potentialities of the modern novel, a post-classical genre (though derived from the epic imagination) rooted principally in the real and generically flexible. As Gyorgy Lukács argued, the evolution of fiction through Romanticism into realism to Naturalism and thence the great twentieth-century social frescoes shows how understanding of the *real* changed from a focus on individual lives and manners to the image and concept of collectivities, that is, the material of sociology, ethnology, and social history. The development further loosened previous formulas for fiction and created openings for non-fictional materials, sometimes incorporated directly. The osmosis between story and non-imaginative materials—history, journalism, social analysis—has enriched the genre, making it at once more factual and more truthful. Austin's tales are interwoven with environmental criticism. Cather's narration of the lives of Jean-Baptiste Lamy and his vicar uses factual sources but fictionalizes them. Marriott evoked the Kiowas by their myths and stories, arranged in such a way that they serve as a chronicle; *The Ten Grandmothers* is almost an ethnological novel. Church wove her autobiography into the story of Warner and of atomic research at Los Alamos. Armer re-wrote the legends of the Navajos. None of these generic measures is radical; what counts is the remarkable adaptation of genre to cultural and literary purposes.[47]

Yet these artists were not vanguardists nor experimenters. While Modernists elsewhere introduced new ways of recounting, including quasi-simultaneous narratives, the interior monologue, and metafiction, these five writers did not practice break-up in language, plot, or logic nor cultivate the aesthetic of shock. It could be argued that viewing the rough and angular settings of the Southwest might lead writers to the techniques associated with the new, fractured vision of the twentieth century; but these settings had been humanized, traditionally, and the task of the five writers was to identify, preserve, and make understood this delicate, but enduring and moving, humanizing of the earth. They wanted to sound their own notes and, apparently, to avoid what had become clichéd. Church tells how Warner, trying to narrate her life in New Mexico, gave up: "After the first few pages it sounded to her too much like the standard adventure: 'White woman moves West. Lives among Indians.'" The point here is not to find shortcomings; on the contrary. As Cather asserted, "To note an artist's limitations is but to define his genius.... A creative writer can do his best only with what lies within the range and character of his talent."[48]

Chapter Two

Mary Austin

Austin's Reputation, Commitments and Achievement

Though "a small, plain, brown woman, with too much hair," Mary Austin can be viewed as preeminent among women authors of the Southwest, the *doyenne*. Once said to be "a woman of genius and no talent," she was considered by other observers to have talent but no genius. William Allen White called her a "strong, overbearing woman," vainer than a flock of "gargantuan peacocks." She wrote about a variety of issues with what one commentator called "a sharp moral vision that continues to invigorate readers a century later." Her oeuvre, which consists of essays, fiction, poetry, drama, autobiography, criticism, and miscellaneous pieces, is large (some thirty-two books by one count, twenty-seven by another) and uneven. Most of her works, even minor ones, concerning southwestern scenes or topics are treated below.[1]

Her reputation illustrates the reader-reception factor noted in the preface, by which producer, product, and consumer (audience) create a triangle; their relationship changes in "an ever unfolding potentiality of meaning, which can be seen as actualized in reception at various historical moments." In other terms, "meanings are constructed within the dynamics of an exchange between participants in a given communication situation." Yet, while what is known about the past is always subject to correction, enlargement, and reinterpretation, with the result that past recorded utterances (to use M. M. Bakhtin's term) can acquire new meanings within the present context, these altered or developed meanings must not be attributed retrospectively unless the new reading depends on newly-discovered past facts. That is, critics must see that some older texts simply do not fit into later contexts.[2]

Austin celebrated two southwestern areas: the California desert val-

Mary Austin, 10 December 1932. Courtesy San Francisco History Center, San Francisco Public Library.

leys, and Arizona and New Mexico, of which John Gould Fletcher considered her an eminent interpreter. Her writing—a way of knowing about "[a] country that failed to explain itself"—was closely connected to those great spaces. (The phrase is curious, implying, presumably, that more fertile areas, with their agriculture and settled communities, show clearly their human purposes and their potentialities.) For a while she lived as a genuine western pioneer; her family, originally from Illinois, settled in California as homesteaders, and she witnessed the hardening experience of struggling with aridity and recalcitrant soil. (Because of this exploitation of the desert, her position cannot be considered solely that of a disinterested observer.) She may have become hard herself. It was said that "the milk of human kindness had curdled in her," that she was an "egocentric loner"; another epithet was "God's mother-in-law." Yet her approach to the wilderness and especially to its inhabitants was caring and moral. "I loved the land so much I couldn't bear not having grown up in it." She understood that the southwestern environment dictated its ways and set limits. Those who loved it grasped, like her Walking Woman, "the naked thing ... not dressed and tricked out ... by prejudices." Like the ancient Greeks, she saw that nature and human nature must be properly connected. She could have endorsed Witter Bynner's statement: "The Southwestern landscape, more than any other in North America, reduces vainglory in a man and enforces his exact, or at least his reasonable, importance. It is at once a humbling and an ennobling landscape."[3]

Aspects of Austin's wide appeal can be surveyed here. She is celebrated today as an early conservationist or "naturist," sensitive to the beauty and value of nature, both immanent and, as she saw it, transcendent. Her environmentalism has become part of the standard narrative, or dominant understanding, concerning her. Her sense of natural beauty developed early, becoming deep respect for the earth. With John Muir, she has been called the first truly *western* nature writer. She gave voice to her surroundings by writing eloquently of the beauty of natural places and the need to preserve them. She was highly sensitive to the connections between the land and human communities. She showed, one critic asserts, how the west could support "forms of idyllic domestic space." While her conservationism appeals widely, it attracts especially eco-feminists and those who call themselves "deep ecologists," who take the natural world as an absolute, having inalienable rights. Many have adopted her as a prophet—a new Jean-Jacques Rousseau, viewing civilization as evil, or at least corrupt, and visualizing a new relationship between nature and mankind made possible by a leveled, egalitarian society, built on the general good, without hierarchy or individual autonomy and eschewing industrialization. One inspired admirer, Barney Nelson, writes of Austin's "deep ecology with a vision of a truly democratic, multicultural, human society ... and an inclusive ecosystem."[4]

Although she often preferred simple living, Austin was not, however, truly a forerunner of the radical environmental movement; she was an anthropocentric environmentalist. A case in point is that she celebrated the pastoral industry of sheepherding, despite its connection to human greed and soil damage; and she was not an uncritical partisan of governmental control of land. Nor was she against irrigation in California; what she opposed was diverting water to Los Angeles. (After *The Land of Little Rain* appeared, the city water authority succeeded in its diversion plan, and Owens Valley agriculture was ruined.) What she meant by *conservation* was not preservation of wilderness but, rather, controlled, suitable use, or multi-use of resources. Land has instrumental utility; it cannot be totally authentic (unspoiled) when it is inhabited by human beings, who turn it to their purposes; and its voice can be only that of human observers, who, it was remarked, contribute to it their meanings. So the question becomes: Who deserves to inhabit and utilize the land, and by what standards should they be judged? Her writings indicate clearly that the semi-nomadic Indians, with no fixed abode, to whom she is partial, deserve consideration; but, for her, whites who live in tents and those who put down roots (houses, agriculture) similarly have legitimate claims. Nature is not entirely benign, moreover. While Indians make their dwellings from wattles and brush and are thus closer to the land, in their later years, as Austin reports, they also go blind regularly from smoke. Settlement presupposes either virgin territory or displacement of earlier occupants.

Should white sheepmen (in *The Flock*) have priority over white tourists in Yosemite National Park? *The Ford* indicts improper use of resources—dangerous oil pumping, monopolizing of water, without which use of the land is impossible.

A further factor in Austin's current fame is her concern for American Indians' welfare. This concern, sincere, but which hostile critics consider imperialistic, reflects romantic primitivism; it suited her expansive, poetic, indeed spiritual sense of nature. It is an aspect of her democratic idealism, generally and rightly emphasized by critics; it may have contributed to her eschewing Modernism and its elitist poetics. Among native tribes she discovered a kind of authenticity that contrasted with the commercial world of whites, their deviousness and untruths.

She did not merely sympathize with Native Americans; she used her pen in their behalf, as a central figure in the movement to make Indian poetry known. She wrote the introduction to George Cronyn's *The Path on the Rainbow* (1918), which she called "the first authoritative volume of aboriginal American verse," and contributed eight translations or "interpretations," stressing "a full expression of Indian thought." Whether her confidence in doing such interpretations sprang simply from her experience with native tribes in California and careful reading, or whether she believed she had insight going beyond such preparation, is unclear. Articles of hers in *The Bookman*, *Saturday Review of Literature*, and *Theatre Arts Monthly* presented native material to a national readership. She was invited by the Yale School of Drama to lecture on Indian dance and wrote the pamphlet on the topic for the New York Exposition of Indian Tribal Arts, to which Laura Adams Armer contributed the brochure on sand-paintings. She protested against laws constricting or regulating native languages, religious practices, and mores, such as hair length, and in the 1920s she campaigned against the proposed Bursum Bill (concerning land titles and Indian claims) and against Indian Commissioner Charles Burke's banning of native dances (following Alonso de Posada's seventeenth-century example). Austin's claim to authority in native matters was, however, challenged by colleagues and some Indian critics. A New Mexico acquaintance, Ina Sizer Cassidy, wrote privately that concerning Navajos and Pueblos Austin knew "very very little, at first hand." Elizabeth Shepley Sergeant asserted that Austin "seemed to work more through intuition than through factual knowledge."[5]

Additionally, Austin was a feminist, according to the standards of her day; she is sometimes viewed as ground-breaking. Denying appeals to tradition, she took publicly a reformer's stand on matters such as women's (especially wives') condition and rights in matters of suffrage, birth control, labor regulations, and sexual freedom. An anecdote related in her autobiography traces to her girlhood her resentment of the male prerogative to make decisions for women. She disliked soft eggs. Her request to have her egg boiled longer was rejected by her mother, who would not take the trouble, and her brother, putative head of the family. Yet, she observed, what harm would be done? To her, his decree was a clear case of arbitrary male authority, or patriarchy, to which she was loath to defer. She had a "grouch" against Jack London, she told him, and other male writers for "missing the essential feminine note of the day." As a young woman, she spoke against a group of white men, some from respected families, who were not charged with a crime after having raped two Indian schoolgirls. Her interest in women's condition continued throughout her life. Yet she would always prefer men's company to women's and wished to be like men intellectually—as she was. Peggy Pond Church even identified an "exploitive side of the masculine in Mary's own psyche, which is the enemy of the land-loving husbandman within her."[6]

Her activism is part of today's standard narrative on her, and her popularity in feminist circles (American literature scholars, women's studies departments, women's organizations) is attested by republications, anthologies, and scholarly studies. She can be compared to the older Kate Chopin, who became celebrated, read in countless classrooms, when feminist critics discovered her. Not many decades ago, however, Austin's accomplishments, and particularly her feminist vein, were obscured. In 1968 only one work, *The Land of Little Rain*, remained in print. In Ellen Moers's study *Literary Women* (1976), composed when the women's movement had already had tremendous effects on literary criticism and publishing, Austin is not mentioned even in the lengthy repertory of names or the index.[7]

Despite this near-eclipse for decades, Austin is now viewed as instrumental in overturning earlier American ideas of womanhood and society. Janis P. Stout asserted that she contributed to "American self-definition" and was central (with Willa Cather) "in the establishment of a new and regendered tradition of visual and literary ... engagement with the West." As a "feminist prophet," Austin sought, another critic stated, "to change male and female attitudes toward both the land and women—to help men get beyond attitudes of dominance ... and women change their concepts of fertility and passivity." A third admirer wrote that Austin "attempted to redefine women's nature, [as] typically inscribed in western conventions

... by altering the traditional perceptions of the Southwest desert as negative and subordinate" and rewriting "certain tropes of landscapes." "She challenged the assumptions about women's inherent weakness and incapacity to cope with the outdoors, their identification with culture rather than nature." She even wished, it is alleged, "to alter the stereotypes of women's nature by redefining the conceptualization of Nature itself." She emphasized "matrilineal creativity in women's lives"—storytelling and material skills, including devalued creative forms such as weaving, basketry, and food preparation. (These are, however, culture, not nature.) Church believed, however, that she was less interested in this human task than in being "a tongue for the wilderness."[8]

Yet Austin cannot reasonably be assimilated to today's radical feminists; she is at most a forerunner and beacon. Her outlook and positions could not have been theirs, given the social, economic, and political circumstances in which she and her contemporaries in America, married or not, carried on their lives generally. Indeed, she has occasionally been taken to task for not being much of a feminist at all. To read her works through the lens of current feminist theory, as if she had been familiar with it, is to misunderstand her time; and what she would have thought and done if alive now is only speculation. Furthermore, she was in some ways conservative; she was proud to keep house and cook, placing herself explicitly in that regard in the lineage of her grandmother and other forebears; and, as it was noted earlier, she preferred men and cultivated relationships with them. As one critic noted in assessing her account of revisiting her childhood home, she held "to a past that was familiar and to a tradition with values that should be retained." Though in the mid-1890s, she denied being a Christian, she nevertheless renewed her membership in the Methodist Church (while denouncing that denomination sometimes and rejecting its tenets).[9]

In essays, often in fiction, Austin was an outstanding stylist, honoring by words, frequently luminous, the greatness and splendor of her land. Critics who emphasize her populism and who associate high style with elitist, oppressive values must overlook the pride she took in fine writing and the importance she attributed to it. Occasionally she took ungraciously others' commendations of her style because they had the effect of under-emphasizing her fictional powers.[10]

Demonstrating the truth of the Count of Buffon's maxim that style is the very man (or woman), she put into her pages her spirit—her generosity and her superiority (not to say arrogance) alike, and what she saw as those of the desert. The afternoon is "that magical moment when the shadows begin to stir and crouch for their evening assault upon the plain, and the burnt reds and thick yellows and pale ash of the desert clear and flash into translucent flame." At a later hour, "the long valley ... filled with lilac light that changed without lessening from moment to moment. The shadows between the hills lifted slowly and shook out their delicate veils." Additionally, she turned psychological insight into crisp formulas. "With women, no matter how free the giving, there is always something to pay for it in the end, and it is easiest paid where it is owed."[11]

Additionally, Austin considered herself a thinker. Her search for authenticity, in herself and her surroundings, brings her close (despite differences) to existential thinkers such as Søren Kierkegaard, Friedrich Nietzsche, and Albert Camus. "The *felt experience of life* must ... always take precedence of [sic] the orthodoxies of science..." (Austin's italics). While this sensibility is frequent among artists, she illustrated it particularly well.[12]

For some readers, however, her achievement is diminished by her romantic transcendentalism, or "mysticism" (her term and others'), which allies her with such figures as William Wordsworth, Ralph Waldo Emerson, and Henry David Thoreau (whom she resembled by her concentration on details in nature). This mysticism, or spirituality, was connected to what she viewed as her extraordinary sensitivity and to her artistic temperament. While she did not define clearly the unifying transcendent principle with which she communicated from girlhood on, she connected it to nature, where "even stick and stone, as well as bush and weed, are discovered to be charged with an intense secret life of their own." Even weather is "the visible manifestation of the Spirit moving itself in the void." She pointed out that Muir, who knew so much about mountain storms, was devout and believed in angels. Myth was "the root and branch of man's normal intimacy with nature." Sometimes she identified spirit with a Paiute deity, Wakonda, or Friend of the Soul of Man. Yet she specified that this indwelling principle was not God. In another sweeping statement, Austin asserted, using italics, that "God *is* the experienceable quality in the Universe." Presumably, she did not intend this view as trivializing, nor mean that everything human beings "experience," whether mentally or materially, was connected to the Deity.[13]

The view is less allied to her family Protestantism (which, it was observed, she rejected in dogmatic terms, if not turn of mind) than to Roman Catholicism, mirroring the Augustinian conviction that earthly beauty is an incarnation of divine beauty, and the Thomistic belief in God's immanence. Catholics, wrote Andrew Greeley, have a religious sensibility that inclines them "to see the Holy lurking in creation." As Dana Gioia expressed it, "Nature is sacramental, shimmering with signs of sacred things. Indeed, all reality is charged with the invisible presence of God." This Catholic worldview, which extends also to a mystical sense of continuity between the living and the dead, is intrinsically communal.[14]

Among critics disturbed by Austin's accounts of extraordinary experiences was Van Wyck Brooks, a friend, who thought her mysticism both a curse and a blessing. (He called her "a lonely disappointed woman with an empress complex.") Similarly, skeptical critics challenge her credulousness about Indian medicines and her understanding of evolution; they see her vision of nature as flawed, through enthusiasm or misinformation—that is, unscientific. For that accusation, she cared nothing. She claimed to know the story of Coyote-Spirit was true because "Basket-Woman told it to me and evidently believed it." Brooks faulted her "adoration of the Indians" for her failure to "establish a real relation with the world beyond the desert."[15]

She owned herself that the effect on her mind and output of the "only intellectual life" she had for sixteen years, centered on Paiutes, was "probably more extensive than I have been able to reckon" and that it had formed the best and the worst of her style. Her claims of clairvoyance likewise may qualify her intellectual standing. She reported knowing that her mother was dead before receiving word, and had "a sense of impending disaster" the day before the great San Francisco earthquake. She was far from alone, however, in such claims; William James, whom she met there, shared her interest in diverse states of consciousness and believed in certain sorts of extrasensory perception.[16]

Austin's Background and Career: Earth Horizon

Mary Hunter Austin was born in Carlinville, Illinois, northeast of St. Louis, on 9 September 1868. Her parents were George Hunter, a Yorkshire immigrant, who had enlisted in the Union army, served in Mississippi, and contracted malaria, and Susanna Savilla Graham Hunter, of French and Scots-Irish pioneer stock. Susanna was a Methodist—duly concerned with sin (rooted in self-indulgence), with "tremendous particularity about behavior." Susanna was active in the Women's Christian Temperance Union, whose members were firm enemies of drink but in other ways surprisingly open-minded; Mary attended meetings at which women's rights were affirmed.[17]

The couple's first surviving child, James, two years older, was favored by Susanna, whose indifference, even coldness, towards Mary never abated, according to her. At no time did Susanna show the least interest in her writing, Mary claimed. Her early literary success "alarmed her mother and infuriated her brother." Two other children, Jennie and George, were born. Her father's death, when Mary was ten years old, removed a source of comfort, affection, and inspiration. Two months later Jennie died, having contracted diphtheria, perhaps from Mary, who had the disease first and, hungry for love, often embraced her sister. Austin felt guilt over the death; her mother, she wrote, cried out against God for taking Jennie. (Why not Mary?)[18]

Austin recorded that at age four or so she became aware of an inner self, autonomous, separate from the social person. She called it *I-Mary*. This powerful awareness, or alternative persona, offered protection against the world's impingement. She later complicated this auto-multiplication by the addition of "Mary-by-herself," an outcast, isolated. In fact, as Church remarked, "the rather insufferable I-Mary" was complemented by "the Mary who walks in the shadow of her mother, in yearning recollections of her father, in sullen envy of her long-dead little sister, in despair of affirmation by her brother (and perhaps the rest of the male world)." The girl appears to have been strongly connected to others by empathy. Susanna chided her for "story-telling" and falsely claiming she had witnessed particular scenes. Not surprisingly, given the time, Susanna, trying to prepare her for a normal life, was highly concerned about what people thought. She forbade her, for instance, to read John Ruskin's *Seven Lamps of Architecture*, since such reading would make her seem "queer"—or *make* her queer or disliked. (Because Mary, who had heavy features, was never viewed as pretty, it mattered that she not call attention to herself.) Thus, despite her empathy, Mary developed behavior that her mother called "not taking an interest." Church saw, however, that it could have been instead (or additionally) "an intense preoccupation with her own inner self."[19]

The same intense awareness led to Mary's first otherworldly, or mystical, experience, at age five. Standing below a walnut tree and observing a bee around wild foxgloves, she felt suddenly a powerful sense of joy, "a pulsing light of consciousness," as her sense of I-Mary strengthened. Awed, she asked herself whether God was present and concluded that He was (despite her statement elsewhere that the unifying principle she sensed was not divine). The awareness occasionally took on religious, or at least pious, feeling; she believed, sometimes at least, in efficacious prayer and had visions of Christ.[20]

Because of the organic connection between I-Mary and her autobiography, *Earth Horizon* (1932), the principal source of biographical information, it can be usefully treated here, out of chronological order. Although one-third or so is devoted to her southwestern period, the emphasis is upon her childhood and youth. The material is slanted in such a way that the artist's vocation is highlighted, along with handicaps and unhappiness—her father's death, her mother's character, the loss of her sister and the domineering voice of her brother. Church pointed out that Austin was "very much concerned about what posterity might think of her, and she worked hard to give the impression of a child who has been overwhelmed by her own grief."[21]

Research indicates that Austin glossed over information that might have made her narrative less dramatic. When she started the book (1929), Anna Burns, her mother's niece, sent details about family history that apparently Austin had never known; the material was not used. She exaggerated her surprise upon learning that the family was to leave Illinois for California; letters from her brother had made the plans clear. The chronology is often blurred, and reported conversations cannot be relied upon.[22]

At the sentence level, Austin's style is impressive and appealing. The composition is questionable, however. She alternates between two grammatical persons, first and third, the *I* voice and *she*, or "Mary" (or "I-Mary" or "Mary-by-Herself"). To overlook this two-voice narration is to miss a central feature. The elaborate multiplying of ego, crafted to portray a psyche as well as recount, and defend, a life, exaggerates the split and gives too much importance to the additional persona. Additionally, it disorients the reader, who looks for sustained identification with the subject. The switch between grammatical persons may be occasional or may recur in the same paragraph. "One day in the Palazzo Vecchio, Mary had a glimpse of a slender woman ... [Isadora Duncan]. Mary followed and lost her. I thought I would go up to Gordon Craig's apartment ... and the beautiful lady came to the door. Mary backed out...." The effect trivializes what psychological truth the division of selves, or *homo duplex*, might have.

The disappointing sales of *Earth Horizon* may reflect readers' difficulties in dealing with the double voice.[23]

With the discovery of her inner, autonomous self, Austin was at the threshold of artistic creation. After schooling in Carlinville, she attended a state normal school, where she had what is called a mental breakdown. Recovering at home, she painted and wrote poetry. She enrolled in Blackburn College to complete her degree, which she took, to others' surprise, in science (knowing she could provide her own literary education). Her knowledge of science, especially botany, served her well in her nature writing. By the time she left Blackburn, her exceptional gifts were recognized. Someone wrote in the *Blackburnian* that her poem "Oak Leaves" was "the work of a genius," soon to be recognized in the literary world. Church, interested in knowing how Austin recognized her unusual abilities, did not deny the genius but found it somewhat off-putting. What Mary called genius was, in Church's words, a force or spirit within her, which "seized upon her, shaping her to its own purposes." The realization was henceforth key to what she undertook. She believed that it would "justify condemned behaviors" and eliminate the responsibility for meeting "current standards of success." As Church comments, "It was, of course, a serious temptation to make such a claim, and Mary would walk the fine line all the rest of her life between humility toward the creative powers and the most outrageous identification of her own human ego with them."[24]

In 1888, Mary traveled with her younger brother and mother to join Jim in California, where he had staked homestead claims in his name and his mother's. They spent time in San Francisco and Los Angeles, then headed to the Tejon Pass area of Kern County (San Joaquin Valley). Mary's account of the last stage in the journey, "One Hundred Miles on Horseback," appeared in *The Blackburnian* in 1889. The homestead where they tried to make a living was near Bakersfield and the vast Tejon Ranch. Mary became acquainted with employees there and its owner, General Edward Fitzgerald Beale, the first Superintendent of Indian Affairs in California, who encouraged her to write about the region. (His portrait is traced in *The Flock*, where Austin relates how, using camels, he traced a wagon route from Ft. Smith, Arkansas, to the Colorado River—a route followed later, roughly, by the Santa Fe railroad, U.S. Route 66, and Interstate 40.)[25]

The late 1880s were extremely dry in their area; nothing was profitable. Mary collapsed after six months, perhaps from malnutrition. After she and her mother moved to Rose Station, a trading post on the Tejon Ranch, she found a teaching position not far from Bakersfield but lost it in December after failing the teachers' examination. She remained on a local dairy farm as a boarder and worked as a tutor. In May 1891, perhaps out of financial pinch, she married a University of California graduate, Stafford Wallace Austin (1860–1932), from a prominent Hawaiian family. They settled in the country, then Bakersfield. Theirs was not a happy marriage. Though not shiftless, Wallace appears to have been impractical, restless; he speculated in land and incurred debt; he moved from one property, one town to another, turning down reasonable prospects (such as a school principalship) in favor of more appealing but less assured positions. The couple was evicted once from its lodgings, and Mary had to cook and sew to pay for room and board. "He had no capacity for concerted action, for coöperation."[26]

Long determined to write, she set to making money thereby. In 1892 her story, "Mother of Felipe," a "slender little sketch," was published in *Overland Monthly*. While sentimental (though not maudlin), it is a persuasive story. Wallace and Mary spent time in San Francisco that year; she met various writers during that visit and subsequently. They left then for Lone Pine (Inyo County) in the Owens Valley, east of the High Sierras, below Mt. Whitney—the territory the Shoshone called "The Country of Lost Borders." Wallace and his brother Frank undertook a short-lived project to provide river water to farmers.[27]

In late October that year, Ruth, the Austins' daughter, was born in Bakersfield, at Mary's mother's house, after an agonizing delivery (perhaps damaging to the child), followed by inadequate post-delivery care. Ruth was significantly abnormal—slow in development, particularly in speech, and uncontrollable. The word *autistic* has been used for her. Mary blamed her husband for not having revealed that there were cases of retardation in his family. Some self-reproach can be detected, also; during her pregnancy Mary had worked very hard, perhaps excessively. She was criticized by neighbors for her apparent maternal neglect. Ruth was cared for briefly by Austin's mother, then by other families; ultimately she was institutionalized. She died in 1918, of influenza, according to Austin. Expressions of maternal feeling and tenderness toward children are frequently visible in her writing—"The Walking Woman," for instance.[28]

Albeit with difficulty, given Ruth's condition and Wallace's preference for isolated places, Austin managed to pursue her literary career. Wallace was not entirely unsupportive, but his impracticality raised barriers and he was often withdrawn. Her mother, from whom she became estranged, died in 1896. Mary taught in various locations, sometimes with Wallace, more frequently apart (in Bishop, for instance, in 1895–96). In 1899 she went to Los Angeles, purportedly to consult doctors for Ruth; she also wished to find employment (as she did). She met Charles Lummis, an editor and sometime photographer, autodidact ethnologist and archaeologist, Indian rights advocate, and historic preservationist, who earlier had lived and worked in New Mexico. (He took credit for giving the term *Southwest* to the area treated in this book.) At his house Austin met other writers, and he supported her literary endeavors, if somewhat condescendingly. In his magazine *Out West* he published stories, poems, and sketches of hers, dealing with sheepherders, miners and their camps, and small towns. Among them is the long story "The Truscott Luck," which displays Austin's narrative skills. A tale of buried treasure, recounted by an adolescent observer, whose point of view Austin handles well, it can hold its place honorably beside work of Bret Harte and Mark Twain.[29]

In 1900 Mary rejoined Wallace in Independence, in the Owens Valley, where she would remain six years. They built a house, with a separate writing refuge for her; she called it a wikiup (an American Indian shelter made of brush). Her first book, *The Land of Little Rain*, appeared in 1903; the whole decade was highly productive. She made money through articles and books and by lecturing. In 1906, leaving Wallace, she settled in Carmel, already a small colony of intellectuals and soon a magnet for other writers, including London and Lincoln Steffens, whom she had met earlier and would see in New York. She built a wikiup in Carmel likewise—in fact, a tree house.[30]

Learning in 1908 that she had breast cancer, Austin traveled to Rome. From Cardinal Rafael Merry del Val and Mother Veronica of the Blue Nuns, she received instruction in prayer, which became her means of escaping pain. She termed this method "the studied attitude of the spirit in transaction with the creative attitude working from within." She credited this therapy and what she called the healing power of beauty with the disappearance of her cancer. She proceeded to England, where, in London, she met literary figures such as H.G. Wells, William Butler Yeats, Joseph Conrad, and George Bernard Shaw. She went to London again in 1921 to promote *The Trail Book*.[31]

In 1910, Austin departed for New York. From there, she went back and forth to Carmel. She became well known in Manhattan literary circles, including the salon of Mabel Dodge (later Luhan), and moved among suffragists. Finally Wallace, having charged Mary with desertion, obtained a divorce (1914). She was honored in 1922 by a dinner at the National Arts Club. Then and later she had numerous male friends; two (Steffens and the botanist Daniel T. MacDougal) have been identified as lovers. Church believed that Austin had "betrayed the land" by her abandon of "primal experience" for urban literary life. Moreover, Church found her interpretations ego-centered and noted that, despite her feminist pronouncements, "her many books are about men and their relation to the land rather than about women."[32]

Austin's first visit to Santa Fe, in 1918, was prompted by her study of Indian lore and history. She was attracted by the aesthetic sense she found everywhere around her. In 1924, tired of Carmel and New York, where she suffered from "boredom," she settled in the New Mexican capital; by the next year her "Casa Querida" was finished. It is possible that she met Carl Jung, whom she cites from time to time; he visited Taos Pueblo (1925). She assessed well her achievements and her needs: "New York had failed to engage the exigent interests of my time.... It lacked freshness, air, and light.... I liked the feel of roots, of ordered growth and progression, continuity, all of which I found in the Southwest.... I knew that my work, which was essentially of the West, ... had a permanent hold on the future."[33]

While writing and publishing energetically in her new home, Austin participated in local artistic and cultural undertakings. An early undertaking was to organize, with help, a community theater. Unconcerned, apparently, with the original aristocratic basis of New Mexican hacienda society (by land grants), she founded, with Frank Applegate, the Spanish Colonial Arts Society (1925) and thus helped protect the continuing traditions of *santos* (saints' images sculpted or painted on wood in characteristic styles) and *carretas de la muerte* (carts with sculpted dead). She rightly credited the Spaniards for their contributions to New Mexico culture: domestic animals, religion, architecture, furniture, and various arts. She was instrumental in arranging for preservationists to purchase the private chapel, built by the Chávez family, at Chimayó (now administered by the Santa Fe archdiocese). "The Spanish-speaking group here is emerging after a long foggy period of Americanization," she wrote (1930). Similarly, she helped develop the Pueblo Pottery Fund, soon known as the Indian Arts Fund. She herself painted; Nell Norris reported seeing her work years later in a New Mexico gallery and pronounced it quite good.[34]

Austin had long been interested in her niece, Mary Hunter, Jim's daughter, and had disagreed with her brother George, the girl's guardian, about her welfare. The two Marys did not always have smooth dealings, but ultimately Austin left her niece a bequest. In the 1920s Mary Hunter went to New Mexico to teach. A school friend of Agnes de Mille, she assisted the dancer when she performed in Santa Fe, and Austin offered wise words to Agnes: "You must let the rhythm of the American earth come through what you do."[35]

Often unwell (with high blood pressure and other ills), Austin died in Santa Fe in 1934, after a heart attack the previous year. Her ashes are sealed in a sarcophagus of native stone atop Picacho Peak.

The Land of Little Rain, Lost Borders *and Other Early Works, 1903–1909*

The Land of Little Rain consists of narrative and poetic essays composed after Austin's return to Owens Valley. Some had appeared in the *Atlantic Monthly*. Critics state generally that they constitute her best work. The book was well illustrated. A second printing came out in 1904, the year following publication. It is now deemed a classic of literary environmentalism. Writing the essays was a consolidation and maturation of her vision, by which she became, poetically speaking, almost one with her desert surroundings. As Melody Graulich observed, "The desert landscape, the western storytellers and drifters, and the Indians helped her develop her voice, her way of seeing, and her art." Often praised as a visionary map for the future, the book concerns, according to Cynthia Taylor, "the possibility for responsible civilized life in the West and the role that women and native people must play in that life." But, as Krista Comer noted, "Austin's is not a nationalist project with great relevance to a postindustrial capitalist economy, one in which limited development is generally a moot question and in which computer literacy is a skill necessary to the most basic service job."[36]

In *The Land of Little Rain*, Austin speaks in her own person; everything is filtered through her consciousness. The style is bold, even confrontational, sometimes arch, yet inviting, as if soliciting suitable readers. Edward Abbey called it "poetical, elliptical, somewhat periphrastical," but found it seductive. Another commentator spoke of "mystical nature sketches in the Emersonian tradition." In the preface Austin tells readers that they may "reach my country and find or not find, according as it lieth in you, much that is set down here.... The earth is no wanton to give up all her best to every comer.... I am in no mind to direct you to delectable places toward which you will hold yourself less tenderly than I." She boasts of keeping faith with the land, annexing "to my own estate a very great territory to which none has a surer title." Her lesson is that it cannot be tamed by the usual methods—cannot be tamed at all, but, if respected, is able to sustain life. That is, environment dictates existence. All Austin's southwestern writing displays this strain of deterministic realism, or Naturalism, somewhat antithetical to the romantic foundation of the whole.[37]

Thus challenged at the outset, readers either abandon the adventure or, being carried where the author wants, ultimately to understanding, allow her to describe the land at will, in factual and human terms. Anthropomorphic and animal imagery is omnipresent. It does not constitute exploitation or delusion; anthropomorphism is the bent of the mind, indicating adaptation and symbiosis. "Desert is a loose term to indicate land that supports no man; whether the land can be bitted and broken to that purpose is not proven." "Mesa trails were meant to be traveled on horseback.... A foot-pace carries one too slowly past the units in a decorative scheme that is on a scale with the country round for bigness. It takes days' journeys to give a note of variety." Soils, dust, air, dunes and slopes, playas and cañons (as Austin writes), coyotes, lizards, rabbits, hawks, owls, shrubs, flowers, and trees are evoked by carefully-chosen details (such as the silky hairs of certain plants). The pull of the wilderness, its "lotus charm," resembling love, exorcizes resolution to leave. Whatever readers on the other side of the nation had imagined the California desert to be—assuming they gave it any thought—was surely dead letter compared to this living, palpitating, seductive, yet reticent, even diffident system of mineral, vegetable, and animal existence. It constituted the American exotic, "an uncivilized, even savage frontier"—strikingly different, yet connected to their own nation.[38]

Austin excels at discerning movement and vitality in what appears static or dying. Of quail, she describes "that peculiar melting motion ... twittering, shoving, and shouldering." On the water trails "they splatter into the shallows, drink daintily, shake out small showers from their perfect coats, and melt again into the scrub, preening and pranking, with soft contented noises." Water is highlighted throughout. Prehistoric pictographs on black rock indicate a spring; a Shoshone circle of stones surrounds parallel lines between which an arrow would be placed, pointing to the precious element. In many desert places potable water lies below the surface; Austin says that those who venture there must know how to look for it.[39]

The economy of desert nature is noted time and again. Scavengers have their role; in most seasons, the landscape is clean. Alas, one animal discards trash that cannot be utilized by others. "It takes man to leave unsightly scars on the face of the earth." "There is no scavenger that eats tin cans, and no wild thing leaves a like disfigurement on the forest floor." Littering is, fortunately, the work of few. But human presence of any sort is noticeable. Even abandoned Paiute campoodies (villages) look ugly, though they are made of brush. At best, human beings do not improve things. The owner of a field near Austin's wikiup expects to make a fortune by dividing it into lots; "but though the field may serve a good turn in those days, it will hardly be happier. No, certainly not happier."[40]

Among human inhabitants of the desert are an old miner, who belongs to the land nearly as much as animals do, and a Shoshone medicine man who remains devoted to his tribe, though he has spent most of his life among Paiutes. According to custom, he is executed when, for the third time, he is unable to cure those struck by disease. Austin depicts also a mining town, Jimville, which lives by a morality (if it can be called that) built entirely on honor, though of a rough, western sort.

The Basket Woman: A Book of Indian Tales for Children, first published in 1904, is suited chiefly to young readers but can be appreciated by adults. The collection has a clear pedagogical purpose, though the meaning of a story need not, Austin argues, be apparent immediately; myth is "a living tissue, which will not bear too much handling," and children are to discover its import slowly. A preface to the school edition (1910) describes three rough categories of material, all mythic by her definition: direct transcriptions from Indian lore; "myths" suggested by her experience among the Paiutes; and "the stuff from which hero myths are made." It is clear that, for her, borrowing of Native American material (here and elsewhere) does not constitute misappropriation. She contends that children are naturally drawn to myths and are myth-makers themselves, like what she terms (using terminology of the day) "the primitive mind."[41]

The tales display a child-like, anthropomorphic and pantheistic vision, which sees spirit in nature—coyotes, rabbits, streams, flowers, trees, as in "The Sugar Pine" (for which "The Streets of the Mountains" in *The Land of Little Rain* affords background). Thought, resolve, even language are the privilege of natural objects; though they may err, nature's funda-

A Shoshone Encampment. From *A Book of Famous Travels* (Boston: Hall and Locke, 1901).

mental wisdom prevails. The eponymous basket weaver—based on Seyavi, a Paiute neighbor, present also in *The Land of Little Rain*—sees everything in rainbow hues and discerns, under a coyote's hide, a man. "The Fire Bringer," in which an Indian boy and a coyote collaborate to steal fire from the volcano-like "Burning Mountain," appeals by its animal mythology as well as explanation of how fire was obtained. Contrasted with native tales are the historical references to conflicts between Paiutes and Shoshones, then Paiutes and settlers.

Certain stories, among the best, emphasize whites, the ultimate audience. Austin introduces Basket Woman by showing how a homesteader's small son learns to trust her and appreciate her tales. Friendship between a white youth and an Indian his age flourishes but brings grief to the Indian—who is, however, proud of having kept a vow ("Mahala Joe"). "The Christmas Tree" features a white boy from the forest who, after making friends with a tree, is sent to school in town, goes to church, and learns the Christian message; his joy at Christmastime is enriched by the presence of his beloved tree, now turned into a symbol.

The finest story, "The Golden Fortune," which concerns a solitary miner and the theme of atonement, can be fully appreciated only by adults, despite its inclusion in a book for children (who would respond well, perhaps, to animal elements and depiction of snow). Having failed his fellow man by turning away a stranger (although the skies bespoke heavy snow to come), the miner regrets his error (symbolized by his failing lode) and seeks to atone for it. Years later, he finds mountain sheep struggling in a huge snowdrift over a dark lake. He is able to rescue the old wether, too feeble to extricate himself. Until the beast can continue alone, the miner "half carried the sheep and was half borne up by the spread of the great horns." Falling in the snow and dying, he has a vision of being led by a stranger's voice to his cabin and lode, again resplendent with gold. The emblematic ram refers back to *The Land of Little Rain*, where Austin similarly describes sheep floundering in rifts of loose, shifty snow, and recounts how a Pocket Hunter (miner), lost in a blizzard, takes shelter under bent-over cedars along with sheep, whose heat preserves him from freezing.[42]

Austin's first novel, *Isidro* (1905), a rambling, melodramatic pot-boiler marked by lyrical description, appeared serially in the *Atlantic Monthly*. The book publishers recognized its appeal; the first press run was her largest. It shows how the writer, like her nineteenth-century predecessors, still believed in the historical novel, and thus in history. To underline, presumably, the historical period (shortly after 1823, when a republic was declared in Mexico), she used a somewhat precious style and diction (*forsooth*, for instance). The California desert, mountains, and mission towns furnish the setting. The tale features such romantic staples as parricide, murder, a death-bed confession, a foundling, disguise (a girl in boy's garments), dramatic disclosure or *coup de théâtre*, treasure, kidnapping, and solemn vows, combined with picturesque local color—sheepherding, mission bells, knives and riatas (replacing swords and pistols). Women's concerns are present—for instance, the silliness of skirts and side-saddles, the distaste and burden of a paternally-imposed marriage—but without feminist rhetoric. Except for peripheral questions of Indian welfare and rights, talk of liberty, and the contest between the Church and the republic, the work has few reforming elements and shows little influence of Naturalism. Nor does it resemble the modern psychological novel; it has more in common with Sir Walter Scott's and Victor Hugo's popular novels.[43]

Susan Goodman and Carl Dawson identify in *Isidro* "titillating scenes of homosexual embraces, miscegenation, and near rape." This response reflects the present cultural context in which they are writing. The goodbye scenes between Isidro and Jacinta, a girl who is disguised (for Isidro and readers) as a boy, are unremarkable, titillating only to those primed now to see them as homoerotic. Such disguises—not true cross-dressing—were commonplace in Romantic fiction. The near-rape was similarly a common plot device. However objectionable might have been to some readers a *mésalliance*, involving caste as much as race, between a Spanish upper-class girl and a mestizo, mixed-blood unions involving Indians and lower-class whites are mentioned in a matter-of-fact way, without concern for miscegenation. The term, coined in reference to black-white unions, does not fit well historically, anyhow.[44]

In a dramatic forest fire, Isidro and Jacinta, now his wife, run for safety, along with Indians, beside frightened animals. In the panic and disorder, Jacinta is brushed by a stag, onto whose body her companions succeed in securing her even as he flees; she is thereby saved. Creatures not burnt or trampled in flight reach a stream with deep pools; even there they feel the effects of the conflagration but survive. On the bank the next day, before departing, Jacinta "waded out to the buck and put her arms around his neck.... She laid her cheek to his throat and blessed him, signing the cross on his shoulders." Here the Christian symbolism is explicit, indicating suffering and redemption, like the medieval prototype (sometimes standing for Christ)—an entirely different religious dimension from Austin's vague transcendental pantheism elsewhere.[45]

The Flock (1906), a long essay about sheepherding, is part textbook (history, animal husbandry), part romance, at once technical and lyrical. On a western bookshelf it is a forerunner to Winifred Kupper's *The Golden Hoof* (1945), a history and description of sheep ranching in New Mexico and Texas. Austin's book is based on her close observation in the Owens and San Joaquin valleys. Understanding certain consequences of land misuse, she proposes remedies. Throughout, she displays her admiration for labor—essential, of course, for survival, but even more, the means by which men are made. She has sympathy for sheepherders, dogs, sheep; her heart is with them more than with the authorities in Yosemite National

Park and particularly what she calls "silly tourists." "The sheepmen were not alone in esteeming the segregation of the Park for the use of a few beauty-loving folk, as against its natural use as pasture, rather a silly performance."[46]

The phrase "natural use as pasture" shows how Austin viewed nature (a meadow and herded, domesticated sheep, in this instance) as being legitimate material for human use. What she meant by "silly performance" cannot be established with certainty, though her arrogance may have come into play when she observed tourists or reflected on the effects of their presence. Tourism had increased significantly from the time when the park was established and developed in the nineteenth century. In any case, she had known and sympathized with sheepmen, and she was clearly bothered by human interference in nature that was directed toward what she viewed as frivolous or greedy ends.[47]

The style of *The Flock* is somewhat affected and the diction occasionally obsolete, presumably to suggest earlier periods and unusual uses. Poetic expression is the norm, as in this description of late-spring twilight, with its anthropomorphic and oxymoronic perceptions: "Night begins close along the ground, as if it laired by day in the shadows of the rabbit-brush or suspired sleepily from thick, secret sloughs.... All the effort of nature seems to withdraw attention from its adumbration to direct it toward the ineffably pure vault of blueness on which the clear obscurity that shores the rim of the world encroaches late or not at all." Describing the Long Trail, along which sheep go northward, hundreds of miles, to summer pasture, Austin writes, again in a poetic vein (with alliteration): "Conceive the cimeter blade of the Sierra curving to the slow oval of the valley, dividing the rains, clouds herding about its summits and flocks along its flanks, their approaches ordered by the extension and recession of its snows." The first metaphor introduces an exotic note, appropriate, as was noted, to the California desert; the second underlines the principal theme of the book.[48]

Lost Borders (1909), building on earlier success, is set in the Owens Valley, where Austin says "the boundary of soul and sense is as faint as a trail in a sand-storm." The book is mostly narrative, its tales, whether invented or drawn from life, by turns tender, dramatic, and psychologically keen. The first-person narration is provided by the author-in the text, chiefly an observer or reporter, though occasionally intervening; and Austin reveals a good deal of herself. Various recurring names tie the book to *The Land of Little Rain*, reinforcing the impression of a particular, dynamic desert world. She describes craters, mountains, valleys, "the coil of a huge and senseless monotony; straight, white, blinding alkali flats, forsaken mesas; skimpy shrubs … starved knees of hills … black clots of pines." The desert is unmovable, yet nonetheless appealing; were it a woman, it would, paradoxically, be abundant: curved and ample, with masses of tawny hair, "full-lipped like a sphinx." The emphasis is on native or almost-native inhabitants—a pronghorn, coyotes, teamsters, homesteaders, miners (and a jinxed mine), drifters, treasure hunters, herders (one wears sheepskin, with leaves in his hair), squaw men, and others "who love [the desert] past all reasonableness … neglect their families because of the pulse and beat of a life laid bare to its thews and sinews."[49]

To what degree the volume, like *The Land of Little Rain*, provides a "visionary roadmap" or blueprint for reform, as certain commentators have asserted, is difficult to assess. There is no explicit proposal. The treatment of women and Indians is realistic, without moralizing, and the mood is deterministic. Indian women appear but remain "in the blanket." Catameneda's love for a white youth, whom she protects in a sandstorm, and her ultimate sacrifice for him of food and water are the work of love, not conditioned and resentful submission. When a miner's wife finds she is better off without him, the discovery is expressed simply, without being a call to rebellion against norms. The abandoned Indian girl in "The Ploughed Lands" resembles victims imagined by Thomas Hardy and other pessimists; the seduced woman in "The Fakir" (a superb psychological study) is an Emma Bovary of the desert. An Englishman's decision not to take home his half-Indian child is less an indictment than a psychological and social study (with recognition that the girl is much better off with her mother). The story of a tainted woman desperate to place her child with a respectable couple is chiefly melodramatic. "Love of mastery," which leads men to pursue wild beasts, is depicted but without explicit blame. The double standard by which fallen women are viewed as "bad blood," whereas a man who accepts their services can nevertheless marry honorably, comes closest to appealing for justice. In short, reforms are suggested subtly, if at all, though today's readers, with decades of social and sexual criticism behind them, may easily read into the stories a reforming intention.[50]

"The Woman at the Eighteen-Mile" is the most modern story in the volume, with foregrounded manipulation of narrative, as in metafiction, and drama mostly implied. The facts are filtered through the narrating consciousness of a quasi-author, who skillfully introduces suspenseful hesitations, postponements, gaps, and multiple sources with which she purportedly struggled (as Austin perhaps did actually) in her efforts to learn the truth. What the "Eighteen-Mile Woman" knew about a certain Lang, whose body was found at Dead Man's Spring and who was connected to a man she knew well (and loved secretly), is ultimately known to the narrator but never disclosed to readers. Nor are they informed why this man told the woman, enigmatically, as he was returning east to his family, that he had *missed her* during the two years they worked together. Finally, it is not indicated why the narrator promised not to reveal Lang's story. The fact-collecting, gaps, enigmas, and reticence overshadow the data and become the chief narrative line. Only the concluding authorial commentary strikes a nineteenth-century note.

The Ford, The Trail Book *and Other Middle-Period Writings, 1911–1923*

The first version of Austin's play *The Arrow-Maker* was written in "the aboriginal type of free measures." What appeared in print (1911) was "what was left of it after a New York production" (at the New Theater in February). The play was very important to the author. It focused on a Paiute *chisera* (medicine woman) whom she had known and who appears in *The Flock*, where she successfully brings rain. Austin's purpose, she said, was to awaken the public to the "enormous and stupid waste" of women's talents. Both text and production—directed by Red-Eagle, of Winnebago and Paiute parentage—were based on research (names, costumes, dances, scenery, and songs). Although many critics scoffed at the stage version, the New York *Times* called it a "splendid public display" but noted that the Indians seemed very sophisticated. Edmond Gosse, the distinguished British critic, read the play and liked it. Clearly, the appeal of the American exotic was strong (other Indian plays had preceded Austin's).[51]

The drama is, however, astonishingly bad. The premises are, as Michael Castro put it, preposterous. The topic of women's rights does not fit well into a play concerning Indians. Worse is the diction. Since true Indian speech could not be utilized, the judicious choice, to avoid distraction, would have been unexceptional English, fitting the expected audience; only bits of flavoring from the local tongue and expressions should have been added. Instead, Austin used archaisms and obsolete language. As T. M. Pearce remarked, the natives talk like Old Testament prophets and "speak in the stentorian diction of Cooper and Longfellow." Rather than contributing to the theatrical illusion, these features call attention to themselves and the shortcomings of the play. A historical drama cannot be successful if the language is alienating; at best, it is a tour de force. The whole is stilted and seems contrived, especially when read against Armer's works featuring Indians.[52]

The Ford (1917), about oil and water interests—also labor unions and women's rights—is a lengthy social novel in the Naturalist vein of Frank Norris and Upton Sinclair. Graulich terms it a "revolutionary novel"— that is, political. It has considerable historical interest and deserves consideration because of its connection to environmentalism and concern with the economic gap between the prosperous and those barely eking out their living. The novel has not aged well, however. It illustrates what time may do to a thesis novel, even when its reasoning remains sound; extrapolation of the thesis from earlier circumstances to the present is usually unsatisfactory. Moreover, fiction that depends on debates, no matter how pressing the issues, will not be appealing later. While the petroleum industry and its practices remain controversial, Austin's depiction of ranchers' and farmers' protests against risky oil exploration are dated, too isolated and small-scale to seem pertinent. As frequent droughts in the U.S. indicate, water similarly remains a vital topic; but past disputes over water rights and usage do not correspond in scale or type to today's water battles. The discussions about women's nature and their rights (including divorce) present little of interest, since the fundamental questions have been set out ad nauseam. In short, like countless others, Austin fails at making out of political, class, sexual, and economic struggles persuasive and enduring human drama. It is unfortunate that her fine style in descriptive passages cannot redeem the rest. If, as Eudora Welty wrote, "morality as shown through human relationships is the whole heart of fiction," nonetheless, "the zeal to reform, which quite properly inspires the editorial, has never done fiction much good." Though it appeared almost ninety years later, and thus in greatly changed circumstances, Joan Didion's *Where I Was From* (2003) offers, more successfully, some of the same criticism of the cooperation between government, furnishing the infrastructure, and large private businesses that created what was essentially a subsidized monopolization of the state, leaving small landowners and businessmen as pawns.[53]

For the setting, Austin created a fictional valley, based on Kern and Inyo counties, "a hard country for women." Numerous episodes take place in San Francisco, the center of attempts to pre-empt valley water. The book partakes of the Bildungsroman, since the third-person omniscient narration includes long scenes involving and observed by a boy, Kenneth Brent, who comes from a family of sheepmen. The language has what Ambrose Bierce called a "tang of archaism."[54]

Powerful, greedy corporate interests are indicted; but those who cannot or will not defend their rights and effectively succumb are likewise accused, defeated in part "by forces within themselves." In Jean-Paul Sartre's phrase, they are half victims, half accomplices, stubbornly independent or as grasping as those who exploit them. "They had only to stick together"; but "the solitary, rural habit which admitted them to a community of beguilement could not lift them to a community of enterprise." The underhanded urban interests are represented initially by a man of "sinister intelligence," dressed in black, who boasts about "fortunes made in a day" and peddles not only mortgage pay-outs but opportunities to invest in oil stocks for recently-opened California fields. Another figure, a local landholder with vast properties, plays his game carefully, conspiring to increase his water rights so that he can demand a high price. Small-scale interests are voiced by the Brents, suffering, like their neighbors, in drought. Austin uses irony to make her point: the night after Brent has sold his spread to city interests, great, healing rains fall. "What is called Business consists largely in taking things away from other people," he tells Kenneth in a pithy and pertinent formula. That, grown up, Kenneth escapes city corruption and ultimately finds a life suited for him—the bride he needs and the soil he loves—is satisfying to readers but does not resolve the larger struggles.[55]

In *The Trail Book* (1918), a sequence of connected "prehistoric trail stories" for children, Austin demanded and gave an example of a new national story for America, a far-sighted vision intended to challenge prevailing narratives and suppositions. The collection can stand as "an alternative national history" or "multi-cultural history of North America," in Graulich's terms; it thus answers decades before the fact complaints from numerous quarters about the "white man's history" that prevailed until recently. The tales sketch pre-Columbian cultures and encounters between natives and new immigrants, or "Pale Faces." The point of departure is the Museum of Natural History in New York, where Austin said she did research. Two visiting children (the narratees, to whom the stories are told) watch as Indians and talking animals, such as Road-Runner, come alive and recount, even relive, their adventures, as in "What the Buffalo

Chief Told." Central figures, motifs, and plots—the coyote, migration, the initiation test, fraternity with animals—are familiar to readers of southwestern anthropology and folklore. Commerce among tribes, development of trails, writing, as at El Morro ("Inscription Rock" or "Signature Rock," in western New Mexico) attest to the industry of the pre–Columbians.[56]

The tales make explicit Austin's far-sighted conviction, anticipating later anthropologists' and historians' positions, that marginal cultures and their products, including oral lore, warrant as much attention in pedagogy as cultures deemed higher (ancient Mediterranean, European, American-European)—indeed, deserve *more* attention, to compensate for oversight. She urged her contemporaries to put away dominant inherited views and forms—"the faded hues of European myth"—in favor of authentic, local ones. (She made the same argument when introducing *The Path on the Rainbow*.) Thus, for instance, she has a native princess relate and comment on the visit of Hernando de Soto and his "Iron Shirts." "It was always an unhappy ending for the Indians."[57]

Austin's book on Indian poetry, *American Rhythm* (1923), containing a long essay and translations (called "re-expressions"), was another major attempt on her part to call attention to underrated, even unknown, native materials. Like various other books of hers, it aspires to make, or identify, art coming from the soil. She bristled when the collection was misunderstood or ignored. Herbert Spinden, writing in 1933, did not include her among the four great recorders of American Indian poetry. While only specialists can assess her contribution properly, even non-specialists may question her analysis of sound and rhythm for children, Indians, and the "Dawn Mind" as well as her historical suppositions about lyric verse, which she traces to magic of the Stone Age. Her disparaging of English verse forms as being derived and, for American speakers, artificial is unconvincing. At best her study reveals considerable speculation about essential connections between land and poetry. Her whole thesis—that "relationships must necessarily exist between aboriginal and later American forms"—is dubious. Bynner wrote, "Your main error seems to be in trying to connect what you call the American rhythm with the English rhythm of your translations of an original Indian rhythm. You could never convince me that your rhythms in translations have anything to do with the American soil in the sense that the original Indian rhythm belongs to it."[58]

Bynner's observations, albeit a bit confusing, are basically sound. Esther Stineman, pointing out Austin's breezy attitude toward others' research even as she considered herself "a creative thinker" and an ethnographer, concludes that Austin relied chiefly on herself. "In her view she had gone beyond scientific knowledge" to present fresh insight into the origins of poetry. Noreen Groover Lape noted that trained anthropologists among Austin's contemporaries often criticized her methodology, accusing her of borrowing information without attribution, disregarding facts, and ignoring methods of collecting. "She opts for intellectual and emotional identification with Indians over the more appropriate role of 'authority.'" Yet Austin did attempt to become informed, through reading and consultation with researchers, and she insisted once that she was the only person doing translations from Indian material.[59]

The Land of Journeys' Ending *and Other Late Works, 1927–1934*

Though published more than twenty years after *The Land of Little Rain*, the essays entitled *The Land of Journeys' Ending* (1924), one of Austin's finest books, complement the earlier volume. As a critic noted, she wisely avoided "ephemera—politics, economics, personalities." Lummis wrote a review "so scurrilous that the editor of the *Saturday Review* refused to print it." (According to Austin, he also sent her an insulting letter when she originally settled in New Mexico. Earlier, he had criticized her mistakes in Spanish and shaky facts.) She attributed his bile to resentment of her meddling in what he considered his territory. Lawrence Powell, in contrast, praised the work as a pinnacle, the "ripest, richest book of all she wrote," embodying best "the essences of the region whose heartland is Arizona and New Mexico."[60]

The land in question lies westward from the upper Rio Grande (including its forests) past the Colorado River and southward. As a kind of practical southern limit, Austin mentions the fields of igneous rock called Jornada del Muerto, southeast of Socorro, New Mexico, and thus introduces subtly the theme of death, adumbrated by the title likewise. Unlike the Owens Valley, she knew the area chiefly by automobile journeys, including a long tour with MacDougal and Ina and Gerald Cassidy of Santa Fe. There are, however, reflections of hiking also.

The collection is varied, using past and present tense: historical pieces that review what is known of the original settlement by Amerindians; descriptions of geological features, flora, and fauna; information on contemporary peoples. Summaries of remote pre–Columbian history, such as the gradual movement of tribes from plateaus to lower plains and valleys, are less detailed than Marriott's, but, like hers, are based on anthropologists' and historians' works and their sources. Like Marriott later, Austin brings information together for non-specialist readers, in a lively style and with her own keen appreciation.

Figures such as Álvar Núñez Cabeza de Vaca, Francisco Vázquez de Coronado, Juan de Oñate, Eusebio Kino, and Zebulon Pike appear, with their journeys traced. Information is provided on the Anasazis, particularly at Chaco Canyon; Apaches; Hopis; Papagos; Rio Grande Pueblos; Zunis; and Spanish villages. Anticipating or sharing the conviction of other Southwesterners, Austin believed that "more streams of human energy came to rest here than anywhere else" within the United States, "because men felt here the nameless content of the creative spirit in the presence of its proper instrument."[61]

The approach in *The Land of Journeys' Ending* is at once poetic and matter-of-fact, even scientific. She depicts conifers (and their cones), cactus (barrel cactus, prickly pear, cholla, and what she calls sahuaro and ocotilla), aspen and creosote bush, agave and yucca. She is concerned with use of water by desert plants and their utility to birds and small animals. She stresses the barrenness of soil between bushes and trees, "each in its inviolate circle of bare earth, bound together by not so much as the roots of grass." Studying the seasons, she observes how, when rain falls, the processes of foliation and floration "are pushed almost to explosion"; the rest of the time, life is quiescent.[62]

Always at the periphery if not forefront is the relationship between human beings and the desert world. Men modify the landscape by their presence and are modified in turn. Imagining drums "far down in the dancing-place," talking with feather-venders, watching the Fire Dance, she evokes the Anasazi of Chaco and Canyon de Chelly. She notes what vegetable matter Indians use—maguey, pollen, juniper. This leads to a vision of human instrumentality in the world as inspired by nature's material potentiality. "The plant world begins to stand to man not for itself but for ideas." The arched boughs of the juniper were, for instance, part of the idea of bow and arrow. By "the long process which leads from the thing to its idea ... the juniper got itself made into bows.... The wild grass and the tree on the mountain yearned toward and made themselves evident in man."[63]

Austin does not overlook great topographical features. One is El

Morro, difficult of access, but which she climbed; she thought she might wish to be buried there. Another is the Colorado River: its wanderings on the Colorado Plateau, Echo Cliffs, Marble Canyon, the confluence with the Little Colorado, then the "Grand Cañon," and the Virgin River. Her geological descriptions, eschewing technical terms, give a human, imaginative sense of the landscape. "Against the steady gnawing of the river, rose the land, as a log is pushed against a moving saw. Below the *entrada* of the Little Colorado, there must have been times when the land rose faster than the river could eat through the marble walls. Here the evidence of its balked fury stuns appreciation."[64]

The posthumous novella *Cactus Thorn*, composed apparently in 1927, was rejected at Houghton Mifflin, where, ostensibly, the ending was judged unconvincing. At least one present critic assumes that it was because of sexual subject matter and "the grittiness of its understanding of the gender politics of heterosexual sex." The work is a spare, well-constructed psychological study. It loses nothing by its concision, and, despite the melodramatic conclusion, the narrative control identifies a master writer. The settings are the California desert and New York, with which Dulcie and Grant Arliss are respectively identified and which constitute moral centers and poles of conflict. The story is reminiscent of earlier French and American novels in which masculine and feminine truths contest with each other "in the eternal war ... between men and women"—almost always to the woman's disadvantage. Until the last, the story is related in the third person from Arliss's point of view; his obtuseness and hypocrisy work ironically to reveal his character. Analepses (flashbacks) provide useful information; prolepses (flash-forwards), one indicating that he will never visit the desert again, foreshadow, with irony, the conclusion.[65]

Arliss has heard that "the desert lays hold on a man and never lets go." Dulcie, beautiful and independent, represents "pure incandescence of the spirit ... the lure of the desert." Her lover calls her a "rank pagan." She honors nature's economy, suitable relationships among life forms, and stewardship. She feels "Something" there. Morality is relative to the person, the situation, the place. "If I were to go against the wild things, something would happen to me." Arliss, a political orator, aspires to office on progressive, though vague, grounds; but even as he denounces exploitation of land and human beings, he uses Dulcie in male ways and discards her when she becomes a liability. Although in California the two establish a warm, understanding, fundamentally honest relationship, when he returns to the east he buries the experience. "The desert that gave had taken again."[66]

The poems gathered in *The Children Sing in the Far West* (1928), attesting to Austin's enduring concern with young people, were the fruit of four decades, she said. The desert country of California was then so new that "there were no songs about it that children could have for their own." At Lone Pine and elsewhere she undertook to provide poems for school use, some in free verse, most rhymed. Their instructional effectiveness then cannot be assessed. While, to adult readers presently, some are irritatingly (if understandably) reminiscent of nineteenth-century didactic verse, others, by their subtlety and suggestiveness, are appealing. Southwestern school children could have responded well to subjects such as wild sheep (which "God doth shepherd"), meadowlarks, pronghorns, sagebrush, saints and prayers, and the Grand Canyon. The range of topics is even wider than these samples suggest, and the Gerald Cassidy illustrations add considerable charm.[67]

Taos Pueblo, a folio album of twelve large-format photographs by Ansel Adams, "described by Mary Austin," was issued in 1930. An Afterword by Weston J. Naef quotes her: "The real mystery of creation resides in things, in the mystery of invisible energies which all our science struggles to resolve, spiritual energies which by their coalition constitute the Thing Itself." Taos (the cradle of rebellions) was, with the Zuni Pueblo, considered the most inviolate New Mexican community. Adams, who predicted later that his friend Austin would be deemed "a writer of major stature," went to New Mexico in 1927 and made his negatives in 1929–30.[68]

The album strengthens her claim as a voice for the region. She traces the history of those known originally as "Red Willow People" and connects them to the earlier pit-dwellers and cliff-dwellers of Colorado and Arizona, stressing their "essential primitiveness" and "vital pagan quality," and speaking of "this still kindling coal of the primitive hearth of society." The photographs are characterized by brilliant sunshine and deep shadow, showing commitment to both light and form. Among them is "South House, Woman Winnowing Grain," where the sole human figure stands against the multi-storied pueblo, its architectural details accented. The old church, destroyed partly in 1847, and new one, erected about 1860, are both included in the portfolio. The final image is Ranchos de Taos Church, made famous by Georgia O'Keeffe in paintings of 1929 (and photographed by Laura Gilpin in 1930 as well as Adams).[69]

Austin's text begins by describing Pueblo (or Taos) Mountain, which "stands up over Taos pueblo and Taos water comes down between the two

"Taos Pueblo National Historic Landmark, New Mexico, 1941," by Ansel Adams, NARA 519984. Dept. of the Interior, National Park Service.

house-heaps, North house and South house." The mountain, "bare topped above, and below shaggy with pines, has the crouched look of a sleeping animal, the great bull buffalo, turning his head away and hunching his shoulders." She was moved by the surrounding landscape and its " quiescent aliveness ... as if it might at any moment wake and leap." "Far out to the north, where the Taos Valley ceases to be valley without having lifted again to hill proportions, there is a feeling of the all but invisible tremor of a sleeping sea." Indian lore, including Plains and Paiute elements (such as "Brother Coyote"), remains part of Austin's vision. She notes the matriarchal formula for social patterns. "Peace and stability, these are the first fruits of Mother-rule." The Taos "Creation epic" stresses the importance of women. She describes tribal dances and other ceremonies—including those for opening of irrigation ditches—in connection with belief. Regretting that all the Rio Grande pueblos except Taos have become Mexicanized, she nevertheless quotes their "Prayer of the Rain Song," which gave her a title:

> All your people and your thoughts, come to me,
> Earth Horizon!

Starry Adventure (1931), a novel, was characterized in the *Saturday Review* as "rich in landscape and customs" and highly praised by Adams. The publisher marketed it as another jewel in the crown of a "major novelist." It attracts little attention now, bypassed in favor of other writings by Austin on women, conservation, and labor issues. It begins as a family story of considerable charm, then develops into a novel of passion and marriages. The action takes place in northern New Mexico (described appealingly); the characters are Anglos, with Hispanics at the edges. Class and color questions are posed—the snobbery of old Spanish families, Anglos' class-consciousness and disdain of anything Hispanic, the marginalization, or near-invisibility, of Indians. Austin's own experience is reflected. Luhan is satirized as Eudora Ballatin, a wealthy, arrogant bohemian who marries an impoverished Hispanic for his old name. A noteworthy compositional feature is the frequent second-person narration, by which Austin has the protagonist, Gard, address himself. This technique, alternating with third-person narration in the same paragraph, adds immediacy and invites identification with the central consciousness but is irritating and suggests psychic division, like the double-person narration of *Earth Horizon*.[70]

The novel offers a fictional counterpoint to *The Land of Journeys' Ending*, since the central character may be considered as New Mexico itself. Austin's characteristic mysticism is displayed again in her treatment of the Sangre de Cristos mountains, flowers, trees, the great starry sky, and the Spanish heritage (artistic, religious). She sees in Indian lore a mode of "investing all things with ... a mystical apprehension of unseen powers at work behind the veil of Things." Mysticism assumes a personal form in Gard's conviction that something "wonderful" will happen to him and that it is organically connected to the place he loves.[71]

Austin's collection of southwestern tales, *One-Smoke Stories* (1934), attests to her abiding interest in folklore and cultures as well as conservation. Though the publisher was skeptical about its appeal, it was praised in the New York *Times* and elsewhere. The title comes from the Indian custom of telling short, well-shaped narratives during ceremonial smoking of corn-husk cigarettes. She drew on Basque tales from California, Zuni and Pueblo tales collected by Frank Cushing and Applegate, and other sources, and worked at shaping the material into a satisfying order. There are intertextual relations among the stories and with other works of hers.

Native American lore, or what purports to be, dominates, but additional southwestern material, some realistic, is included, and there are modern notes (the Great War, for instance). Totem animals are again featured; native wisdom appears in ancient sayings and moral conclusions. The unity of the universe is stressed. "All things are one, man and the mire, the small grass and the mountain, the deer and the hunter pursuing.... Man can hurt nothing without also hurting himself."[72]

The collection includes Christian fables and tales. In accordance with the dialectic whereby the last shall be first, a poor man believes in the apparition of the Archangel Michael and asks for his blessing, whereas the archbishop and a rich man reject the evidence of their eyes and ears ("La Visita"). "White Wisdom," subtitled "The Telling of Twice-Bitten, the Gray-Eyed Ute," concerns a man believed to be a half-breed, educated as white, loving a white woman, but unaccepted by her and her family. The ironic fact, known to few, that, though reared by a Ute woman, he has no Indian blood merely underlines the force of perception and prejudice. "The wisdom of the Whites is such that even the Whites are sick with it." In this and other stories, the author's sympathy goes to assimilated natives, victims of hypocrisy and missionaries' proselytizing.[73]

Certain tales show that, though moralizing, like her mother and, presumably, other forebears, Austin was not always serious. A delightful example of humor is "The Devil in Texas," an elaboration on the traditional conceit that West Texas is not very different from hell. The Devil, visiting, is tormented by a sandstorm; his mouth is burnt by chiles; by mistake he shoves a prickly pear pad into his mouth; he is kicked by a longhorn and lands in a cactus patch. "The Bandit's Prayer," set in New Mexico, is another instance of humor, allied, in this case, to clever revenge and the fleecing of a priest.

Austin's Southwestern Legacy

Notwithstanding numerous flaws in her oeuvre, Austin's accomplishments in writing about the Southwest remain striking. Her abundant production, albeit uneven, created a vision of the desert and other natural beauties that could not be ignored, reinforced by her strong presence on the literary scene in California, New York, and Santa Fe. It will be recalled that one critic chose *The Land of Journeys' Ending*, her "ripest, richest book," as the work that represented best the writing of the region. Another asserted that while the majority of her work was in shadow, the Indian works endured. Austin obliged readers (fewer than she had hoped, though) to take note of the moral value of the desert—its seriousness as well as its beauty, its topographic and weather features, the strange symbiotic relationship its inhabitants (plants, beasts, human beings) must develop with it, its importance as a resource. The continuing appeal of her southwestern essays attests to their insights as well as the seduction of her style. Her legacy is centered there—not in her egoism, eccentricities, trances, resentments, fascination with Indians, or activism for various causes, but her expression for others of the intimacy she established with an extraordinary natural and human community.[74]

CHAPTER THREE

Willa Cather

Cather as an American Writer

As an adult, Willa Cather made her home in the east—first Pittsburgh, thereafter New York City—and circulated in the literary world there. Stephen Miller places her among those attracted by the "magnet" of New York, drawn by "Manhattanism," an undefined but recognized culture that appeals to the deracinated and those who want to live independently. (Cather was not truly deracinated, nor did she wish to be isolated—her family and friends meant a great deal to her; but she was autonomous.) Her fiction frequently involves northeastern scenes and characters (as well as Londoners and Virginians). Other novels and stories, including the most famous, are set on the Great Plains, where she lived as a girl. She was not thus principally a southwestern writer. But three works, including what is considered a masterpiece, *Death Comes for the Archbishop*, are set wholly or partly in the desert Southwest. They are sensitive depictions of the region, with fine shadings of tone and color. Cather hoped to do a non-fiction book (perhaps a rival to Mary Austin's similar work) on the Southwest, for which she would use photographs of pueblos near Española, New Mexico, and of Mesa Verde, lent to her by the president of the Denver and Rio Grande Railroad; she broached the subject with her editor at Houghton Mifflin.[1]

Current scholars are greatly indebted to the 2013 publication of Cather's *Selected Letters*. With short commentaries but without extensive annotation, the letters take up nearly 700 pages. Most of this material, from scores of archives, was known, if at all, only through summary, since in her will Cather forbade publication of her correspondence, in whole or in part. Some was deliberately destroyed, and it was long asserted that most had been burnt or otherwise disposed of, by her or her friends, notably Edith Lewis. That seems not to be the case; about 3000 letters are known to exist. The following examination of her career and publications draws on this lengthy correspondence. Recent commentaries on her southwestern writing are similarly taken into consideration.[2]

Background, Career and Interests

Wilella Cather, who went by Willie or Willa—occasionally, at her initiative, by Will—and was known later as Willa Sibert Cather, using a family name (slightly emended), was born to Charles and Mary Boak Cather on 7 December 1873, near Gore, Virginia, at the state's northernmost point. In her adulthood she felt "very deeply" that she was a Virginian. "She did not come out of Virginia for nothing," noted Eudora Welty. Bert Wyatt-Brown considered her removal from the Shenandoah Valley to the featureless plains "an erasure of personality." Cather was the eldest of seven children. She died on 24 April 1947. She subsequently altered her stated birth year, first to 1874, then to 1876. Her ancestry was Irish on the paternal side; the name may be Welsh. On the maternal side, uncles had fought for the Confederacy, and her grandfather had served in the Virginia House of Delegates. The women of her family and area were entirely proper but vigorous and did not correspond at all to the image of the fainting belles on Tidewater plantations. Her grandfather Cather raised sheep. In 1874 he and Willa's grandmother left for Nebraska, where their son George had already begun to homestead. Willa's parents then moved to the grandparents' property to oversee the sheep operations. The grandparents went back to Virginia briefly, but in 1877 returned to Nebraska to stay. In 1883, following the disastrous burning of the Virginia sheep barn, her parents likewise left for Nebraska. The first home was on the Divide, a plain between the Republican and Little Blue rivers. After eighteen months, her father took his family to Red Cloud, a division point on the Burlington and Missouri railway line, very near the Kansas border.[3]

While still in Virginia, Cather, a tomboy, spent much time outdoors, roaming the hills and streams or helping her father herd the sheep. If one takes as a self-portrait Vickie, a character in the story "Old Mrs. Harris" (the text invites such a reading), she believed she was not pretty. Her first ambition was to study medicine. She was closer in temperament to her brothers than to her younger sisters. Her dealings with her mother were sometimes unpleasant, but later Willa showed her love and devotion. Early in her girlhood Willa began developing an idiosyncratic self-identity. She cut her hair short, keeping it shingled through part of her college years, and sometimes wore mannish clothes.[4]

Her life can be called unconventional. Her closest friends were always women. More than one of these relationships was doubtless *une amitié amoureuse*. Others may well have been physically intimate. Her longest association was with Lewis, likewise from Nebraska, her companion or partner for nearly forty years, with whom, beginning in 1908, she established a household in New York City. Earlier, her close friendship with Isabelle McClung in Pittsburgh, initiated in 1899, was countenanced, reluctantly, by the girl's parents, whom she admired, especially Isabelle's father, a judge. Cather spent long periods at their house, starting in 1901, supposedly as a temporary guest but in fact living there. "No other living person cared as much about my work, through thirty-eight years," she wrote of Isabelle. James Woodress called the friendship "a great love that lasted a lifetime"; Janis P. Stout noted that it did not matter whether it was "physically lesbian, since it was, clearly, emotionally so." Isabelle's marriage in 1916 was a blow; at first Cather could not abide her husband, Jan Hambourg, a British subject of Russian Jewish extraction. But the women's friendship endured, and later Cather sailed with the couple to Europe and visited battlefields in their company. (Any anti–Semitism on Cather's part was subsequently corrected, at least somewhat, by her warm friendship with other Russian Jews, the Menuhin family, whose children, including Yehudi, were dear to her.)[5]

Cather was not interested in politics or social causes such as laborers' or women's rights, unlike many contemporaries, including her friend Elizabeth Shepley Sergeant and her near-contemporary Austin. Current admirers may praise her unconventional life but, even by earlier standards, cannot claim her legitimately as a crusader, a militant. "I became disillusioned about social workers and reformers," she wrote. She was convinced that to create literature as a means of social reform was to denature and abuse it. In her fiction she apparently did not wish to treat attachments between women, and she seemed indifferent, despite living with another woman, to what have become today's questions of gender identity and definition, though it has been observed that she often showed how men's and women's traits and roles were not so rigid as commonly assumed.[6]

Yet she was a feminist in her way, believing in women's prerogative to arrange their own lives, independently, as they saw fit, living, if they chose, in a man's world. She had what a reviewer in the Pittsburgh *Press* called (1897) "the true progressive, western spirit, that fears neither responsibility nor work ... plenty of 'grit.'" A *Century* magazine advertisement for the Women's Political Union would have had her approval: "Is marriage the highest destiny of women? Or is it achievement?... Women are refusing—and must refuse—to accept the old ideals of the relations between men and women." Early in her career, as an associate editor and columnist for the Lincoln *Courier*, she wrote about women novelists, suggesting once that women authors should take up male topics—adventure and war.[7]

Like Laura Adams Armer, what she cared about most throughout her career was art, that is, aesthetic values. "There is no God but one God and Art is his revealer." Painting, literature, and music, especially opera, were essential for her. She admired Gustave Flaubert and Guy de Maupassant, those preeminent craftsmen of fiction, but did not celebrate the decadent aestheticism characteristic of *fin-de-siècle* France. (Nor did she adopt the mode of French or American Naturalism, too harsh an outlook for her.) In 1895 she wrote that "to feel greatly is genius and to make others feel is art." She likewise appreciated John Ruskin's aesthetic morality and knew by reproduction the works of Edward Burne-Jones and Dante Gabriel Rossetti, though, seeing the originals in England, she found that their colors were unpleasant, the paintings "mouldy" or touched with a bit of mud. Two other beacons were "the Georges": George Sand and George Eliot, each of whom excelled in the male literary world and led an unconventional life—shocking and, in the case of the young Sand, very publicly so. She doubtless approved of their literary success; she may have thought of them also as models (though Sand's reversion to grandmotherly character—"la bonne dame de Nohant"—may have been disappointing).[8]

Cather matriculated at the University of Nebraska as a preparatory student when she was not yet seventeen (1890) and graduated in 1895. Shortly after her courses began, she abandoned her plan to study medicine; instead, she took up literature and resolved to be a writer. Her reading background was already substantial; her family owned sets of major English and American authors. She published essays in school and city newspapers and elsewhere and launched a career as a reviewer of plays and operas. She likewise wrote essays and poetry. *April Twilights* (1903; republished in 1923, enlarged and considerably revised), a collection of mostly youthful, derivative verse, was admired by some. Her early fiction appeared in local publications and even Boston.

In 1896 Cather moved from Nebraska to Pittsburgh, accepting a post as editor and book columnist of the *Home Monthly*, where she published her own fiction. A year later, she resigned, then took a job as drama critic on the *Pittsburgh Leader*. She also taught (Latin and English) for five years. By traveling to Red Cloud, she stayed in touch with her family. The list of her journalistic and literary activities in Pittsburgh years is remarkable. Her active social life there allowed her to develop numerous acquaintances and prepared her for life in New York, where she settled in 1906 as an editor for *McClure's Magazine*. (In her magazine work she met both Sergeant and Witter Bynner.) She traveled abroad, savoring France.

Throughout her career she would remain highly successful at placing her work in periodicals and finding book publishers; she lived chiefly on her writing income from 1912 on. It has been observed that she was "a skilled self-marketer" and clever at shaping her self-identity and persona, that of the woman artist. "In my business one has to advertise a little or drop out." She was forthright and bold, even provocative on occasion (as in elaborate dress), carrying over what was perhaps her prairie gumption into an urban and cosmopolitan literary and journalistic environment, where she held her own well. She had little diffidence and thus differed markedly from her older friend Sarah Orne Jewett and Emily Dickinson even earlier, who both maintained reserve and stayed close to their native New England. In 1922 she won a Pulitzer Prize, for *One of Ours*, concerning the Great War; that same year she left the Baptist denomination, along with her parents, to join the Episcopal

Willa Cather at the Palais du Luxembourg in Paris, August 1902. Courtesy Archives and Special Collections, University of Nebraska–Lincoln Libraries.

Church. She was awarded honorary degrees by various institutions, including the University of Nebraska and Columbia, Yale, and Princeton universities.[9]

Features of Cather's Work

Cather was always a keen and sensitive observer, and she had imagination for character and human relationships, which are "the tragic necessity of human life." She identified her ability to be interested in people, scenes, events as the source of her literary strength. She knew also the cost as well as benefits of such a close embrace of others and their experience. "As for me, I have cared too much, about people and places—cared too hard. It made me, as a writer." Her sensitivity to and concern for the disadvantaged and those on the edges of society appear often in her life and work. An instance is her emotion, as a girl, upon witnessing the return to Virginia of a former slave whom her grandmother had smuggled to the North via the Underground Railway. This incident was the inspiration for the epilogue in *Sapphira and the Slave Girl* (1940). In Nebraska, Cather was sympathetic to the plight of many immigrants—Bohemians, Swedes, Norwegians—who survived there under difficult circumstances. Her sensitivity similarly allowed her to draw refined portraits of Hispanics and Indians.[10]

Her powers of invention were not, however, tremendous; she created no broad, Balzacian human panorama. Her work depends considerably on material provided by familiar models—her own life, that of her Nebraska neighbors, others met in the Northeast and during her travels, her reading. In fact, she remained characteristically so close to her material that friends and critics recognized the models of her characters (sometimes herself). Following this pattern, though they may seem impersonal at first glance, her southwestern works turn out to be dependent in considerable part on her experiences while traveling there.

Cather did not become a Modernist—she dismissed Modernist fictional modes—or an ironist or sophisticate like Ernest Hemingway and F. Scott Fitzgerald. In fact, she cultivated the past—the old, not the new. She included explanatory passages and commentary of a sort later novelists eschewed as unneeded or violating authorial remoteness. She retained the vocabulary of nineteenth-century romantic optimism and undifferentiated spiritual feeling. Of Anton Dvorak's symphony "From the New World," the heroine in *The Song of the Lark* (1915), thinking of her childhood years, reflects on "the amazement of a new soul in a new world, a soul new and yet old, that had dreamed something despairing, something glorious, in the dark before it was born; a soul obsessed by what it did not know, under the cloud of a past it could not recall." While Cather's style may be unpretentious at times—her characters' plain, direct speech—her diction is often similar to that just illustrated, marked by nostalgia and rapture, and her lyrical prose frequently has feminine overtones. This romantic style and the expansive vision it implies served her well in writing about the Southwest.[11]

Cather created outstanding feminine characters, but her principal personae are often men. Jewett told her that when a woman wrote in a man's character it was always "something of a masquerade," but Cather demonstrated that the rule did not hold true for her strictly; yet there is something to it. She noted in 1916: "The trouble about this story is that the central figure must be a man, and that is where all women writers fall down. I get a great many bouquets about my men, but if they are good it is because I'm careful to have a woman for the central figure and to commit myself only through her. I give as much of the men as she sees and has to do with—and I can do that much with absolute authority. But I hate to try more than that." She violated this principle often, however, as in two works considered here, *The Professor's House* (1925) and *Death Comes for the Archbishop* (1927).[12]

Experiencing the Southwest

Her first visit to the Southwest (spring 1912) lasted approximately three months. Her discovery of the region was, in one commentator's words, "the principal emotional experience" of her adult life. She took the train to Winslow, Arizona, where her brother Douglass worked for the Santa Fe railway. The trip constituted a holiday from work at McClure's and a chance to consider her future. The visit affected her greatly by exposing her to different people (though she did not like many, except the Mexicans), different landscapes, and pre–Columbian history as written into the cliffs and canyons. The experience cleansed her, even changed her as an artist. "I did no writing down there, but I recovered from the conventional editorial point of view." She quoted a sentence from Honoré de Balzac: "Dans le désert ... il y a tout, et il n'y a rien.... C'est Dieu sans les hommes" [In the desert ... there is everything, and there is nothing.... It is God without men]. The desert was a human revelation. "People are the only interesting things there are in the world, but one has to come to the desert to find it out, and until you are in the desert, you never know how *un*-interesting you are yourself." Cather does not suggest that such altering experiences are mystical or even eerie—not even in *The Song of the Lark* (although the heroine is named *Thea*). Only Tom Outland, in *The Professor's House*, experiences what the author calls a "religious emotion."[13]

In Arizona Cather amassed material, such as facts about railroading, which would feed her writing. Her brother's cook, whom she liked, would serve as the model for Henry Atkins in *The Professor's House*; another acquaintance, H. L. Tooker, a brakeman who irritated her greatly at first but whom she learned subsequently to appreciate, inspired in part the characters of Rodney Blake in that novel and Ray Kennedy in *The Song of the Lark*. A young Mexican man in Winslow fascinated her; glimpses of his charm appear in the latter novel. She attended a Hopi Snake Dance, visited the Painted Desert, hiked, and camped with Douglass and a friend of his. In addition, she visited cliff dwellings in Walnut Canyon, constructed by the pre–Columbian Sinagua natives (1100–1250). This was an important moment. She had known of cliff-dwellers since she was a girl and, with her brothers, had speculated on them. She said in a 1925 interview, "When I was a little girl nothing in the world gave me such a moment as the idea of the cliff dwellers, of whole civilizations before ours linking me to the soil." On the return trip to the northeast, she stopped in Albuquerque. New Mexico was "the most beautiful country I have ever seen anywhere."[14]

In 1915, she and Lewis spent the summer in the Southwest. They traveled by train to Denver, then by narrow-gauge tracks over La Veta Pass to the southwest corner of Colorado. The Anasazi dwellings of Mesa Verde impressed her greatly. For hours they explored Cliff Palace, the most famous of the structures there. She met one of the brothers (probably Clayton) of Richard Wetherill—by then deceased. One day, while Cather and Lewis, with an inept guide, toured the difficult canyon terrain in order to reach a still-unexcavated site, they got lost; the women were stranded for several hours while the guide went to get help from the camp of Smithsonian archaeologist Dr. Jesse Walter Fewkes. Lewis later wrote that those hours were the "most rewarding of the trip" for Cather, who said she had never learned "so much in any other twenty-four hours." A few days after that ordeal she was on horseback again (she was a good rider); she wanted to return to the canyon. The two friends then went to Taos, not yet the vibrant artists' colony it would be later, but full of interest. Willa was struck by the Catholic presence everywhere. With the painter Ernest Blumenschein, she rode horseback around the countryside, visiting villages in the mountains and valleys, looking at churches, the decorations of which—frescoes, *santo*s, carvings—appealed to her greatly. In Santa Cruz Cather met Father Halterman, a Belgian priest, who shared with her information on the northern New Mexico pueblos. Cather and Lewis then went to Santa Fe and the surrounding area, then visited Isleta Pueblo, near Albuquerque. The two friends returned to Santa Fe and Taos in summer 2016. She wrote to her brother Roscoe: "Taos is a beautiful place ... forty dreadful miles across canyons from the railroad; all Mexicans, no whites, wonderful Indian pueblo near the Spanish town."[15]

Another significant visit to the Southwest, again with Edith, took place in 1925. Willa was at work on the proofs of *The Professor's House*. They stayed on a guest ranch on the Rio Grande, then at in the "Pink House" at "Los Gallos," the house of Mabel Dodge Luhan in Taos. The two travelers also went to Canyon de Chelly in Arizona. The following year they returned, visiting the Zuni Pueblo, Ácoma Pueblo, and the Mesa Encantada or Enchanted Mesa. Cather must have been struck by the growing vigor of the New Mexico literary and art communities. She again accepted Luhan's invitation to visit Taos. Tony Lujan, Mabel's husband, took Cather on long drives; she admired his driving skills. She visited the Lawrence Ranch, some miles north of Taos. Willa had already met D. H. and Frieda Lawrence and Dorothy Brett in New York. She later stated that she had known Lawrence "very well." Two years previously, he had published *Birds, Beasts and Flowers*, which contains poems connected to New Mexican places and features; if he read selections to his visitors, Cather would have been interested. Cather and Austin similarly knew each other in Manhattan before crossing paths in Santa Fe. They had taken tea together; both were invited to a large dinner in 1912 honoring William Dean Howells; and Willa wrote thirteen letters to Mary, from 1921 through 1931. She told her brother Roscoe that she should like to have a house in Taos. After 1925, however, she did not return to the Southwest for lengthy visits.[16]

Cather was impressed by the famous light of northern New Mexico, praised by Lawrence, for which the elevation, latitude, and aridity are responsible. In the short piece "Light on Adobe Walls," she wrote of "a conception of clouds over distant mesas." When she was elsewhere she missed the vast spaces and huge skies, which give the spirit "wider range."

Willa Cather at Cliff Palace in Mesa Verde, 1915. Courtesy Archives and Special Collections, University of Nebraska–Lincoln Libraries.

"The sky was as full of motion and change as the desert beneath it was monotonous and still—and there was so much sky, more than at sea.... Elsewhere the sky is the roof of the world; but here the earth was the floor of the sky. The landscape one longed for when one was far away, the thing all about one, the world one actually lived in, was the sky—the sky!"[17]

"The Enchanted Bluff" and The Song of the Lark

"The Enchanted Bluff," published *in Harper's* in 1909, an early short story concerning the Southwest, warrants consideration for its imaginative dimension—a southwestern landscape as dreamt, not seen. It shows how fixed her thoughts could be on her surroundings and foreshadows rich depictions later. One critic calls the story "a comic subversion of the quest romance adventure." This reading overlooks Cather's own quests in the Southwest, utterly serious (if poetic) in both her life and their literary transposition. It overlooks likewise a common feature of stories featuring boys—the juxtaposition, even conflict, between imagined or half-lived adventures and the reality of life, especially as manhood comes. Nor do the adventures lose their moral value by being unrealizable.[18]

The story evokes a mesa with prehistoric ruins. She may have found her model in reading about Enchanted Mesa (strictly speaking, a *butte*), 430' high, just north of Ácoma Pueblo. Its sides are nearly vertical. Since prehistoric artifacts have been found there, though no traces of building (destroyed by time and weather, presumably), it must have been accessible, probably by natural cliff-side irregularities on the southern side, eliminated subsequently in a landslide. Cather may have had in mind likewise El Morro, farther west, 200' in elevation, where pueblo ruins do exist still and there is ample water. When she composed the story, she had seen neither site but obviously knew of them or similar mesas. She attributed great height (900') to her imaginary bluff and made it difficult of access, with the top, like a mushroom, extending over the approach. She imagines that the natives, depicted as hunters, disappeared, probably exterminated by hostile, and less civilized, Indians.[19]

The first-person narrator is a boy (he appears later as a man). The story, essentially romantic, is an effective character study. Set in Nebraska, along a sandy river like the Platte, it evokes the mesa but only as an *image* in the minds of six boys, who have heard reports of ancient peoples there

Southwest Point, Mesa Encantada. Photograph by George Wharton James, ca. 1900. University of Southern California and the California Historical Society. CHS 4624.

and resolve to be the first whites on top. Adulthood smothers their "long, long thoughts"; none carries out his resolve, though one man plants it in his son's mind. But the boys' imaginative evocation announces Cather's enduring fascination.

The Song of the Lark, begun in autumn 1913, is a long novel of development containing important episodes set in the Southwest. The title refers explicitly to a painting by Jules Breton in the Art Institute of Chicago. It shows a peasant girl listening to the bird's song, that is, awakening to beauty. Cather's British publisher, Heinemann, rejected the book (after it appeared in the United States), asserting that Cather had tried to tell too much about everyone. Later, she acknowledged that "art should simplify ... so that all that one has suppressed and cut away is there to the reader's consciousness as much as if it were in type on the page." She pointed out that Jean-François Millet's numerous sketches of peasants sowing grain led to a single image, "The Sower," so ideal that it seems inevitable.[20]

The story of Thea Kronborg, a singer, is told by an omniscient third-person narrator, who remains close to the heroine and her thoughts. While the model was a professional performer, Olive Fremstad, whom Cather knew well, the heroine's background and psychological and artistic development reflect the novelist's own, including awareness of her individuality and her artistic vocation. Cather spoke in a 1913 interview about hearing larks on the Nebraska prairie the first time she was driven there (in a wagon). "Every now and then one flew up and sang a few splendid notes.... That reminded me of something—I don't know what, but my one purpose in life just then was not to cry, and every time they did it, I thought I should go under." (The bird was perhaps the North American horned lark or, more likely, the western meadowlark, of a different family, whose song is richer and stronger.)[21]

Thea's life begins in a Colorado town (modeled on Red Cloud), located near Denver, among sandy hills, like the Sandhills in Nebraska. There are southwestern suggestions in the surroundings: yucca, sagebrush, Mexicans. But the Southwest is represented chiefly by "Panther Canyon" (the title of part iv, set in the San Francisco Peaks, north of Flagstaff, Arizona). Episodes there, crucial for the heroine's trajectory, constitute about ten per cent of the novel. The young woman's enthusiasm for the area and her sensitivity are Cather's own; Fremstad had not visited Arizona. Thea is young—not yet twenty—but, after difficult months spent in Chicago working as a singer and accompanist and taking lessons, she is greatly in need of rest. With the support of a Chicago friend, Fred Ottenburg, who is in love with her, she goes to spend some weeks on a ranch, part of the vast lands his father owns. She sleeps well, hikes, explores a canyon and cliff dwellings (based on those in Walnut Canyon), and reflects on the "Ancient People." Among the cliff-side structures, in a well-preserved room, she makes for herself a little day-house, which she furnishes with Navajo blankets. This high ruin suggests her lofty aspirations. It also underlines subtly the domestic impulse of even an artist such as Thea; moreover, it can be viewed as a "reproach to the messiness in which we live." Pinyon pine and western cedar, birds, wind, sunlight, and blue sky, the cliffs at morning and at evening—all appeal to her imagination. The author renders her impressions in rich, luminous language.[22]

These landscapes are seen by some critics as eroticized. Krista Comer writes of the way they "link artistic creativity to representations of the female body and the land, and ... express something of Cather's frustrated lesbianism." The novelist herself stresses, however, their connection to art and the past. Letting the natural features speak to her, absorbing her present surroundings, which one critic calls "a kind of sacred space," Thea empties her mind of ideas and words. Yet the past is eloquent, since evidence of the lost pre–Columbian culture is visible in the architecture and bits of relics she collects. (Like the Native Americans, however, she was superstitious about potsherds and preferred to leave them in place.) "It was the Cliff Dweller ruins that first awoke [Thea's] historic imagination," Cather wrote, adding that there Thea "began to find herself." Bathing in a canyon creek and reflecting on ancient water jars, she sees herself in a great stream of time and relates its passage to art. "What was any art but an effort to make a sheath, a mould in which to imprison for a moment the shining, elusive element which is life itself?" Decoration on the pottery shows her how the utilitarian alone did not, and could not, suffice. Though surrounded by evidence of death and ruin, Thea is exhilarated by her reflections; the past seems to impose on her a duty to carry out the age-old impulse toward transcending one's condition. Thus the girl's experiences lead from passive appreciation into a resolve to continue her singing, to make a career and a mark.[23]

When Ottenburg comes to visit her, she has gathered her strength and resolve. Providence, she understands, will do nothing for her; circumstances *may* help her; but she is herself the driving force. Fred's devotion and assistance belong to the circumstances. Thus she agrees to go to Mexico with him. There she learns of *his* circumstances—he cannot marry her because he already has a wife, in a sanitarium. The discovery will not, in the long run, be crucial. She is, however, disturbed, reproaching herself, and she needs help. Yet the will is in her, the will to emulate "the bits of frail clay vessels, fragments of [the cliff-dwellers'] desire." Much later, at the height of her success, she tells Fred that from Panther Canyon she drew the sense of truthfulness and other ideas for her art, "for the heroic parts ... out of the rocks, out of the dead people.... They taught me the inevitable hardness of human life."[24]

The Professor's House

The Professor's House, a short novel set partly in the Southwest, was serialized by *Collier's*, which paid Cather $10,000, a handsome sum; it was then brought out by Knopf. She wrote of "the really fierce feeling that lies behind the rather dry and impersonal matter of the telling." After *Collier's* ran it, readers whom she called "old hard-boiled publishers and solemn professors" wrote to her that the story "gave them a pulse." Lewis considered it the most personal of Cather's novels, reflecting her enthusiasm for the Southwest and derived in part from her experiences there. Tom Outland's death (which recalls that of Cather's cousin G. P. Cather) during the Great War introduces a note of violence and cultural disaster. In addition, the value assigned (explicitly by Outland and indirectly elsewhere) to art and natural beauty mirrors once more Cather's high estimation of aesthetic values.[25]

The Professor's House is tripartite, but the parts are of unequal length, leaving an impression of imbalance. Cather, who struggled with it, claimed it was modeled on the sonata form (a three-part composition). Welty praised the "compression and strength" of the middle part, a simplicity "never surpassed" by Cather, and found artistic excellence in the work as a whole. Austin found fault with the structure and with Cather's treatment of the Southwest. "The best she could do was split her story wide open in the middle and insert a green bough of New Mexico in such a fashion that I suppose nobody but myself really knew what she was trying to do." While Austin may have viewed Cather as an unwelcome competitor, the criticism is not unjust. Austin acknowledged, however, that the public appreciated the New Mexico section more than the rest. (Rightly so, it may be added.)[26]

The first part consists of seventeen chapters, the second of seven (an embedded narrative, about a quarter of the book), and the third of only five, very short. The structure corresponds roughly to what the author noted as a French and Spanish fictional technique: inserting a *nouvelle* into a *roman*. Begun in 1916, apparently complete by 1922, the book was intended as "full of love and hate." Featuring Outland and recalling the Panther Canyon episodes in *The Song of the Lark*, the central section could have become a novella or a novel, with Outland the main character. In fact, it was initially conceived as a separate work, for which Cather took notes, to be called "Blue Mesa." An early essay on Mesa Verde has been labeled by one critic as "Tom Outland's Story in Embryo."[27]

Cather illustrates here some kinship with modern, innovative novelists, since a framed tale impinging on an outer one through psychological effects is a feature of post–Romantic, post–Naturalistic fiction. The design had been illustrated brilliantly around 1900 in France by Pierre Louÿs, in *La Femme et le pantin* (1898) (*Woman and Puppet*), and by André Gide, in *L'Immoraliste* (1902), where a long embedded confession so draws in the listeners that they become implicated, as it were, incapable of judgment. Cather may have had in mind Gide's masterpiece in writing that "the commonplace way to do it is so utterly manufactured, and the only way worthwhile is so alarmingly difficult!" She may have thought also of Joseph Conrad's *The Heart of Darkness* (1902), in which a long oral account, given to a ship's crew preparing to sail, *may* affect the listeners. In 1924 she told a correspondent, apropos of "the story of action," that there was "another kind of story that ought to be told—I mean the emotional story, which tries to be much more like music than it tries to be like drama.... That is what Conrad tried to do, and he did it well."[28]

Whether this avoidance of the commonplace in *The Professor's House* by an unusual structure was a successful strategy is questionable. The author seemed pleased with it: "I thought the unusual structure was sufficiently bound together by the fact that the Professor's life with Tom Outland was just as real and vivid to him as his life with his family, and because Tom Outland was in the Professor's house so much during his student life. He and the atmosphere he brought with him became really a part of the house—that is, of the old house, which the professor could not altogether leave." It is true that Outland's personality, dominant in part two, also colors the narrative in parts one and three and contributes to the plot. Compositional flaws remain, however, including imbalance and insufficient narrative interdependency.[29]

It is useful here to distinguish between "story," or points on a forward-moving time-line (what the narratologist Gérard Genette called *histoire*), and "order of telling" (Genette's *récit*). The latter has kinship to mental time, in which the mind moves forward and backward with ease, subsuming past and future into a constant present. Cather's order of telling is elaborate; the reference points on the time-line vary. There are frequent analepses (flashbacks) with respect to *changing* chronological points of reference. Parts one and three are recounted by an omniscient third-person narrative voice; part two is a first-person retrospective account. Part one begins *after* all the action of part two has been completed. Even in part one, the order of telling does not follow the story but depends on analepses, introduced through scenes and summaries, including Tom Outland's puzzling allusions (such as a bank account he will not touch) and the professor's reflections. There is also a proleptic element (flash-forward), as his wartime death is alluded to even as scenes of his arrival are recalled. One flashback is the episode of Tom's arrival at the house of the professor (on the faculty of a university in the industrial Midwest), an episode that the latter replays in his mind and in which Tom first gives, selectively, facts about his past, mentioning pinyons, rock trails, and ruins, and displaying turquoises and samples of ancient pottery. When, later, he offers an intact pot of unusual design to the professor's wife, his gesture is a compliment to the family's hospitality and the warmth of their household (a sign of contemporary civilization); the attitude contrasts with his dim view of museums, keepers of the institutionalized and remote past.[30]

Of additional facts concerning the professor's family, the most important is that one of his daughters became engaged to Outland and that he left her a large inheritance gained from an enormously successful engine he invented, with assistance from another professor. (The subsequent dispute over credit for the invention can be viewed as peripheral, though the claim might suggest shadiness.) The daughter has since married someone else. By the end of part one, readers know that Outland had come to the university to study with the professor, whose main field of interest as an historian is the Spanish in North America. Outland was a brilliant student. There is also mention of Blake, his New Mexico partner, who has disappeared, and of "Tom's mesa." Meanwhile, the professor has had full knowledge of Tom's past because he was the listener in part two, which for readers expands on fragmentary information given before, filling in gaps and coloring differently the character of Outland.

Throughout part one the story continues to advance along its own narrative line, involving, among other things, the legitimacy of the legacy and how it has changed the family life. There is an element of suspense, along with dramatic irony, keeping readers unaware of what Tom knows, or knew, and what the professor learned. Though readers are in ignorance, there is no obtuse central consciousness; that is, Tom has not been without awareness, except insofar as he cannot know the hour and manner of his death nor assess its effect, feeling only that he must somehow pay for what happened in New Mexico.

Part two is Tom's story proper as told to the professor. An orphan (belonging to no one or everyone, or the land or the past), he worked for the railroad before falling ill with pneumonia. After his recovery, he is hired as a cowboy, along with Blake. (The latter's name has positive overtones for the author, anticipating a character in *Sapphira and the Slave Girl*, Rachel Blake, whose name in turn evokes Cather's strong-minded maternal grandmother, Rachel Boak.) Outland and Blake first tend the herd on its summer range, a sagebrush plateau. They then move to winter camp, at the foot of Blue Mesa, a prominent, imposing formation rising purple as the men approach. (Cather identified the model as Mesa Verde, cut by twenty-six canyons; the little town in the book, Tarpin, is based on nearby Mancos. The story, however, puts the mesa in New Mexico, a tactic adopted doubtless for practical reasons.) Hearing from old settlers that the mesa has never been climbed because of a river winding around it and innumerable canyons, Outland and Blake resolve to get to the top. Their employers warn them, however, that, by fording the stream, the cattle could escape there from the herd and join bands of wild cattle.[31]

While Blake tends the herd, Outland swims the high water with his horse, makes his way through canyons, and glimpses high, intact cliff-dwellings, including a fine tower, granaries, and what is revealed as a funeral chamber. The complex is preserved "like a fly in amber." Evidence suggests that the inhabitants did not plan their departure and yet were not exterminated in their dwellings; perhaps they were annihilated by a hostile tribe as they worked their irrigated fields in the valley below. Outland concludes that they were pacific.

Old as it is, traces of their civilization, now silent, reduced to artifact, suggest not ossification of human possibility but rather the realization of potential for social organization and culture. The beautiful, well-preserved pottery, irrigation channels, and burial usages speak of a culture perhaps superior to its coevals. While the cliff-dwellings seem like a city of the dead, Tom is in fact not disheartened but magnetized by the discovery, the way Cather was thrilled by cliff houses in Walnut Canyon and at Mesa Verde. Outland and Blake return to the site, explore further, and eventually build themselves a small cabin there. They remove and store many valuable artifacts. (Although the Antiquities Act of 1906 forbade mishandling of such and removal except by authorities, during the following twenty years pot-hunters still stole much.) The men's intention is to donate the artifacts to the Smithsonian Institution. Using their joint funds, Tom goes to Washington in an attempt to attract the authorities' attention. (This episode is based partly on the Wetherills' fruitless efforts to interest the Smithsonian in excavating the Mesa Verde ruins; officials were friendly but noncommital.) After more than six months, for his pains Tom has nothing but disappointment and an empty wallet. Cather's description of routine-bound office workers and the petty, self-serving ambitions of museum authorities shows her own dislike of Washington, where she had lived briefly in 1900–1901; *that* at least is not civilization.[32]

Returning to New Mexico, Tom learns that Blake has sold most of the artifacts to a German trader who will ship them to Europe via Mexico.

Willa Cather on the balcony of La Fonda Hotel, Santa Fe, with the cathedral in the background. Courtesy Archives and Special Collections, University of Nebraska-Lincoln Libraries.

Outland is enraged. As a purist, he never viewed them as sources of income; they are sacred. Blake protests on practical (or interested) grounds; since the Smithsonian refused the gifts, and selling artifacts in the U.S. is difficult at best, he was right in accepting an offer from a foreign trader. Outland remains angry, and the two quarrel. Profits from the sale have been put into a bank account in Tom's name, but he considers the money contaminated. Blake leaves in anger, crossing the river in high water. It is learned ultimately that he reached town and bought a ticket to Winslow. What happened to him afterwards is unknown (hence the professor's notion in part three that he should go look for him). Tom then departs for the university. The remainder of his story has been related previously by one means or another.

The final burden and effects of his acts are visible in part three, by means of the professor's reflections on himself after his wife, daughters, and sons-in-law have gone to Europe for the summer. He is content but has aged. His second youth, in the person of his favored student, an agent in his life, ended with Tom's death. The novel is now the survivor's story. "Tom Outland had been a stroke of chance he couldn't possibly have imagined.... His devotion, his early death and posthumous fame...." The professor believes that he has himself fared well with fate through knowing Tom; that knowledge is one way he endures and moves from middle age into another stage of his life.[33]

In part one and even part three, many details seem excessive. True, the basic portrait of the professor is needed, since it is through him that Outland becomes connected to his daughter and since he is among those changed by Tom's presence. Readers need to know likewise something of the professor's daily life. The attic retreat where—though his family has moved elsewhere—he spends his study hours, in discomfort, often cold, but in welcome solitude, indicates his attachment to the past (like Tom's). This garret appears to be based on Cather's similar room during her girlhood; it recalls Thea's room in *The Song of the Lark*. It may symbolize aspirations, but the cramped conditions cancel out suggestions of loftiness. Such details as the dress mannequins that occupy part of the attic study (a note inspired perhaps by Anatole France's novel *Monsieur Bergeret*, which the professor mentions) may be viewed as suggestive of his character. Similarly, the almost-unvaried routine of the family life, along with the overcrowded and stuffy conditions, provides an intentional contrast to the sense of a wider life, or "fresh air," that Outland conveys when he speaks of New Mexico.[34]

In both *The Song of the Lark* and *The Professor's House*, the scenery and other details—ruins, artifacts, history—are means by which Cather's characters discover and reveal themselves and move from one moment in their lives toward others. There is implied value in what enables them to develop thus, because what they move toward—respect for the past, beauty, awe—is, in the rhetoric of the novel, held as important, both for individuals and culture as a whole. It is clear, moreover, that Cather herself was touched, inspired, and energized by the ruins as well as the landscapes, sun, and air of the Southwest; her response, as contrasted to the bureaucratic, machine-like existence she depicted in Washington, is an implicit cultural judgment. Cather has Tom Outland reflect that what he felt on the mesa was a "religious emotion." But the story in these novels is not that of the pre–Columbian Southwest itself. The voices heard are those of European-Americans of the nineteenth and twentieth centuries, whose understanding is an outsider's. No belief in native mythologies and customs is implied or stated, unlike what one finds in writings of Austin and Armer, who embrace the Southwest so closely that it seems to speak through them.[35]

Death Comes for the Archbishop

Death Comes for the Archbishop won the Howells Medal, awarded by the National Institute of the American Academy of Arts and Letters. It appeared the same year (1927) that Laura Gilpin published her album *Mesa Verde*. Cather worked on her book in Austin's Santa Fe house, available to her because Austin was away. The latter, a "gossipy defender of local mores," according to one commentator, later showed guests the chair Cather had used. One can speculate that pride was a source of this gesture—more precisely, the desire to insert herself into the literary history of the book and claim her own important role. A review by Austin, which bothered Cather greatly, appeared in *The World*. Austin, devoted to the Hispanic heritage, complained of the Eurocentric tone in the book and was irked to discover that Cather had given her allegiance to the French blood of the archbishop and sympathized with his desire "to build a French cathedral in a Spanish town." Austin added that the bishop's influence had "dropped the local mystery plays almost out of use," along with other Spanish customs. The great honor Cather paid him underlined for Austin the foreignness of French style and the cultural damage for which it was, in her view, responsible. Such extra-literary criticism, directed not to the writing but to the central figure of the book and cultural preferences (his and the author's), reflected, probably, Austin's annoyance and rivalry with her contemporary. Whether the local traditions were truly, or properly, endangered by the French influence, especially the Romanesque revival style of San Francisco Cathedral, is uncertain and not strictly pertinent. The archbishop could not, of course, have endorsed or encouraged the natives' persistent heathenism (as sketched below), harking back to their pre–Christianization; the best he could do was tolerate it. Cather was annoyed at Austin's remarks and what she considered a violation of her privacy, and denied that any part of the book was written in the Santa Fe house. Yet in the copy given to Austin, she wrote, "For Mary Austin, in whose lovely study I wrote the last chapters of this book."[36]

Cather's title was borrowed, she said once, from Albrecht Dürer's *The Dance of Death*. Elsewhere she gave the source as Hans Holbein's series by the same title. The first scene (prologue) was inspired by a painting she had seen in the Louvre, by Jehan Georges Vibert, called, according to Cather, "The Missionary's Return," showing a group of cardinals, at ease with their wine, and a worn, obviously road-weary priest reporting to them, "his face all alight." (The actual title may be "The Missionary's Adventures," ca. 1883; a Vibert canvas by that name is nearly identical to the one she described.)[37]

She wrote that she "loved" her central character and loved working on the manuscript. She was aware of its literary worth, believing that, together with *The Professor's House*, it would "stand the wear and tear" (of time) better than her other books; she successfully negotiated with Knopf for higher royalties than usual. It sold 30,000 copies almost at once. Yet reviewers were confused or a bit put out by its generic unconventionality. It is usually termed a novel, following Knopf's label; Cather called it a "narrative," a useful term. It has a general chronological line (with analepses), beginning with an arrival and ending with a death, but does not have a plot otherwise; and it is driven by character, not action. A common response is to find it "episodic, nearly plotless." In essence, it is a retrospective and imaginative documentary or re-creation, incident by incident, held together by the protagonists, with fidelity to basic data but also fictionalized by invented scenes, dialogue, and attributed thoughts. Although Cather's characters are renamed, they are based on historical figures—Jean-Baptiste Lamy (1814–88), the first bishop, later archbishop, of *New* Mexico, and his vicar general, Father Joseph Machebeuf. Cather inverted the order of their death: Lamy died first, but she makes her Archbishop Latour survive his friend, Father Vaillant, so that the narrative concludes with his own end, in 1888. Involving as it does an exotic culture, hearsay (concerning Fray Baltazar Montoya), and the Christian marvelous—a sense of wonder, the possibility, perhaps reality, of miracles—the work also bears resemblances to the generic European *romance*. (Cather wanted to do something "in the style of legend," akin to what the French muralist Pierre Puvis de Chavannes did with the life of Saint Geneviève.)[38]

The work consists of a prologue and nine books, divided into chapters. Each book concerns one aspect of the bishop's undertakings, the vicar's, or their joint activities, or one incident or group of characters. The story begins in the mid-nineteenth century, after the Mexican-American War, when new ecclesiastical administrations had to be established for territory ceded by Mexico. Cather had learned much from Father Haltermann about the apostolic appointee, replacing the bishop of Durango, and his vicar. She also read a publication concerning the life of Machebeuf, by Father W. J. Howlett, based on interviews with Machebeuf's sister in France and letters she gave to Howlett, which revealed in detail the life of the two priests. (Cather wrote that she had "come upon" informative letters, not indicating they had been published.) Lewis wrote of Cather's encounter with it: "In a single evening ... the idea [of her book] came to her, essentially as she afterwards wrote it." She borrowed from Haltermann's volume some phrasing and various details and episodes—such as the frustrating attempt to get a driver and coach in Taos and the accident in which Vaillant's horses and carriage slip off the road over a precipice. The story of the white mules was drawn from life (though Howlett calls them "bay").[39]

That she did not acknowledge such borrowing—nearly-verbatim reproduction sometimes—was noticed by Howlett and others. She addressed the matter in an open letter published in the Catholic weekly *Commonweal* (which had reviewed the book), in which she stressed that other elements of the narrative came from her experience and her father's. Elsewhere she acknowledged that in her story "many of the incidents are invention" but added that others "are used almost literally as they happened." "What I got from Father Machebeuf's letters was the mood," she wrote. An acknowledgment of Howlett as a source would have been courteous; but fiction writers find their pollen where they can and make of it their own honey. Some overlaps with Howlett's narrative are simply facts, known to others, such as the paucity of water (experienced on the bishop's first trip to Santa Fe, via West Texas from San Antonio). Similarly, Cather's data on the origin of the bell in San Miguel church was not specifically Howlett's information. Scenes such as those where the vicar must pronounce the excommunication of priests at Taos and Arroyo Hondo were doubtless fed by accounts in Howlett's book, but in the 1920s old people in Taos still recalled what they had heard about the two priests, their behavior and schismatic church, and the Taos rebellion of 1847, in which Governor Charles Bent and other Americans were murdered. (Taos, the northernmost and easternmost of the New Mexico pueblos, also the fiercest, was, as noted in chapter two, a crucible for resistance against Spanish and Anglos alike.)[40]

Cather's membership in the Episcopal Church allowed her, presumably, to appreciate, in spirit as well as historically and aesthetically, the Roman Catholic presence in New Mexico—churches, crosses, canonic names, an omnipresent faith. She honored the Episcopal ritual, akin to that of Rome, and the church's role in early Virginia and elsewhere; moreover, its attachment to the past, through the Book of Common Prayer and the Apostolic Succession, was important to her. She had admired the statue of Lamy in front of the Santa Fe cathedral. She feared, however, "nothing so much as seeming a sort of stage Catholic." She was pleased that the *Commonweal* reviewer did not portray her in such colors.[41]

Cather evokes well the exotic character of New Mexico, a state that, as observed earlier, remained almost entirely foreign to Americans well into the twentieth century. Her work doubtless helped popularize the young state to northeastern readers by evoking its beauty and singularity and imparting something of its history, landscape, populations, and other features. Her depiction of the life of the two priests and the friendship between them is tactful and sensitive. Latour and Vaillant (the names bearing the obvious suggestions of a tower of light or faith, and of courage), the principal personages, are heroes (of a rough, modest heroism), but in the narrative design, their faith is the larger agent, along with the anonymous people who share it and whom they serve—the Church as a body. Thus, as Latour suffers from thirst in the desolate wilderness, he finds a stream and verdure, and then a welcoming family that provides shelter and food for him. This "miracle," as he terms it, is a sign of an invisible presence, to which the priests are but servants.[42]

Death Comes for the Archbishop omits the cowboy, that iconic figure of western writing, but portrays the frontiersman Kit Carson, with whom the bishop becomes friends. Peripheral characters are mostly Hispanics and Indians—Pueblos, Navajos, Hopis. In the course of the story, the Sisters of Loretto arrive to settle in Santa Fe. An occasional cutthroat appears—the bishop does not hesitate to threaten one with his pistol nor to lead the authorities to him—and there are two abusive priests, including the historical character Antonio José Martínez, accused of fomenting the Taos rebellion and known for high living and, perhaps, breaking his vow of celibacy. He had been married during his first youth but, after his wife's death; had been ordained; it was rumored, however, that since his ordination he had fathered illegitimate children..[43]

The northern New Mexico settings—mountains, sagebrush plateau, and desert to the west—are well evoked. Particularly striking is the episode called "The Lonely Road to Mora," with its evocation of the Truchas Mountains in wintertime, the heavy rain and icy wind—as well as the priests' close escape from death at the hands of the cutthroat. (The model for him may have been one Noel, of Mora, who had a common-law wife, whom he beat, and who perhaps poisoned a priest.) The priests not only succeed in getting him apprehended; they also help save his terrorized wife. Names of pueblos and other locations add their appeal to the narrative: Santo Domingo and Tesuque pueblos; Ácoma, the sky city, with its great church, the materials for which (including huge beams) were carried up the mesa on human backs; the Laguna Pueblo; Enchanted Mesa; Chimayó; the Pajarito Plateau; Taos and Mora; Arroyo Hondo and Questa; the Colorado Chiquito or Little Colorado, Oraibi, Tucson and the beautiful church of San Xavier del Bac; even Cripple Creek, where Father Vaillant goes to minister to miners. The apricot trees at the bishop's lodge in the red hills almost bear fruit on the page. Taos Pueblo, Santa Fe, and Los Ranchos de Taos are described as they appeared in 1850, or as Cather imagined them. Cactus, rock, turquoise, and parrot feathers add local color (parrots are raised locally but Cather notes that before the Spaniards came, Pueblo tribes sent traders for them down to Mexico). The human beings seem to belong to the landscape, as to its history. "Two Zuñi runners sped by.... They coursed over the sand with the fleetness of young antelope, their bodies disappearing and reappearing among the sand dunes, like shadows that eagles cast in their strong, unhurried flight."[44]

Ecclesiastical markers are everywhere. Ranchos de Taos and Taos Pueblo churches are well evoked. The Church of San Miguel, Santa Fe's oldest, plays its role, even as the archbishop plans for a cathedral in a "Midi-Romanesque" revival style. The prevailing viewpoint on indigenous peoples is not without charity and respect but is fundamentally Catholic: they are essentially different; they are heathen. "Neither the white men nor the Mexicans in Santa Fe understood anything about Indian beliefs or the workings of the Indian mind," reflects the bishop (expressing a singular attitude which may or may not have been Cather's). Latour reflects that he cannot transfer to the natives his European memories, behind which "there was a long tradition, a story of experience, which no language could translate." The bishop acknowledges the piety of some Indians but understands that their enduring paganism, marked by the Snake Root ceremony and other signs, cannot be eliminated during his time. The gods of wind, rain, and thunder, the sun and the moon are painted above the altar in the Laguna Pueblo church.[45]

Cather's bishop is nevertheless concerned with injustices against ethnic peoples. As an old man, he takes pleasure in knowing that black slavery has been abolished. In Zuni Pueblo he meets an outlawed Navajo chief and hears him plead for his people's return from the Bosque Redondo exile to Canyon de Chelly, their sacred homeland. Although they do not adapt easily to white ways, including religion, he finds in Navajos a strength surpassing the Pueblos,' and he is pleased when they can return to their native lands. As for the Spanish-speaking flocks, they are superstitious but devout and are highly resentful of the invading Americans. According to one man, "They say at Albuquerque that we are all Americans, but that is not true, Padre. I will never be an American. They are infidels." The bishop himself is considered by some in the novel (as by Austin) to be a foreigner, a gringo—though not an American (Protestant)—-since he is neither Mexican nor Indian and since he opposes Martínez and eventually excommunicates him.[46]

Death Comes for the Archbishop shows how, like Austin, Cather respected the cultural past and nature. She too was a conservationist of the time, and her environmentalism is viewed by one critic as being "integral with consciousness itself." Her characters offer models for proper care of their surroundings. Tradition is important; Indians and Spanish generally "disliked novelty and change." They honor their forerunners, the Anasazi, and leave ancient sites undisturbed. The landscape is similarly regarded as almost sacred, not to be violated. There is little over-use, little craving for domination; people content themselves with little. "They seemed to have none of the European's desire to 'master' nature, to arrange and re-create." A Mexican family's relationship to nature is happy. "They spun and wove from the fleece of their flocks, raised their own corn and wheat and tobacco, dried their plums and apricots for winter.... They had bees, and when sugar was high they sweetened with honey." Before Father Vaillant and his Navajo companion Eusabio leave the spot where they have camped during their return from a visit to Arizona, Eusabio removes all traces of their presence. The very dwellings of the Indians belong to the landscape: "The Hopi villages that were set upon rock mesas were made to look like the rock on which they sat.... The Navajo hogans, among the sand and willows, were made of sand and willows."[47]

Sight and Insight

Although Austin's principal writings on desert life appeared first, preceding one by one Cather's southwestern works and contributing significantly to introducing readers elsewhere to the historical and natural importance of the region, Cather drew further attention to the Southwest by rendering aspects of it in two outstanding narratives, which had wide distribution. She brought to bear on her topics the insights drawn from close observation and reading, her sensibility, lyrical gifts and stylistic abilities, and a keen understanding of character, as well as her sense of space and familiarity with harsh living on the plains. Additionally, her acquaintance with the New York literary world must have given her a sense of what would be successful there. Like Austin's, thus, her writing helped to extend American readers' familiarity with the Southwest. Historically important, her contribution has a permanent place in the literary canon, a singularly moving project, beautifully achieved.

Chapter Four

Laura Adams Armer

Armer as Writer and Artist

Laura Adams Armer (1874–1963) came late, not to artistic vision, but to her literary vocation, writing about the Southwest, which she first visited in 1902 but did not know well until later. Most of her books appeared in the 1930s; they are thus contemporaneous with the first mature poetry publications of Peggy Pond Church, her junior by thirty years. She began writing after cultivating painting and photography, in which she won prizes and an international gold medal. (She was called "possibly one of the finest photographers California has ever produced.") Her literary works are focused on the Navajos and Hopis (whose land is surrounded by the Navajo Nation). An outsider, she became nonetheless an eloquent exponent of their customs and arts.[1]

Her literary work consists of two non-fiction volumes, four novels for juveniles—which adults also can appreciate—and short writings, all with numerous interconnections and illustrated by her or others. The novels could be classified now as Young Adult fiction, provided it be understood that sexual matters play no role whatsoever. *Waterless Mountain* (1931) won the 1932 Newbery Award (given by the American Library Association) and the Longmans Green prize ($2000), both for juvenile fiction. *Southwest* (1935), a searching and artistically-conceived collection of personal and historical essays, furnishes information on Native American traditions. *The Forest Pool* (1938), a short book for young children, which she wrote and illustrated after visiting Mexico, received an "Honor" in 1938 for the Randolph Caldecott Medal (recognizing the best illustrator of a children's book combining text and pictures). Whatever the medium, she considered herself always an *artist*, devoted to the beautiful (*nezhoni*) and believing in "the power of beauty." Beauty was its own justification. Yet she did not pursue art for art's sake. She knew, in sculptor Carl André's words, that "the essence of art is human association."[2]

Armer's vision, like Mary Austin's, was painterly, poetic, moral, and religious (in the broadest sense). Resembling Mary's "land of little rain" and "land of lost borders," her desert presents similarities with Anne Morrow Lindbergh's ocean in *Gift from the Sea* (1955). Armer's pages are often like prose poems, as she describes landscapes, voices, faces, and depicts her intimate relationship with the territory and people she came to love. Natural features are drawn delicately, but with almost-imperceptible dynamism. She describes thus an afternoon on a mesa top, a place "suspended between heaven and earth, where the air was clean and pure, the sparse shrubbery pungent with health-giving incense.... How blue were the distant hills! How imperceptibly they became blue. From my feet resting on pink gravel, the desert stretched away pink and soft gray-green, and then it was blue with a blue sky above it. The blueness was vibrant with vitality descending and ascending from sky and earth." Her cosmic sensibility often resembles D. H. Lawrence's but without the sexual element except in the most symbolic manner (Mother Earth and Father Sky). Her style, which shows no influence of Modernist tendencies and yet does not hark back to nineteenth-century usages, is remarkable for its evocative power.[3]

As Mary Austin wanted to comprehend, by words, "[a] country that failed to explain itself," Armer took up writing as a way of understanding. She noted her initial response to the desert. "I went first as a painter, trying to explain the inner longing for the intangible in a land that is cruel and impersonal." She sought illumination beyond the brilliant light, in the mystery of the land, its "sense of the hidden." "The secret does not lie thinly veiled. It is deep down at the heart of things." A moral dimension, even a religious one arises from, or inspires, such an approach. "Art is a prayer of thanksgiving, born out of the deepest experiences of a people ... at once retrospective and prophetic." Painting was not sufficient, though. Ultimately, she took up her pen: "'Don't worry,' I found myself saying out loud, 'when you are an old woman you will write what you fail to paint.'" The two media were, for her, different ways of thinking. "I've been writing books in my mind for the last thirty-five years. *Waterless Mountain* was merely the first one I put down on paper." She did not cease painting and drawing, however. That the connection between her graphic word and writings is organic is shown by her book illustrations but also, more subtly, through visual effects in her prose. *In Navajo Land* (1962), a beautifully-cast memoir, was perhaps ekphrastic. She could have agreed with Marcel Proust's assertion that "style is a question not of technique but of vision."⁴

Background and Career

Armer, whose writing is closely bound to her experiences, is ill-known, barely mentioned or absent in books on southwestern literature. Her life should be of considerable interest to those who study women artists. Laura May Adams was born on 12 January 1874 in Sacramento, California, the youngest of three children. She was proud of her family. Her father, Charles Wilson Adams, from New Hampshire, had crossed the plains, driving an ox cart, from Missouri to California, after a failed venture in Illinois. It was claimed that he was related to the famous Adamses of New England. For him, "nothing turned to gold," Laura wrote. He tried mining but broke his leg, and his claim was jumped; he then worked as a laborer and carpenter. Her mother, Maria Henry, likewise from New England, later joined him, with their first-born. Maria "fought the perils of Sacramento river floods, went through the daily drudgery of caring for her children born on the banks of the river." Her great skill as a seamstress was illustrated in the wedding gown she created for Mrs. Leland Stanford. Laura recalled her rustic childhood bedroom, with "a bed quilt of log cabin design in shaded tones of brown and pink, a braided rug beside the bed, a white porcelain wash basin and pitcher."⁵

Laura spent her childhood in San Francisco. "Always my mind approaches that shore by the western sea." She learned to love nature and remembered well the green hills above the city. Her formal schooling was irregular, owing to uncertain health and "puny" build; her parents, believing she was too sensitive to pursue high school (or perhaps coddling her, as the favorite child) had her tutored (French lessons were included). She was viewed as "dreamy" and indeed called herself "a dreamer" later. An early photograph shows a "strong, almost masculine look" and "a determined scowl in her large, protuberant eyes"—somewhat unattractive. She was later described as having "considerable beauty of face and figure," but her character showed masculine traits, including a venturesome spirit and forcefulness. Her motto, written in a copybook, was "Let us then be up and doing / With a heart for any fate" (from Henry Wadsworth Longfellow's "A Hymn of Life"). Though as an adult she considered herself "delicate," she had tenacity and boldness, illustrated in her willingness to camp out and explore the terrain and to be alone (she often wanted isolation for her painting). Yet she did not create for herself a quasi-masculine identity, unlike Willa Cather, and the daring quality in her character did not lead to the sort of public literary life cultivated by Cather and Austin.[6]

Supported by her uncle Fred Adams, who was clearly in favor of careers for women, Laura studied from age 19 to 24 at the California School of Design (today's San Francisco Art Institute), guided in particular by Arthur Mathews, considered a master of the Decorative style, who had done the murals in the rotunda of the state capitol. He advised her to keep away from systems and "academic training." With her uncle's assistance, she opened a photography studio. She did portraits of society figures and celebrated local and international figures, and she displayed art photos at exhibitions, including the San Francisco Photographic Salons of 1901, 1902, and 1903. She was among the most successful photographers in the Bay Area, with admirable shots of San Francisco, notably Chinatown. She won four awards in the Kodak competitions of 1904 and in 1906 traveled to Tahiti for a shooting assignment. She provided eight illustrations for Theodore Elden Jones's *Leaves from an Argonaut's Note Book*.[7]

In 1900 she published in the *Overland Monthly* (to which Cather and Austin likewise contributed) an article entitled "The Picture Possibilities of Photography." Pictorialism, also called naturalism, was a late-nineteenth and early-twentieth century reaction against "art photography," which had adhered closely to painters' techniques and aesthetics. Yet Pictorialism similarly called on art, enhancing the real through soft focus and manipulations of light and dark. With "creative insight and technical skill," Armer used the style for portraits, which she wished to individualize (deploring the uniformity created by fashions in attire); she retained certain Pictorialist features in her later work. (Ansel Adams was familiar with the style but would react against it subsequently.)[8]

She continued to work in oils when she found the time, particularly landscapes and seascapes, and her canvasses won ribbons. In painting and drawing, she favored curved lines and subtle shadings. Her stylized representations, including human figures framed within or set against a leafy or figured background, have affinities with the work of the French artists Gustave Doré and Henri Matisse, Mexican artists such as Diego Rivera and José Clemente Orozco, and American painters Georgia O'Keeffe and James Swinnerton. In *The Forest Pool*, the kinship with Rivera is visible.

At age 28 Laura wed Sidney Armer (1871–1962), likewise Mathews's

Unknown photographer, *untitled* (*Laura Adams Armer at Little Theater, Berkeley*), July 1952. Photograph, 13 × 9.75 in. Collection of the Oakland Museum of California. Gift of Mr. and Mrs. Austin Armer.

student. They had known each other for eight years but had postponed marrying. She moved her studio to the house they built in Berkeley. There she processed her film and gave classes for women and children. Sidney, reputedly once the highest-paid commercial artist in California, began his career at the Dickman-Jones Lithograph Co. and later worked for Traung Lithographs. He provided the Sun-Maid Raisins design, the Turk of Hills Brothers Coffee, and the Del Monte shield. Reproductions of his work were sold as fine art prints. His oils, like his teacher's, tended toward the somber; but later he did bright watercolors of California plants and flowers. In his retirement his botanicals sold well, and he was called "the Audubon of the wild flowers" (though he viewed such praise as "flim-flam"). In drawings such as the illustrations for Laura's *Cactus* (1934), he clearly aimed at fidelity to nature, through delicacy of line and accuracy of observation (sizes, shapes, surroundings). Laura later wrote that he "put every spine in the right place and just the right number of spines." They often worked together in book design.[9]

The Armers' marriage may have been "an uneasy partnership." Sidney, a Jew, was an active member of the Socialist Labor Party. He was accommodating, she, demanding, tenacious, and authoritative to all those around her—"tyrannical," according to one observer. The fact that she used her maiden name as part of her publishing signature may suggest pride in the Adams family but also may represent her stance of stubborn independence. They shared many interests, however, including good literature and beautiful objects. He was an avid horticulturist (gardens are a frequent motif in her writing); she liked interior decorating. She collected Navajo rugs and Zuni and Hopi pottery. The couple traveled, together or separately, and led an active social life, though not generally among the literati. Sidney knew Jack London well, however, and Laura met Mary Austin during a visit to Carmel, where she had gone to take painting lessons with William Merritt Chase. They had one son, Austin Adams, born in 1903, who was the nude child in many of her art photographs until he declined to model further. An infant daughter died shortly after birth in 1905. Laura was said to be a difficult mother, domineering, yet somewhat neglectful and without understanding, particularly as the boy grew older.[10]

When Laura, in her sister's company, paid her first visit to Arizona, including Tucson (spring 1902), she was smitten by the "desert delirium." She subsequently wrote articles on the Southwest, illustrated by her photographs, for *Sunset*, to which she contributed a cover photograph, and *Overland Monthly*. Later a ten-part series of articles appeared in *Desert*

Magazine. Samples of her southwestern photography, including shots of Canyon de Chelly, are in the Wheelwright Museum in Santa Fe.[11]

By 1918–19 tensions in the Armers' marriage resulted in Sidney's emotional breakdown; thenceforth they were often estranged, living in different areas or under two roofs on their property. Financial difficulties (Laura was spendthrift) and her domineering personality may have been to blame. He spent a month with a sister in Pasadena. The family then went camping in the desert, stopping on the Agua Caliente reservation and exploring the environs. This visit was crucial for Laura, "the beginning of the second and deeper half of her life and her success with the rest of the world." *Cactus* perhaps had its origins then; it shows specimens from the Mojave Desert. From 1923 until 1936, she spent long periods in the Arizona desert. Those experiences are explored below.[12]

In the early 1930s Armer became familiar with Carl Jung's principles of psychology through an analyst who was interested in black-and-white drawings arisen, he thought, from her unconscious. She underwent daily analysis and was said to be harder than usual to live with. Work for Sidney became scarce; she, meanwhile, had her prize money from *Waterless Mountain*. For two years he worked in Brooklyn, then spent five months in Detroit, where Austin Armer and his family had settled. Laura once spoke of divorce, and she may have been attracted by someone she met at a party at Mary Austin's. These currents are not, however, expressed in her writing, which, though drawn from her deepest self, does not disclose personal dramas. The couple collaborated on books. Physical separation may have increased their estrangement but more plausibly reduced it by alleviating her anxieties and demands.[13]

In the mid–1930s Laura expressed a wish for her own home in the wilderness. "The desert called and the desert claimed me." Using some prize money, she and Sidney had a Navajo named Klitso build for them a modified hogan (with the requisite eight sides but without the center pole) at Black Mountain, just west of Chinle (spelled then *Chin Lee*). It had no electricity, no telephone. Sidney collected cactus to plant near the house, and the two completed *Cactus* there. Unfortunately, Laura had no ownership rights to the property; in 1936 she was obliged to abandon it.[14]

They were never truly prosperous thenceforth, and Sidney had to sell his carefully-assembled jade collection. She spent her last years researching sand-paintings but published only (at age eighty-eight) her memoir *In Navajo Land*. This decline in productivity may be related to separation from the territory she loved. The couple sold their Berkeley house and moved to Crescent City, near Redwood National Park and Oregon; Laura wrote *Farthest West* in a redwood studio she built there (on others' property, however). They eventually settled in Fortuna, close to Cape Mendocino, the westernmost point of the California coast, where they lived for seventeen years and Sidney had a renowned garden. After his death, at age 91, Laura moved to Austin's house, then to a nursing home in Vacaville; she decorated her room with Sidney's oils, photographs of hers, and Navajo rugs. She died following a stroke in 1963.[15]

Life in Arizona; Photography

When, after some twenty years, Laura returned to Arizona (summer 1923), she may have become familiar already with Navajo and Hopi songs through her son, who, as a flutist, accompanied Derrick Lehmer, a mathematics professor who had transcribed some and sang them publicly. The continued appeal of the Southwest for her was indicated by her attire for a costume party; she dressed as the "Painted Desert."[16]

The return journey was undertaken with Sidney, Austin (then a university student in Berkeley), and a friend, Paul Louis Faye, an anthropology instructor who rented their garden cottage. She left her brushes at home. They camped out some. Sidney gave her $500 to spend on herself. Austin was at the wheel of their Buick; she and Sidney did not learn to drive. (Austin said his mother simply expected others to drive for her.) She stressed how "physically difficult" it was to enter the Navajo domain, "in a part of my own country" but foreign. Some fourteen years later she stated that she would "rather be in Arizona in the 'Back-to-back month' [October] than anywhere else in the world." Later, during a drought, Sidney joined her in trying to assist the Navajos (or The Tinneh). Though he was not so keen as she on the desert, he saw well that "it's the poverty of the desert that makes life so rich." She wrote of the "nakedness about the Southwest, a bald truthfulness which allows for no subterfuge, and brooks no flattery."[17]

During the 1923 tour she acquired a fine pair of turquoise earrings—a stone then less frequently collected and worn by non-indigenous women than now. It had lured her earlier, after she read of Coronado's adventures. "It was the glamour and romance of these tales of turquoise that first sent me to the Southwest and which finally led me to search for the old pits in the Turquoise Mountains east of the Death Valley Region." The earrings were not for sale new or as pawn; she bought them from the wearer, a Navajo man. Her appreciation is artistic and historic, tinged with romance: "The turquoise was cut in triangular form with rounded corners and sides. The blue gems glowing against brown skin spoke of romance of the Southwest, recalling old tales of Spanish conquistadores who, seeking gold, found turquoise; told of Montezuma in regal splendor of turquoise; told of secret desert mines where the life-giving stone awaited the primitive miner." She asked Faye what she should offer the Navajo for his earrings. "If they are the heart's desire, pay what equals the heart's desire." From her purse she pulled a bill and gestured. Her mute offering clearly delighted the owner. "Thus began the turquoise trail which was to lead to the house of happiness among the cliffs."[18]

Thenceforth she was frequently known as "Turquoise Woman." (Another name, bestowed later, was "Hard-Working Woman.") Since the stone has high symbolic value, figuring in Navajo cosmology, to many her choice signified friendship; some, however, objected to what seemed like expropriation. On one occasion, she listened as an old silversmith explained sand-painting designs. When a surly observer objected, since she might get monetary gain from the lesson, the silversmith protested, adding, "She ... loves the beautiful. She wears the turquoise." Armer recalled what happened: "Spontaneously we two clasped hands as artists." Turquoises remained important to her as material and symbolic objects and as a literary motif; *In Navajo Land* begins with a chapter entitled "The Turquoise Trail." Of the color, whether in stone, bird, or sky, she wrote that "it is replete with life-giving energy."[19]

In February 1924, Armer rented a one-room stone house in Oraibi, a Hopi village. (The name is used here to indicate both the modern village, build by the government, at the foot of Third Mesa, and "Old" Oraibi, on the mesa.) She taught art to children and used an empty schoolroom as her studio. The artist Joseph J. Mora had previously described Oraibi as being "from an artistic standpoint, paradise." Natalie Curtis, who visited in 1903, found every act of life "ceremonial, poetic, symbolic." Armer's purpose was to establish closer contacts with the natives, after having encountered harshness and indifference and struggled to give, in her painting, what she called "the feel of the deep-down impersonal religion of the aborigines." She spent more than six months there and became well acquainted with Lorenzo Hubbell, the local trader.[20]

Lorenzo was the elder son of John (Juan) Lorenzo Hubbell (1853–1930), known as J. L., Don Lorenzo, or sometimes "Father." A sympathetic friend to the Navajos, J. L. had created circa 1878, and owned (land and buildings), the famous Hubbell Trading Post in Ganado, Arizona Territory, the oldest continuously-operating such place in the nation. The operations were subsequently expanded; the empire included as many as twenty-six trading posts. Lorenzo, who was functionally trilingual, had begun his trading at Keams Canyon, at the edge of the Hopi reservation, around 1902. He became Laura's mentor and exercised a profound influence on her. It was he, with other traders, who helped her obtain a federal permit allowing her to spend extended time on Navajo territory. He was described as a wonderful, lovable man. Armer became acquainted with J. L.'s other children—Barbara, Adele (or Adela) and Roman, who had begun managing the Ganado post in 1911, left, but returned. Apparently Laura also knew well their cousin George, who managed another post; he and his family appear in *The Trader's Children*. *Waterless Mountain* is dedicated to "Lorenzo Hubbell, whose faith inspired this book."[21]

Armer came closer than most other visitors to entering into native life. This impulse, part of the mind-set of romanticism, is visible similarly in the "cave-man" drive illustrated by western explorers, trappers, and miners who, while making a living in the wilderness, also adopted the rugged outdoor way of life as a personal ethic. (Ernest Hemingway embodied later this ethos of ruggedness, which may be related in certain cases to an imperialistic drive to dominate terrain and creatures.) Armer showed how a woman in the twentieth century could do something similar, driven, however, by spiritual need and aesthetic impulse, not by desire to dominate. She was determined but not confrontational; her approach did not spring from defiance or what some might see as the impulse toward cultural transgression.

A photograph shows her seated on the ground in front of "Hillside House" (the Betatakin cliff dwelling ruins, now part of Navajo National Monument), where she had gone on horseback with her husband and son; clad in a loose, flowing garment, robe or shawl, she could pass for a middle-aged tribal woman anywhere, except for her visible striking white hair. The flowing garb contrasts with the rough textures, stark cliffs, and right-angled ruins. She does not suggest appropriation of the scene, belonging to a distant past; rather, she is part of it, like Cather's Thea in the cliff house (*The Song of the Lark*). In another photograph, Laura is attired in ample sleeves, a long skirt or loose trousers, and a dark, flowing cape, seated on sand at the foot of cliffs whose wavy strata and lithic textures continue the sand patterns. The photograph suggests nomadism, entirely appropriate, especially since the Navajos had remained partly a nomadic people, even as grazing areas for sheep became overused.[22]

Trusting the Indian men, she was rarely apprehensive when she was alone. Once she hoped to find a place, having a view and a spring, near Lonely Dell (Lee's Ferry), a desolate area south of the Vermilion Cliffs and what is now Glen Canyon Dam. She could not find a suitable house there (though her requirements were modest). During a trip southeast to St. Johns and Greer, near the headwaters of the Little Colorado, she was by herself. In 1925 she camped in Blue Canyon—a dramatic, desolate box canyon thirty miles north of Oraibi—to which Lorenzo took her. His uncle Charlie Hubbell was a trader near there. Alone except for a Navajo woman helper, she arranged her art paraphernalia and personal belongings in two tiny tents. "Optimism sets me down under a rainbow-colored cliff." Hubbell had said, "If this moon place is not wild enough for you, send word to Oraibi and I will try to find you what you want." Asked if she was not lonely, she replied that she was not hampered there by trivialities; she was closer to the spiritual world. She made beauty from scarcity.[23]

She took many photographs, conveying facts and meaning, with integrity. Human subjects have strong presence and are portrayed with generosity, not patronizingly, as curiosities. There is no blurring of natives' identity. Their accouterment suits them without appearing quaint; Armer knew how to avoid giving an impression of artifice. Nor does the matter of white guilt and native innocence enter into the picture. The question of the larger truth value and suitability of her shots must, nevertheless, be raised. Critics often challenge such images, given the widespread view that photographing or drawing human subjects or their property, even with their permission, constitutes ipso facto an invasion of privacy and springs from a condescending attitude that treats them as picturesque, perhaps inferior. (The belief that reproduction constitutes theft of the person, even the spirit, endured in some quarters.) Even with the subjects' consent, did Armer's actions—those of an outsider, a white, a successful artist—constitute an invasion, a means of control, an imperialistic gesture? Did she take what belonged to a marginalized people, dominated, sometimes mistreated, by the national government, or romanticize her subjects for a patronizing public? Did cooperating natives betray their people by posing for her? However one answers, it is certain that, to her, knowledge was not expropriation of others or a gesture of control.[24]

The issue of cultural plunder arises again in connection with turquoise jewelry, as with sand-paintings and dances. In each case she took items—and the beliefs behind them—partly out of context, by wearing, copying, or writing about them. (Other authors treated here similarly seized upon native lore or materials.) Yet her respect for indigenous objects and traditions was enormous. She understood how through art human beings could harness natural forces symbolically, making and shaping the world "through the power and magic of the word."[25]

By reading, listening, and observing, Armer gained information on Navajo mythology, derived from their ancestors—Athabascan aborigines from the north—and influenced by Pueblo Indian lore and elements of Anasazi culture. Her written sources included *An Ethnologic Dictionary of the Navajo Language* (1910), prepared by the Franciscan fathers of St. Michael's, Arizona; James Stevenson's account of the Night Chant or Night Way; and reports by Washington Matthews, an army surgeon stationed in the 1880s at Fort Wingate, Arizona, including *The Mountain Chant* (1887), *The Night Chant, a Navaho Ceremonial* (1902), and his anthology *Navaho Myths, Prayers and Songs* (1907), with "A Prayer of the Night Chant," which ends, "In beauty it is finished." He likewise published "Invocation to Dsilye N'eyeani" (or Dsilyi Neyani, a legendary wandering hero), belonging to the Navajo "Beauty Way" cycle, with the final words, "It is done in beauty," repeated four times. "Finished in beauty" became Armer's mantra. She studied examples of native arts, including basketry and pottery of the Navajos' forerunners. She marveled at the inborn abilities of the native people.[26]

That Armer, like Austin, used the word *primitive* cannot be held against her, although recent anthropologists and cultural critics avoid the term as being judgment-laden. Sensitive to the peoples around her, she still retained the older ethnological vocabulary. She appears to have differed with anthropologists who contended that cosmic problems were not of interest to primitives, since they had no love for thinking.[27]

Sand-Painting and Ceremonies

Armer's most important contribution to art history and ethnic studies is her work on sand-paintings (also known as dry-paintings), connected to sacred healing ceremonies. They had generally been protected from curious eyes. In Oraibi she interviewed Medicine Men, learning the significance of colors and forms. In return, one named Ashi visited her to study her oils based on Navajo myths. (Some were shown subsequently in Los Angeles, New York, San Francisco, and Chicago.) Through an inter-

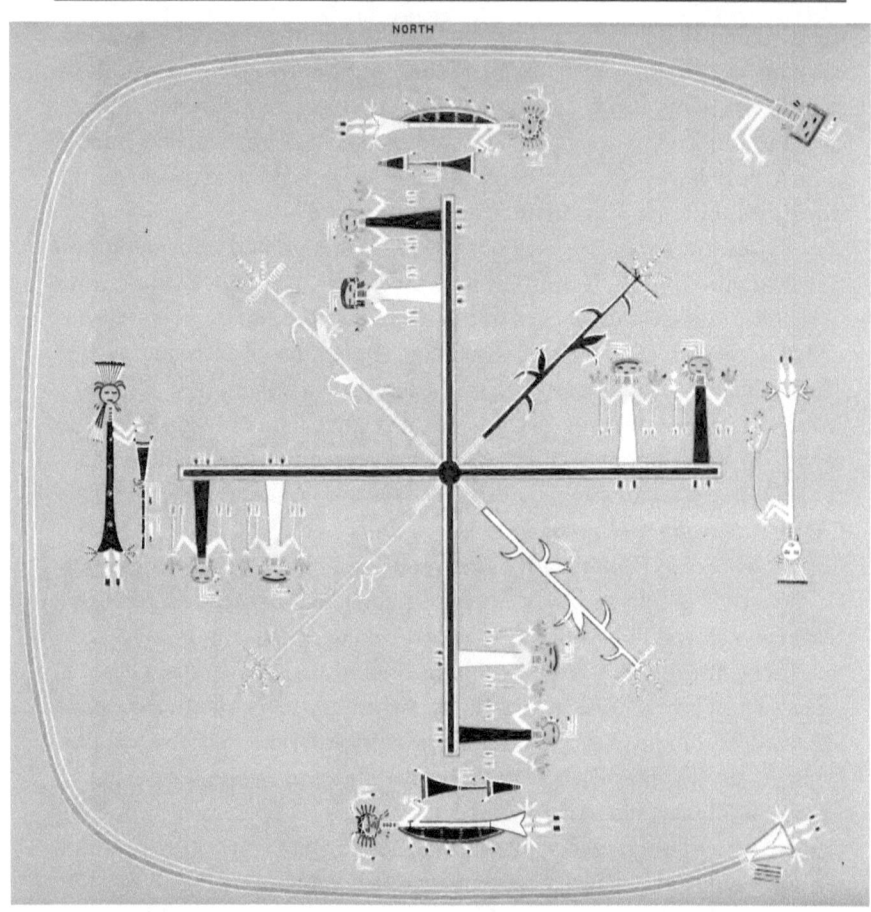

Sand-painting of the Whirling Logs. From Washington Matthews, *The Night Chant, a Navaho Ceremonial*. Memoirs of the American Museum of Natural History, vi: Publications of the Hyde Southwestern Expedition (New York, 1902).

preter, she asked him to make a sand-painting for her. He refused, but returned to re-examine her paintings, which he admired greatly. "The white woman paints strong medicine." When she asked again for a sand-painting, he replied that the art was sacred. "Because of the pollen," he explained. She suggested that pollen could be omitted; he finally agreed, calling her "white sister." He used yellow sandstone, lumps of charcoal, and red sandstone from a cliff two miles away.[28]

Thus she became the first white woman known to have had a sand-painting prepared for her. She later took photographs of the process and finished creations, reworking many in oils. She also copied rugs (the designs of which, in modern times, were based on sand-paintings). She believed there were more than 400 such dry-painting designs. Her copies—more than 100—have documentary value; she knew that the meanings of certain designs, explained in chants, were fast becoming extinct even in the 1920s and 1930s. "The sand-paintings, representing very old traditional art, are a direct outgrowth of religious emotion." She added, perhaps inaccurately but with fervor, "They are the only uninfluenced examples of aboriginal American art produced today."[29]

Ashi's painting for Armer was attested by Oliver La Farge, a Harvard-trained anthropologist who won the Pulitzer Prize for his novel *Laughing Boy* (1929). In August 1924, he and a companion, visiting Oraibi, learned of it and, albeit dusty and unshaven, went to see her. As La Farge wrote, it was entirely authentic, with prayer-sticks around the edges. Though doubting she would accept, the men invited her to their camp to share their meal of goat's ribs. She was not deterred by dust, she said; she had lived in Oraibi for six months. (They cleaned up a bit before she arrived.) La Farge believed that she had won over the Navajos by her tact, persistence, and artistic temperament, love of nature, and unusual understanding of things the Indians did not expect whites to grasp. She saw native beliefs as valuable, productive, and vitally true and embraced their vision. She was also supported by "one of the wisest and most sympathetic of the Navahos' friends" (Lorenzo), as La Farge wrote.[30]

In addition, Armer was invited to ceremonial dances, including the Squaw and basket dances, a kiva bean dance, the Yeibichai Dance, part of the Night Chant, and dancing connected to the Mountain Chant, which she witnessed in 1927. Like sand-paintings, dance was an essential part of Navajo culture, but, as was noted in Chapter One, at risk from outside cultural pressures.[31]

Witnessing the Night Chant required permission from both the Medicine Man and his patient. One of the Hubbells interceded for her. He was asked, "Why should we allow the white woman to see ceremonies which our own women do not see?" When this was reported to her, she said, "Tell them not to think of me as a woman but as an artist." A message came back: "Let the white woman come because she wears the turquoise." She was even permitted to apply pollen to the sick man's lips and head, offer it to the sky, then photograph the sand-painters' hands and copy their patterns in water colors.[32]

In the company of La Farge and Lorenzo Hubbell, Armer witnessed a Hopi snake dance, performed at Hotevilla. There they encountered a "pale creature" with red whiskers, wearing a flat black hat of the sort Mormons favored. This was D. H. Lawrence, present along with Frieda Lawrence, Mabel Dodge Luhan, and Tony Lujan (their chauffeur). Laura had a cracker box reserved as a seat; Lawrence sat in front of Laura, on her feet in fact. He later described the ceremony in detail. Far from denying evil, she, like him, recognized its potency; the snake dance constituted a confrontation with dark powers and defiance of them. In *Southwest*, she quoted his impressions, adding that the dance was a "most understanding study" of Indian religion and that "the creative flow of life had brought him understanding." Seated next to him was Louisa Wetherill, the wife of John Wetherill, a trader at Kayenta and a brother of Richard Wetherill, the Mesa Verde explorer; Laura chatted with her. During their earlier automobile explorations, the Armers had followed John's track across the desert to the great green mesa.[33]

In 1928, with the help of Lorenzo and Roman Hubbell, Armer made, at Canyon de Chelly, a silent full-length film on the Navajos, *The Mountain Chant*. It featured "The Crawler," Na Nai (discussed below). She had no experience at making motion pictures, but persuaded Lorenzo, Roman, and her husband to invest in it, $10,000 each. After studying Matthews's description of the ceremony, she wrote the script, hired two camera men, directed the film, and edited it. The Hubbells assisted her. Filming was done inside a hogan, with magnesium flares as the light source. No rehearsal was possible. The event included sweat baths, incantations, and sandpainting. The patient was induced to tell his dreams, which the Medicine Man interpreted. Subtitles were used to convey meanings. Attempts to market the film in Hollywood and elsewhere failed. It was viewed, properly, as an art film as well as an anthropological documentary. It was shown at the American Museum of Natural History in New York and elsewhere. Because some public screenings included a narration in Navajo by a member of the tribe, it has been considered as the first all-Indian film with an aboriginal language.[34]

Views on Native Beliefs

Like numerous other artists, Armer suspended disbelief concerning religion—in her case, native religious lore and ceremonies. She could respect and understand the Native Americans' beliefs, thanks in part to sharing their understanding of beauty; but to say that she *adopted* their beliefs is too much, although a New York *Times* reviewer described her as being naturally a "pagan mystic." She saw them apparently in both their local context and a broad one provided by mythologies, such as creation myths, with which she was familiar, and by Judeo-Christian traditions, although the Armer household paid no attention to religion or even festivals such as Christmas. "Mythologies preserve a tribal ideal." "That is a good religion, as good as Christianity," reflects Slim Girl in La Farge's *Laughing Boy*. Myths had their ultimate basis in nature, which was, to Armer, animated. A chapter in *Southwest* is titled "On the Summits of the Clouds I Sought the Gods and Found Them." Denying that she had true religious faith, her son (himself a Unitarian) wrote, "Awe of the natural and supernatural—faith in miracles—profound belief in extrasensory perception, etc., she had aplenty." (Her belief in extrasensory perception is a point of resemblance between her and Mary Austin; but one does not find in Armer's work the Christian convictions or Christian God to which Austin's mysticism pointed.) Upon leaving Betatakin, she felt that she had been under a "spell," albeit a "flight of fancy." She asserted that "man's unconscious mind goes back to the time when he was brother to the animals," adding, "I knew that I had touched early animistic belief." Yet gaining understanding is not easy. "One must win his own place in the spiritual world, painfully and alone. There is no other way of salvation. The Promised Land lies on the other side of a wilderness."[35]

Her writings reveal thus someone without fear of being thought credulous. While not ignorant of modern scientific knowledge, she accepted, and used in her writing, poetically and even spiritually, tales of the Sun-Bearer and Turquoise Woman (who lives on an island in the wide water of the west), seeing that such stories had value in native cosmology. She emphasized recurrence in nature, through natural processes such as rain and evaporation, birth and death. She may have known the principle of the conservation of energy. She also saw in Navajo and Hopi teachings valuable ethical principles, which she likened to The Way of Lao-Tzu. "Awareness, wariness is the first virtue in primitive man's morality." She showed sensitivity to native mythologies emphasizing the contrasting and complementary positions between the masculine and feminine impulses. She used the term *collective unconscious*, doubtless learned through Jungian analysis. A psychologist friend (male) remarked one day while gazing with her at the Mojave Desert: "Those desert mountains are the collective unconscious." Her objection that they were there before men evolved made no difference.[36]

Furthermore, her acquaintance with paleontologists' discoveries and theories concerning the arrival of archaic Americans over the ocean and the Bering Sea land bridge reinforced her understanding of native lore about ancestors arriving from the great western water and crossing deserts fiercer than where they themselves lived. Armer also knew that Mesoamericans had been as far north as the Sonoran desert, bringing with them copper and feathers of tropical birds, whose images were preserved in petroglyphs. Such knowledge enabled her to appreciate mythic figures, including the Plumed Serpent or Quetzalcoatl, known to the Anasazi, who endures in Navajo mythology as the great horned serpent, thus tying the tribe to their distant relations in lower Mexico. Her illustration "Where fantasy was born out of jungled chaos" features a native woman, with fruit, against a background of entwined branches and two macaws.[37]

Her willingness to take these teachings on their own terms and honor them made many friends for her. One title given to the "white-haired medicine woman," as she called herself, was *Shama*. The word means 'mother' but, to non-native readers, it suggests powers of healing; and indeed, one Navajo believed she had healed his sick pony. She, meanwhile, called the wise natives *Shamans*—meaning, roughly, priest.[38]

Waterless Mountain

From the mid-1920s until after 1936, Armer devoted herself to writing about the Southwest and her experiences there. Her narratives are not marked by strong plot lines or complex social relationships. She did not *create* characters so much as evoke, often poetically, what she had seen. Though remaining close to what had inspired them, her stories achieve the desired effect, creating a world both true and imaginative. "The best form is that which makes the most of its subject—there is no other ... meaning of form in fiction," wrote Percy Lubbock.[39]

Waterless Mountain, composed in Berkeley, with a preface by La Farge, has been reprinted countless times, owing partly doubtless to the Newbery Medal. An anthropologist called the book "a direct, simple story, movingly told. It is human, it is good Indian and authentic Navaho." It showed that "the Indian is no longer a dummy to hang our own romanticism on, but an interest and appeal in himself." Like *Tom Sawyer* and *Treasure Island*, it interests readers of various ages. A *Harper's* reviewer called it "an exquisite prose poem." The New York *Times* noted that the "beauty and mysticism" of the book would appeal primarily to adults. Laura's daughter-in-law, Alberta, who admitted feeling "gall" when the award was announced, unkindly suggested that the art work, not the text, earned the prize. (Of course Laura did the illustrations also.) The prose alone warranted the prize, however; the story may easily have won over the selection committee. A list of Newbery winners for the period shows titles suggesting exotic subject matter that would broaden young readers' horizons. (In the same period, Laura Ingalls Wilder published her first books in the *Little House* series.) With a large vocabulary, however, and treating matters of culture, beliefs, and spiritual development, Armer's book is doubtless beyond many young readers today.[40]

The first draft, which required rewriting, was initially directed toward adults. It included a romance between Hard-Working Woman and the Big Man—based on herself and Lorenzo Hubbell. (No evidence of such a romance, denied by her family, is available, but they were certainly close friends.) In recasting the manuscript to concentrate on the Native Americans, as the publishers wished, she wisely omitted that plot line. The resulting work inspired a friend to suggest she enter it in the Newbery competition. By the author's calculations, as of March 1960, more than 50,000 copies had been sold. A recording was released in April that year and sold well. Admirers pointed to the work as one of two masterpieces that Longmans Green had published (along with *Robinson Crusoe*). In 1996 the book was chosen for the "Perpetual Mirage" exhibit at the Whitney Museum of American Art. Peter Palmquist called it "a derivative of a photographer's preoccupation with both photography and painting; ultimately it is the spiritual combination of these two media with the written word." After having adhered to the photographic conventions of her era, Armer "felt empowered," he added, to record situations "which she subsequently translated into thematic 'illustrations' for an increasingly wide audience."[41]

The full-page pictures, in shaded black and white, are based on her Arizona paintings (she had done more than thirty by that time). For each chapter Sidney did inhabited initials, woodcut-style blocks incorporating Navajo designs, plants, and animals. The frontispiece and dust jacket follow an Armer painting based on two of her photographs, one a close-up image of a Navajo woman leading her pony, laden with rugs to sell, in Canyon de Chelly, the other an imposing vertical view of the cliffs and ruins there, the lower part of the photo having been cropped.

According to Armer, the title mountain really exists. An Arizona web site places it on the Kaibab Plateau, north of the Grand Canyon; but that is so far from other locations mentioned that one suspects she applied the name to another formation or had in mind a homonym. Or she may have deliberately blurred geographic lines. The local trading post is doubtless modeled on Hubbell posts; the arroyo is perhaps what Hubbell called Pueblo Colorado Wash, north of Ganado. The mountain is said to be without water, but, as the epigraph notes, it has hidden resources. This suggestion of concealed wisdom reinforces associations with mysterious or holy mountains of other traditions. "Below is the deep heart of things." The phrase emphasizes mystery, secrecy, darkness, not as threatening or evil, but as other side of what appears, a store of wisdom. Knowledge is not complete, however; "none of us knows what is at the heart of things."[42]

Navajo mores and beliefs are illustrated throughout, and the element of the marvelous is strong, arising from seeing (and naming) natural phenomena, objects, and abstractions in such a way that they inspire wonder, expressed by song, prayer, story. Armer stresses the connectedness and basic goodness of all things. Inspired particularly by Navajo cosmology, she emphasizes colors (connected to the solar cycle) and cardinal points, white (east), blue (south), yellow or coral (west), and black (north), expressed as mineral matter also: "the four sides of the world, where men of turquoise, white shell, abalone, and jet sparkle in their strength, upholding the heavens above...." White Shell Woman is the younger sister of Turquoise Woman and related to water. Two other directions appear, above and below. *Toh* (water) is a constant motif in a land that resembles Austin's "Land of Little Rain." Too little water usually; occasionally a flood.[43]

The story is centered on a boy (modeled on the son of Pretty Woman, whom Armer knew at Blue Canyon) with a vocation to become a Medicine Man. Armer gave him the name Dawn Boy, whose legend goes back to the Anasazi. (That legend had helped suggest the route she and her companions took in 1923.) The name must not be pronounced often; it is too precious. Instead, he is called Younger Brother. He is a child of White Corn, wandering in the House of Happiness. Omniscient third-person narration is used; thoughts and dialogue give insight into his inner life. While fiction arranged around a child's perspective is often somewhat forced, the child unnaturally wise, that is not the case here. The portrait demanded on the author's part close acquaintance with Navajo life, great delicacy, and a fine imagination. In his preface, La Farge noted that it was a "daring subject," but that Armer had come as close to painting a true picture as anyone could do save a Medicine Man himself. "Many readers will question the high religious ideas, the constant talk of beauty, the mysticism" that she ascribes to the boy and his uncle, a Medicine Man; La Farge assured readers that Indians held such beliefs. The text is rich in lore, including creation tales; some legends highlight the cultural connections between Navajos and paleolithic peoples who came to North America.[44]

When the story begins, the boy is only eight years old. His development is traced until he is almost a young man. While he is a distinct person, the legendary name creates for him a status that goes beyond individuality (and that white boys would not have available to them). His appreciation of nature and life is stressed. During an initiation ceremony, he perceives a Yay (figuring a god), masked in deerskin, with a collar of spruce. The Yay subsequently comes to him in dream. The boy feels that he is the son of a star, that he is called by wind, clouds, and rainbow, that he has a connection with Yellow Beak (an eagle). Indeed, as a sign, the eagle sends down for him a tail feather. Similarly, a bumblebee deposits in his hair a golden ring of pollen. When he reports that he has seen Deer People dancing on the stone floor of a high cave, his priestly uncle knows he has been blessed with a vision. That evening the child sings a new song, and his uncle calls him Little Singer; but that too is a sacred name, not to be used until he has achieved the stature of healer. The uncle teaches him to use colored sand. (Avuncular status may be conferred by blood or otherwise.)

Chance, or destiny, provides additional signs of his calling. A packrat removes his piece of black petrified wood, hidden in an Anasazi cave, but deposits a white pebble in its place; a lamb, which the boy rescues from an anthill, catches a garnet in its wool. When he is old enough, the boy leaves on his pony to travel the "trail of beauty" to the west, a symbolic journeying into his adulthood, intertwined with the mythological traveling of Turquoise Woman to the western waters. As he searches for understanding, he encounters ruin and grief, in the form of an eclipse that brings a flood, wreaking havoc, destroying most of a woman's sheep and other property, and killing her handsome husband. Why does such evil exist?

He then joins the trader and his family to travel by train to the coast, a "place of many hogans," so that his mother can teach weaving there and his father demonstrate silversmithing. The youth is able to see the wide waters—frightening, at first—and make a pollen offering to Turquoise Woman on her island. Subsequently, his vocation is sealed when he discovers in the packrat's cave four large jars containing sacred deerskin masks. His uncle recounts how his own uncle, a Night Chant singer, had succeeded in concealing them before leaving on the "Long Walk"—the enforced deportation in 1864, by federal order, of all Navajos to Bosque Redondo, near Ft. Sumner, on the Pecos River, in eastern New Mexico. The boy and uncle disturb nothing that the Anasazi left in the cave, but the Navajo jars and masks are recovered, and the masks can be used in the Night Chant, with the boy assisting his mentor. The nine-day ceremony, which Armer describes, is a second initiation for him. For the first time he participates in making a sand painting, illustrating the Yeibichai story of the Whirling Logs.[45]

The impinging of the white man's world is not depicted unfavorably. While she was fully aware of historical wrongs, Armer's view is not Manichean, the evil whites, or Pelicanos, contrasted with the innocent red men. A great dragonfly (an airplane, incongruous in the Navajo world), which allows the boy to soar in the clouds, is used by engineers who will pipe water down to the valley. The train, which the young hero's family takes to California, is not depicted as invasive. The trader (Big Man) does an enormous amount of good. A white youth of fifteen whose car has broken down is not mocked or criticized, whereas two greedy Indians are depicted as horse thieves. One steals valuable pawn and sets fire to a trading post.

Dark Circle of Branches, Southwest *and Other Writings*

Dark Circle of Branches (1933) was illustrated by Sidney. The inhabited initials resemble his elsewhere; his full-page pictures recall Laura's in *Waterless Mountain* but are more detailed, with less curvature. She wrote the story partly in an apartment in Winslow, Arizona, during the severe winter of 1931, which she describes, when hundreds of sheep and some Navajos died; she completed the manuscript in Oraibi. The story concerns the Long Walk and the historical figure Na Nai, born without feet, the singer of the Mountain Chant. The action begins during his boyhood, in 1862, in Tsegi Canyon, near the cliff-dwellings of Kiet Seel. Na Nai became a renowned Medicine Man, whose ritual performance Armer witnessed in 1928.

As a historical reconstruction, the work resembles Cather's *Death Comes for the Archbishop* (Na Nai appears under his own name, however);

Navajo deerskin masks. From Washington Matthews, *The Night Chant, A Navaho Ceremonial*. Memoirs of the American Museum of Natural History, vi: Publications of the Hyde Southwestern Expedition (New York, 1902).

religious belief inspires central figures in both. Scenic re-creations and imagined dialogues serve as exposition. Unlike Cather, Armer had no detailed written sources from which to quote but had the advantage of knowing Na Nai when he was old; an interpreter questioned him for her. *In Navajo Land* contains a photograph of him smiling, his face wrinkled by age but shining with deep understanding. Whether she devised episodes cannot be determined at this remove. To convey his boyhood to white children in the 1930s was a challenge; what Edith Wharton called "the historical novel with all its vices" is especially tricky when the central figure appears as a child. Na Nai is born to be a spiritual leader and is gifted in understanding the natural world and its meanings. Learning is imparted to him by his uncle but also seems to come without intermediary other than "That Which Stands Within Me" (mind). The uncle's constant refrain is "May all things live in beauty."[46]

The title phrase refers to the final Mountain Chant ceremony, during which evergreen branches or saplings are arranged in a circle around a bonfire. Na Nai's uncle emerges from a medicine lodge and sings, as the fire burns and dancers, daubed for protection with white clay, circle the fire and whip each other with brands. The rites are intended to heal Na Nai's sick sister.[47]

Various conflicts, some bloody, are sketched, notably between Navajos and Mexicans from the south; there is friction likewise with Utes and the blue-coated Pelicanos. But within Na Nai's family, harmony reigns, as is appropriate, given that "medicine," or healing, consists in recognizing and following the ways of nature and the cosmos. Two Mexican boys, kidnapped by others, are well treated by Na Nai's family and become friends with him and his sister, thus illustrating the harmony that is possible between the two ethnic groups, despite warring in the past.

Navajo life is evoked: cooking, fetching water, weaving, hunting, sheepherding, hogans, attire. To be noted are cactus species, one of which, the twisted-heart, is mentioned in *The Trader's Children* and described in the Armers' cactus book. The text is enriched with Navajo mythology: creation stories, stories of the sun and stars (the Star-Gazer tells of them), White Shell Woman and her loom in the west, "the great horned serpent of the upper darkness," and the tale of Dsilyi Neyani, bearer of beauty, who on the fourth day of the Mountain Chant appears in a sand-painting (or "magic art"). Na Nai creates a charcoal porcupine, with white quills. On the ninth day, Navajos from miles around come to camp and witness the final events. The sister recovers, and all seems peaceful.[48]

It is then that the Pelicanos, Kit Carson at their head, come to drive out the natives from their canyons and mesa-tops, destroying their fields and peach trees and stealing their sheep (worth one dollar each) and horses (thirty dollars). Armer quotes from early testimony on the ordeal. Carson, a decent man, tries to protect women and children, but the destruction is wanton—he may have been responsible for felling the trees—and the subsequent exodus is very difficult. The Star-Gazer dies en route. At least the Mexican boys are returned to their family. Life on the Pecos River is nearly impossible—the conditions are poor, the Navajos are too numerous and not accustomed to large-scale farming, and drought and plague kill what crops they manage to cultivate. Moreover, they are raided by Comanches. Na Nai's mother does not survive. The government finally admits its mistake and allows them to return to Arizona.

Armer does not allow the story to end in sorrow. Back at Tsegi, one of the Mexican boys, now a grown man, returns to visit the family and tells how he has been to school in a great city (Santa Fe) and learned to make silver jewelry; he then announces that he will open a trading post among them. Na Nai learns more songs and makes splendid sand-paintings, the visual equivalent of his singing.

Southwest (1935) is devoted primarily to Arizona, with glimpses of the California desert, Mesa Verde, and Mexico. By its mixture of poetic description, historical summary, and personal responses it resembles Austin's *The Land of Journeys' Ending* (without being derivative). Lorenzo Hubbell and Na Nai are both portrayed. "To him [Na Nai] I owe more debt of gratitude than to any other Navaho, for it was he who shared with me his knowledge of ancient lore. He blessed my trail.... He prayed to the Sun Bearer not to hide the light from the Hard-working Woman." A healing ceremony is summarized. Myths (creation stories, White Shell Woman) are intertwined with botanical and zoological observations and word-paintings—of mountains at dusk, for instance. Armer recounts the building of her hogan.[49]

The illustrations, based on her oils, emphasize the spiritual dimension of her vision. The end papers depict sand-painting figures, Mother Earth and Father Sky, "from the Shooting Chant of the Navahos." The frontispiece, a fine stylized image of Navajos singing, is captioned "Song mounts to the clouds in a moving elixir of life." In another picture, large curves and spirals and stylized leaves entwine around a pensive woman's face. In a third, pieces of fruit on a plate are foregrounded at right, with a squatting woman toward the left and, behind, two enormous stylized toucans. That illustration accompanies paragraphs on the Mayas and Aztecs and especially Quetzalcoatl (the Plumed Serpent). Armer recounts a descent into a coal mine and visits to Cuernavaca, El Paso, and the caverns of New Mexico (Carlsbad). Challenges such as erosion control and the building of Boulder Dam emphasize the importance of water.[50]

Beauty, while justified as itself, is also connected to goodness and truth. As Armer and Mary Austin both remarked, in the Southwest, no subterfuge is possible. The hierarchical relatedness of things, corresponding to the Great Chain of Being, is stressed; Klitso, the builder, remarks on the interdependency of life levels, by which every created thing has power over others. Something, he observes, must be higher than man. What is it? Human intimations of the divine depend on, or call forth, images, both natural and stylized by artistic imitation. "Those holy animals which we call bears, coyotes and badgers, and who live among us today, are not the real people the Medicine Men mean when they sing about them. Who knows what the real ones are? They are beyond man's knowledge. Man invents their images." This insight is almost Platonic: the visible points to the invisible, the ideal. Speaking in her own name, Armer recalls a song of the sun that concludes, "On a trail of beauty, my mind / Approaches the border of earth."[51]

The Trader's Children, with Laura's photographs and inhabited initials by Sidney, appeared in 1937. She may have conceived the book, composed in their hogan, while taking the photographs; or the text may have come afterwards, shaped to the images. It offers a tender and well-written family portrait, with real models and incidents but arranged artfully. The action, which lasts nine months, takes place at Black Mountain trading post. Waterless Mountain reappears. The unnamed trader, whose four young children are featured, is modeled apparently on George Hubbell, the trader at Piñon and cousin to Lorenzo (called "Uncle"). The grandfather may be based on J. L. Hubbell. They are all Nai Kai, that is, Spanish-Americans (light-skinned, according to the photographs). Laura and Sidney are "Aunt Mary" and "Uncle Joe." Navajos play a significant role.

Turquoise stones and carvings, both ancient and modern, are associated with the sky, hence rain, a constant need and a theme here. Numerous washes line the valley; on one, a dam is under construction. (In spring 1912 a federal law had authorized creation of the Ganado Reservoir, perhaps a model.) There is friction between government engineers and native employees because excavation has turned up fossil Phytosaur bones and teeth, which the Indians, more by fear than to honor the remains, refuse to remove. A boy helps mediate the dispute, with the help of three pesos and negotiation skills, and the work concludes. The skeleton and teeth will be sent to an anthropologist in Berkeley. "That is finished, finished in beauty." The dam is, unfortunately, washed out by a great cloudburst, but eventually another is successfully built at a site selected by the natives.[52]

Though not centered on Navajo mythology, the book contains a creation myth and other local lore. Native arts are prized: earrings, necklaces, a silver hat band, a gray saddle blanket with red swastikas, a small fetish, described as *nezhoni*, which resembles a mountain lion ("Soft-footed Chief," a good-luck animal that appears also in *Waterless Mountain*). The Navajo workmen pawn many of their best pieces, pending payday. "The beams in the store were draped with turquoise and silver, waiting to be taken out of pawn." Other prized creations include weavings, pots, and sand-paintings; Aunt Mary copies some in drawings. A Medicine Man explains one involving eagles, eaglets, and a beggar-boy named "He-Who-Picks-Up." She makes a beautiful quilt, with woolen batting, in a cactus flower pattern, as a surprise gift for Uncle Joe, who returns from California for Christmas.[53]

The holiday celebration, which she organizes, includes the trader's family, many Navajos, and the engineers; it is a cordial syncretic event honoring the Nativity and also the return of the sun. When Loud Talker, Mary's new helper, brings his newborn daughter, Mary is thrilled. Invented or not, the child is a reminder of the daughter Laura and Sidney lost as well as the babe of Bethlehem, a motif highlighted by the names *Mary* and *Joe*. In other episodes, the trader's small daughter departs for school in Santa Fe and a Christmas tree is chosen far up a canyon. During a visit to Canyon de Chelly and the White House cliff dwellings, Uncle Joe explores a cave, difficult of access, in which he finds a small shell (a reminder of White Shell Woman) and an ancient basket, preserved from the Basket-Maker era.

Two sons of a figure depicted sued the author successfully for "demeaning his character." The suit was settled by a payment of $750 (by the publishers) and withdrawal of the book from commerce. From internal evidence it seems that the plaintiffs' father was the figure named Hasteen Akako (perhaps an alias). Dealings with him are generally favorable, and he acts as an informant on native matters, in addition to cutting logs for the eight-sided house. One of his daughters does domestic work for Aunt Mary. He is, however, resentful. In need of money, in order to redeem pawn, Akako demands ten dollars from Aunt Mary. She gives him what

Navajo riders in Canyon de Chelly. Photograph by Edward S. Curtis, ca. 1904. Library of Congress.

she has, five. The sum being insufficient, he goes to Gallup and buys liquor from an unscrupulous white man, having in mind resale, with profit. He is caught with a gallon of it. It is a disaster for his family. In an attempt to free him, his daughter walks to the distant *calabozo*, through cold December rain. That the incident took place exactly as recounted is uncertain but plausible.[54]

    Farthest West (1939), an instructive tale for young readers, with illustrations by Sidney, did not, despite its charm, achieve commercial success, as Laura acknowledged. Though not concerned with the Southwest, it deserves mention here for its conservation message, similar to that expressed by Mary Austin, Theodore Roosevelt, John Muir, Ernest Thompson Seton, and others. The book is dedicated to members of the Save-the-Redwoods League, "that far-seeing group which knows the need of serving Earth our Mother." Earth is a home; human beings are its stewards, responsible for it, sharing it with other species. "Greed is a monster," and a purely utilitarian attitude, with no further concern, is disrespectful, indeed, sacrilegious. Armer's hopeful vision (a successful children's campaign to prohibit development near "Pigeon Creek") strikes one now as simplistic (like Austin's *The Ford*) but does not invalidate her commitment.[55]

In Navajo Land

The Navajo cosmology and legends that contributed to Armer's tales are the product of hope, belief, and acceptance of human life in its natural dimensions, with a metaphysical vein. Goodness, truth, beauty are written in the sky, to which human beings aspire. Like happiness, the earthly counterparts of these intangibles are imperfect always, just like life itself, as the trader in *Waterless Mountain* tells the boy. Armer's commitment to aesthetic values, whether in nature or the arts (including her beautifully crafted sentences and appealing images), was her manner of reaching toward the ideal. *In Navajo Land* recalls nostalgically her final departure from Arizona, on Christmas Day: "In my lotus-flower house of eight walls, which I was to leave forever.... I could feel the blessing which had descended upon us.... The fire of desert comradeship still burns in my consciousness. It lights the trail of my mind as it travels to the Old Age River." The book was her adieu to literature, and to life itself. *Nezhoni*, "finished in beauty."[56]

CHAPTER FIVE

Peggy Pond Church

Church's Achievements and Place in New Mexican Letters

The poet Peggy Pond Church (1903–86), who was born in New Mexico and spent nearly all her life there, celebrated its land, skies, traditions, and peoples, Spanish, Indian, and Anglos. While she did not have what might be considered the privilege of discovering the region in adulthood and being moved by its singularity to new vision, she had the advantage of knowing it, as she might have said, in her bones. As an author, she had regional identity. She was called "one of the American west's major poets"; in New Mexican letters of her era, her achievement rivals that of Witter Bynner. Stanley Noyes, a Santa Fe author, spoke of her "significant American voice," possessing "the integrity of the true artist, a capacity for looking with clear eyes at unpleasant realities as well as at beauty." The critic Lawrence Clark Powell called her "one of the few poets to grace the Southwest"—as contrasted to numerous "versifiers" there. She had "a place in our literature beyond the regional"; she belonged to the Southwest but was not parochial. W. David Laid named her "The First Lady of New Mexico poetry, who should be in all poetry collections." Her stature is not, however, that of certain other western poets whose names come to mind. They include Richard Hugo, Theodore Roethke, William Stafford, and two Californians, Robinson Jeffers and Yvor Winters, who both spent time in New Mexico also.[1]

As examination of Church's verse later in this chapter will make clear, it was rooted in nature, to which she was highly sensitive from her earliest years. She sought truth, not fancy; as Andrew Elkins observed, she did not "succumb to the temptation to use the earth as imagination's plaything." She had vision in the poetic sense and, according to some, the spiritual one—"a mystical affinity with the natural world." "Her poetry is as evocative a testament to the sensuality and spirituality of the land as has ever been written in the Southwest," wrote one commentator. She made hers a phrase of Mary Austin: "Beauty-in-the-wild, yearning to be made human." She excelled at details, using a close-up lens. The poem "Blue Heron" gives a sense of her precision with natural scenes: "...the heron was half hidden / in a background of bare branches, yet I saw him fishing // immobile as though he had been rooted there forever / among the willows, long legs stretched and limber, / the serpentine neck poised, sheathed in quiescent feather..."[2]

Church was also a poet of landscapes and of wholes. The Alaskan poet John Haines wrote, "I believe there is a spirit of place, a presence asking to be expressed." When Church was asked about her poet's credo, she replied, "It's the land itself that wants to be said." The "land" included water and air, "which after all is the medium in which the human organism is rooted far more than it is on earth." May Sarton wrote to Church, "You are rare in the depth of your roots in that landscape," adding, "which goes deep into the past." Mabel Dodge Luhan observed of Church: "Her eyes always had a direct, long-range expression, as in one who gazes from a mountaintop across wide valleys to a far-away distance. And always she had time." Church's verse is also an auto-portrait, less direct than oblique, however, with a Whitmanesque blending of self and world. She could have said, with Alfred Lord Tennyson's Ulysses, "I am a part of all that I have met."[3]

Church's world is not, as a critic observed, "tainted by the traditional male attitudes of hierarchy and control." She believed that her approach was not men's. "To the men of the age the land exists only to be exploited ... the attitude of man toward nature has been to possess it." Such an approach was not confined to males; as noted in chapter two, she identified "the exploitive side of the masculine in Mary [Austin's] own psyche, which is the enemy of the land-loving husbandman within her."[4]

Church published prose as well as poetry. Her entwined portrait of Edith Warner (1892–1951) and herself, called *The House at Otowi Bridge* (1959), won the Longmont Award and was praised by Lanford Wilson in the *New York Times Book Review*. She did an Afterword to a reprint of *Interlinear to Cabeza de Vaca*, by Haniel Long (1888–1956), a friend. Another prose work, posthumous, is *Wind's Trail*, her study of Austin's early life.[5]

Church also kept journals, including "Journal of Death" or "Terminal Journal," composed as her husband was dying. Some diaries she burnt. In autumn 1986, she gave portions to Shelley Armitage for sorting, editing, and possible publication as nature journals or autobiography. Though Armitage's edition (*Bones Incandescent*) is unsatisfactory, the original material is rewarding—poetic, philosophical, and personal. The bold, imaginative gropings toward understanding allow readers to see between and behind the lines of Church's poetry. She sometimes used the third person, calling herself "She," and also imagined an alter ego, Quince (the name chosen as unusual)—as Austin had used the I-Mary. The style is reflective and often fine, yet not pretentious or excessively flowery: "The moon last night made a porpoise or dolphin of the black cloud and haloed it with silver. Today is the most shining green and gold early autumnal day. I walked down to the mesa at noon and heard the wind like the swish of a long taffeta skirt in the corn.... I sat at the edge of the growing field of winter rye and saw it moved by the wings of quick little birds and by the wind." Metaphors come as though naturally and carry considerable weight. Needles and thorns prick but give pleasure: "Life is like sucking honey off the thorn." Church recalls that the finest needle for a photograph record is a cactus thorn, giving the best sound—but too delicate.[6]

Church's desire to preserve the natural world was paralleled by concern for the often-fragile creations of its Native American residents, past and present, for whom she felt enormous empathy. Albeit shared by many of the opposite sex, this attitude of empathy is viewed as particularly feminine. To her, indigenous cultures were not closed; they were available to Anglos also. She would write later: "The white man's wisdom has resulted only in the atomic bomb.... We have made a god of man, and that is not good." When someone told her friend Warner that the country was so old "it does not matter what we Anglos do here," Warner countered: "What we do anywhere matters but especially here. It matters very much. Mesas and mountains, rivers and trees, winds and rains are as sensitive to the actions and thoughts of humans as we are to their forces." For Church, the world was "sacred." She agreed with the Pueblos and Warner that all nature was alive with spirit. "To live here we must not only think the mountain is holy but know it—think of its holiness each time we look at it—focus upon it the spirit of all holiness which we feel in us." She spoke of her "personal ecology." "It is the duty of all living men to maintain the harmony they are aware of in the world around them." In the Southwest, the "great powers" that move between sky and earth were close, she thought, and available. "The land itself indoctrinated me with what the Indians both had learned from it and taught it." Yet, like Warner, she resisted "the temptation to idealize the Indians." Though they were often victims, she knew there was no innocence in history: "Not one [nation] but which is, in its way, a piracy."[7]

Background and Life Until Marriage

Margaret Hallett Pond was born prematurely on 1 December 1903 in Mora County, Territory of New Mexico, near Valmora, not far northeast of Las Vegas, east of the Sangre de Cristos mountains. She was the first child of Ashley Pond, Jr., and Hazel Hallett Pond. The latter, thirteen years younger than her husband, was the granddaughter of a former Arkansas governor who in 1878 settled in northeast New Mexico. Born in St. Louis, Hazel later lived with her parents in Los Angeles; she and her brother went every summer to stay on their grandfather's ranch, the Clyde (named for his Clydesdale horses). Pond, the son of a wealthy Detroit attorney, was a sickly boy, suffering especially from bronchitis. He attended Yale, matriculating late because of interrupted schooling; he did not graduate. He enlisted with Theodore Roosevelt's Rough Riders but before seeing action fell ill with typhoid fever. He returned to Detroit but, in 1899, his father sent him to New Mexico to continue his recovery. He met and married Hazel and planned to open a school. To that end, he bought property a few miles east of Watrous, renovated buildings, erected an additional structure, and hired staff. The project came to nothing. In October 1904, the swollen Mora River weakened an embankment of the Santa Fe railroad; when it gave way, water flooded the property, and Ashley barely had time to carry his wife and child to a higher barn.[8]

The Ponds returned to Detroit, where two other children were born. Peggy first learned to appreciate nature at the family house on Three Mile Lake. Pond, whom his daughter thought of as "restless," 'a dreamer," "an idealist," and whom others called "kindly and good-hearted," had not forgotten New Mexico, however. His father's death left him with an independent income and allowed him to take his family first to California, then Roswell (southeastern New Mexico). In 1914, he and four Detroit partners (automobile executives and bankers) established in Pajarito Canyon a "club," a private affair, principally for fishing. (The canyon is part of the Pajarito Plateau, a complex of canyons and mesas of volcanic ash approximately thirty miles to the northwest of Santa Fe, near the Jemez Mountains, the highest elevation of which is 11,561 feet.) Pond moved his family there and managed the property. After the second summer, he relinquished the management and announced that he and his family would leave. The water supply was inadequate (he had been misled by a wet year); in addition, his "improvidence" made the Detroit partners unwilling to continue their support.[9]

Pond invested in mining stocks, worthless, then, at an inflated price, bought another property, just a few miles away, on the plateau. There he opened Los Alamos Ranch School (named for nearby cottonwoods). The first student arrived in January 1918. The facilities were rustic; cattle were run until 1922. Peggy resented the fact that the school was for boys only. It was originally conceived as more "ranch" than "school" and was intended, in part at least, for weak boys, particularly tubercular. One former student wrote that at least twenty boys (out of forty or so, later) were there for reasons of health. While the statement may be inaccurate, he himself had tuberculosis, and one student died. Alice Marriott, who became familiar with the school just before it closed, wrote that it was run by "extraordinary and gifted people." After the arrival of A. J. Connell, the first director, Pond withdrew from the management and returned, with his family, to Santa Fe. (He shortly went overseas with the American Red Cross. Some years later he helped organize and was chief of the Santa Fe Fire Department.)[10]

Peggy was a shy, sometimes "difficult" child. She struggled against low self-esteem (like her father, whose dominating father had controlled him). She spoke later of "a paralyzing shyness and reticence." She believed that she was plain, without her mother's charm, less attractive than her blonde sister, and the least loved of the offspring—particularly less than her brother. (Church's childhood bears resemblance to Austin's.) Like many gifted girls, she was convinced, not entirely without reason, that her parents did not understand her; they showed her little love, apparently, and she witnessed considerable family discord. (Pond once sued his wife for divorce; the two were sometimes estranged.) "The imp is what we try to suppress in all children, but the imp, the rebel, is part of the creative personality." Peggy experienced ambivalence about women's situation; masculine authority, or patriarchy, will, and power bothered her as early as the Detroit years. "Everything spontaneously gay and feminine must subdue itself in the presence of the great ruler of the household" (her grandfather). But she reacted also against her father's impracticality and "chaotic tenderness," which she explored in her notebooks.[11]

She also experienced embodiment in ambivalence and anguish ("the animality of the body"). "The child always envying men their strength, their freedom ... they can go freely into the wilderness. And ... for them there is no dread of rape." The ambivalence is pertinent to her poems on conjugal difficulties. She viewed sexuality as bondage and, as an adult, wrote of awkwardness and unpleasantness in intercourse, humiliation in childbirth and nursing. Her phrase "One's body is one's own" expresses a strong sense of ontological autonomy but wishful thinking, practically. She reacted against her mother's devotion to order and "essential common sense ... which I, alas, scorned, preferring my own flight of fancy, and so came to hate my resemblance to my mother and to fight against it." (The picture reflects her mother's *animus*—that is, the inner masculine part, or authority, by which she "castrated the father psychologically.") The girl's recoil from aspects of feminine embodiment and rejection of resemblance to her mother, as well as her mother's domestic order, may be read, if critics choose, through a feminist screen or a Freudian one. Church appears not to have seen herself in those terms, however; her self-image lay elsewhere.[12]

Unsurprisingly, Peggy was an outdoors girl, scorning dolls. With her siblings, she explored the Pajarito surroundings—sagebrush flats, caves, Anasazi ruins—gathering arrowheads, observing plants and topography. At age five or six, she saw a golden cowslip, "alluring, far-off," in a boggy cow pasture; she longed to approach it, even in her bare feet, but dared not for fear of being sucked in by "the center of the black muck/ she dared not wade through." "But the cowslip is still there, inside." She was keen on riding. At her father's insistence, she first rode bareback. Having himself fallen off the same horse from which she was tossed, he relented. She later used a saddle that had belonged to her great-grandfather, then mother. Even as a child she knew how to groom her horse. She honored animals, recognizing, as Sharon Snyder puts it, that "each animal had a kind of wisdom all its own." Throughout her life she loved hiking.[13]

Her education was erratic. During their canyon year, the children had a governess, who taught them names of wildflowers and mesas. Thereafter Peggy attended various schools in New Mexico and on both coasts; she grew accustomed to long train rides. She apparently did not feel homesickness, perhaps because she became accustomed to change or because home was unhappy. She had dance lessons and learned to play the piano; music brought her much pleasure later. She read for hours, devouring Greek mythology (to which her verse alludes often) and Andrew Lang's fairy tale volumes. In summer 1921 she attended a camp in Vermont, where she won an award, thereby gaining much confidence.[14]

There were, occasionally, good moments in family life. Her father read aloud from Robert Louis Stevenson's *A Child's Garden of Verses* and Edward Lear's verse; her mother recited Rudyard Kipling's "The Ballad of East and West." Peggy "cut her teeth ... on the poets whose geography is timeless." She memorized William Cullen Bryant's "Thanatopsis." At age twelve she composed "Ode to a Flower," identified as her first poem, quite acceptable for the era. (She had practiced earlier; at age eleven she tapped out a rhythm and wrote a couplet.) Her first publication was in *St. Nicholas* magazine. She won an *Atlantic* prize of $50 for a poem; for a story there she was awarded second prize and $50. Her poem "Sangre de Cristo" is an honorable effort for someone aged seventeen. Yet it is alleged that her family discouraged her from writing, though in Santa Fe later her mother was a member of the Little Theatre—an art-oriented undertaking.[15]

Peggy attended Smith College for two years (1922–24). While she was "extroverted and happy" there, as in Vermont, she missed New Mexico. "Years of Eastern boarding school and college had not cured me," she wrote—particularly of her love of horses and mountain trails. She composed there her first poem about fishing, which she had enjoyed with her father. She had with her Alice Corbin's *Red Earth* (1920). It will be recalled that Corbin (1881–1949), a former associate editor of Harriett Monroe's *Poetry*, moved to Santa Fe in 1916 with her husband, William Penhallow Henderson, an accomplished painter and architect. Ill with tuberculosis, she had expected to die. Instead, she got well. She continued to act as advisor to Monroe until 1922. (She published as both *Corbin* and *Henderson*.) *Red Earth* is replete with New Mexican scenes and figures. Church may have admired the interplay of consciousness and landscape, as land offered correlatives of passion and will. "My body is here in the valley"; "My body flows like water through the stream in the canyon." But Corbin's collection is marked by sentimentality; Church's verse is, on the whole, stronger and her production larger.[16]

In summer 1923 Peggy met Fermor Spencer Church (1900–75), a Harvard graduate from Connecticut, who had gone to teach at Los Alamos. He maintained, according to one student, "a deep and abiding dedication to the education of young people." In June 1924 the two were married, precipitously, in order to take advantage of a vacant mountain cabin called Camp May, belonging to the school, where they wished to spend their honeymoon. "The birds had the world to themselves, and the call of the towhee was like a string of jewels let down among the dark branches of the fir trees." They rode along nearby trails, she attired in a

Stetson, chaps, and spurs, using her great-grandfather's saddle. One ride took them to an old Indian shrine overlooking an extinct crater, now part of Valles Caldera National Preserve.[17]

Subsequent Life and Career

In Peggy's own words, she did not love Fermor in any way; she married for love of the Pajarito Plateau. (Her writing shows, however, that she came to care for her "companion" greatly, and her friend Corina A. Santistevan believes that the marriage was entirely right.) His calm and stability—"a quiet harbor"—attracted her; she wrote that "he was the stone, she was the rippling water." In addition, she was proud of herself for having outwitted her father, in a sense, by joining the school community. The couple lived on the school premises, in a stone-and-log cabin, where they reared three sons, Theodore, Allen, and Hugh. Ted graduated in the last class (January 1943). She continued to ride and hike; she knew, she said, every trail within seven miles. Initially, she had few domestic skills, and unlike Austin did not write about her culinary achievements. What may appear as a feminist stance—resentment of woman's domestic role—was perhaps more closely associated with her artistic temperament.[18]

Yet she was lonely. Her husband was constantly occupied by duties, and she missed feminine company. Connell's sister May, an artist, came to the plateau in 1929, but there is no indication of friendship between the women. Peggy resented the rule that forbade her to go riding with students. Connell disapproved of her activities and gave her no credit for her outdoors skills; he envisaged for women only domestic life and vexed her by saying she needed more to keep her busy. Rearing her boys was demanding, and writing was often put aside. Fermor may not have understood well the poetic soul he had on his hands. Given to depression (of some variety) since her girlhood, she was easily discouraged and sometimes almost ill. Like many other artistic women, she discovered how opposed her aspirations, emotional demands, and poet's discipline were to the practical requirements of daily life—deploring, as Virginia Woolf put it, that women do not have wives. Nevertheless, she did manage to write some in the 1920s. At the request of Santa Fe artist Gustave Baumann (a leader in the revival of color woodblock in America), she did a series called "New Mexico Santos" poems, intended to accompany woodblock prints of his (neither poems nor prints were published). A "poem cabin," built in the mid-1930s—her equivalent of Austin's wikiup—gave her private space and quiet.[19]

In addition, she found marriage relationships difficult. "She needed to express the love she held inside and to be worthy of love ... but imagined herself falling short on both counts," in Snyder's words. Her five-quatrain poem "Whom God Hath Joined" (1954) asks whether "ancient hungers stirred and fed" in the "act of flesh" led to the joining, speaks of "the aching times we lay / lonely in marriage bed," and then inquires, in the central stanza,

> Why then the struggle and the tears,
> the two in conflict ceaselessly,
> oneness so perilously born
> out of the you and me?

Such reflections appear frequently in her poems and their titles. Yet there are acknowledgments that the union was close, if imperfect: "...struggle each for his own soul / was struggle side by side."[20]

In 1932 her father fell ill of influenza, then encephalitis, finally encephalomalacia; he died the following year. She suffered what has been called a "breakdown" and a "schism" in her marriage. While such experiences can contribute to a writer's insecurity, they may also lead to eventual healing and increased confidence. Peggy was hospitalized in New Haven in autumn 1933; her married sister lived in the area. She had a brief affair there, deeply satisfying and moving; it functioned as one element in her recovery. She and the man planned to marry; she would divorce Fermor. The latter, meanwhile, had become involved with a local woman. Peggy and Fermor were reconciled, however, after a visit to an aunt in Tucson and a short period of living apart. The same year she also had a brief sexual encounter with her poet friend and mentor Long.[21]

As another aspect of her recovery, or development and working out of her personality, Church became interested in the psychology of Carl Jung, whose work she first discovered in 1934. She studied her dreams, recording many in journals and poetry, as in these lines from "Shattered":

> I came out of my dream
> and found the stars had moved
> only a handsbreadth down the indefinite arc...[22]

Beginning in California, where she had accompanied Fermor in 1938 during his leave of absence to study at Stanford University, she pursued Jungian analysis for years; she returned for sessions in 1959. (One of the poems in *This Dancing Ground of Sky* is titled "On Receiving a Bill for Nine Hours of Analysis.") She and Fermor also pursued biblical studies, especially on the Gospels. She likewise read Sir James Frazier's *The Golden Bough* and once said she was "up to her ears" in mythology. She accepted Jung's theory of ancestral or collective memory, formed of inherited characteristics, intuition, and wisdom. On the mesas, she felt kinship with unknown ancestors, "the ancestors of a race not even my own." Like Jung, she believed that art sprang from the unconscious activation of an archetypal image coming from the collective unconscious. "It seems the collective spirit of the world enters into us." She wrote of a "familiar moment of childhood—a childhood that belongs to us all, though farther away and longer ago than our memories."[23]

Authors to whom Church turned at various times included William Blake, Colette, Doris Lessing, Thomas Merton, Pablo Neruda, Kathleen Raine, Rainer Maria Rilke (whom she read in German), and Eudora Welty. She translated Neruda's poem on Machu Picchu (1973). She became acquainted with Sarton, probably sometime in the early forties, when Sarton visited Santa Fe to lecture and read from her work. This acquaintance led to an exchange of some forty letters (1948–86). Church also corresponded with Denise Levertov.[24]

Peggy Pond Church at Otowi Bridge. Courtesy Kathleen D. Church.

Poetry brought Church regional and national attention. Her first and second collections, *Foretaste* (1933) and *Familiar Journey* (1936), were published by a Santa Fe cooperative called Writers' Editions, established to give "a significant voice" to the New Mexico literary community. These books were followed by a half-dozen others. Her work appeared in the *Saturday Review of Literature*, and in April 1936 *Poetry* printed five poems (following ten by Robert Frost) under the collective title "The Unceasing Fountain." Church was an occasional participant in the Poets' Round-ups of Henderson and Corbin, whom she met in 1931. But she could not have attended frequently, in view of her family responsibilities and driving conditions from Los Alamos to Santa Fe, over long and tortuous mountain roads, with narrow bridges.[25]

Moreover, she lacked the self-confidence needed to pursue a career as a public figure. To write poetry was "no life's work but a form of intellectual (or spiritual) ... exercise...." She was in many ways conventional, using her husband's name in publishing as well as daily life; certainly, as Armitage observed, she was not radical. Noting that Church's talent (meaning, perhaps, *achievement*) was inferior to Sarton's, Armitage attributed the difference to Church's "shyness and commitment to a marriage and children." Despite attraction to the artist's life, Church admitted, that "something in me could never be 'bohemian.'" Put perhaps more accurately, she did not have the sort of ambition that overrode other considerations, the "deep drive for recognition" that Powell detected as crucial in Austin. Her friend Santistevan believes that, though Peggy was "a very strong woman," she did not push herself ahead; she may have remained suspicious of the *animus*, or masculine part (perhaps even in the Jungian sense), fearing what Armitage calls "the prospect of an ego-driven career." Kathleen Church (Hugh's wife) adds that her work "was from the heart, and when it was unappreciated, the criticisms of careless editors broke her." It is significant that in 1929 Church wrote to Austin, whom she had met, sending poems and asking for advice. The *grande dame* of letters in Santa Fe (as she styled herself), reputedly generous to other writers, was not encouraging: "You write very well, but you don't have anything to say." If this assessment was justified at the time, it soon became less so, poetry being a young writer's skill, an older writer's art.[26]

In any case, from the time Church married and thus re-established herself in New Mexico, she was ill-placed to lead the sort of literary life that Austin and Willa Cather had. While novelists from the South and West could sometimes gain fame in the Northeast, poets who achieved recognition there were largely from New York and New England. As Rodney Nelson, reviewing Church's *New & Selected Poems*, put it, "The curricula of modern American literature evolved in New York," where other poets established Greenwich Village as "a spiritual home detached from place." Nelson wondered whether Church "chose obscurity by remaining close to her New Mexico birthplace." In her later years she sent little to publishers, notwithstanding that some of her strongest poems were written in her seventies and early eighties.[27]

In 1942 Church made the acquaintance of J. Robert Oppenheimer, who is quoted in *The House at Otowi Bridge*. Unacquainted with his research, she still suspected that his presence at Los Alamos was connected to war, as was the case. Whether she knew of his Communist Party sympathies when he was in California is uncertain. Peggy was not immersed in politics, but in the thirties and forties anyone who listened to the radio and read newspapers could not be unaware of such political matters. Oppenheimer and his wife shortly became friends of Warner and dined at her little house, along with other famous physicists, for whom Warner put out black plates and bowls made by María Martínez. As a youth, he had spent many weeks near Terrero, northeast of Santa Fe, and had ridden on the Pajarito Plateau; later he had owned property in the area. In the 1920s he had written to a friend, with ironic foreshadowing, "My two great loves are physics and New Mexico. It's a pity they can't be combined."[28]

Late in 1942 it was announced that the school would be closed in order that the Manhattan Project could be carried on there. It was a radical uprooting in Church's life, close to traumatic. Plans were secret; officially, the site and the undertaking did not exist. A joke circulated to the effect that Los Alamos was a submarine base. Yet the veil was not so impenetrable that locals, knowing something of the personnel who had visited earlier, could not penetrate it. A student recognized Oppenheimer and Ernest Lawrence, another physicist, as they toured the property. A celebratory pamphlet on the school, published later, for which Peggy and Fermor wrote the narrative, includes lines from the Mexican ballad "Cuatro Milpas," recalling "the happy hours we spent in that place." What angered her chiefly was the research on the atomic bomb and its testing and use. Having the elements of tremendous destruction on the very ground where her family had lived brought about a conversion experience. (Cather, who had written her regrets over the Great War into two novels, similarly deplored the destruction brought about by the bomb, wondering why science was used for such great ills.) Carrying out implications of her personal creed—humanism and respect for nature—Church became a pacifist, and in 1948 she and her husband joined the Society of Friends.[29]

At Christmastime 1942, Peggy left Los Alamos with her younger sons; her husband and elder son stayed into January (the end of the term). She rented a house in Taos on Camino de la Placita, next door to her brother, Dr. Ashley Pond III, who had settled there in 1936, and not far from her mother. The Churches later moved to Espinosa Road. Peggy was already acquainted with members of the Taos writers' and artists' colony, and she made new friends, including Santistevan. She knew Helen Blumenschein, the wife of Ernest Blumenschein, and Andrew Dasburg, a European Cubist and an old lover of Mabel Dodge and friend of John Reed and Louise Bryant; Dasburg appeared in *Reds* (a film about them). His European outlook—he had visited battlefields during World War I—and leftist political views may have reinforced Church's pacifism.

In the second half of the 1940s, when Fermor was offered a position at a private school in Carpinteria, California, he and Peggy left New Mexico, but, homesick, returned a year later. He rented the Sagebrush Inn, just south of Taos, and opened a school there; they lived in an old adobe house in Ranchos de Taos, with earthen floors, which she cherished and improved. Because of low enrollment, the school closed after one year. To survive, each spouse did various odd jobs; Peggy worked for a time at the Harwood Foundation and the Taos Bookshop. She was able to spend the summer of 1952 in England.[30]

In 1956 Fermor found a position as a field engineer in Berkeley, and for five years the couple lived in the Bay Area. After returning to Santa Fe, they became involved in the life of the city and took pleasure in drives and hikes out of doors. They climbed up Enchanted Mesa—its talus and the "cleft in the rock." Peggy calls it "a winged rock"—borrowing the Navajo term for Shiprock. In 1964 she visited Chaco Canyon. A "healing picnic" took place in 1965, and she traveled to Spain and Egypt that year. Fermor died in 1975. She gave many readings, including one in Taos the year before her death; she attended events at Ghost Ranch (one of two Georgia O'Keeffe properties) and St. John's College. She was honored in 1984 by the Governor's Award for Excellence and Achievements in the Arts. She moved to El Castillo, a Santa Fe retirement compound. On 23 October 1986 she died by her own hand, according to the precepts of the Hemlock Society, to which she belonged. She had suffered from defective sight, inoperable, and loss of hearing, as well as allergies or "chemical sensitivity." She is buried in Los Alamos, next to "Ashley Pond," named earlier for her father (a natural depression filled with water, piped from above the ranch). At her memorial service, nearly two hundred people sat around a simple table, serving as an altar, decorated with stones she and Fermor had gathered on their hikes.[31]

Features of Church's Poetry; Her Collections

Church has been called the "only New Mexico native to take an active part in the Modernist poetry movement that flourished in Santa Fe from the 1920s through the 1930s." If *Modernist* is interpreted broadly, the label is justified. Nonetheless she was not a bold innovator in the vein of Ezra Pound. For one thing, her writing was not nurtured by European vanguardist influences, chiefly French, as were his and T. S. Eliot's. Her aesthetic was not that of surprise, shock, rupture, and Cubist-like poetic collages, though she did use dreams, like the Surrealists writing in France in the twenties and thirties. Her artistic ideal was clarity and communication. Moreover, the direct presentation of the natural world in her verse distinguishes it from that of high Modernism as illustrated by Pound, the earlier Eliot, and Wallace Stevens.[32]

Yet her mature writing is not fraught with nineteenth-century baggage. There is no hint of Tennyson, Algernon Swinburne, or others who finished off that century poetically. Nor do her diction and forms resemble Cather's, nor Austin's verse for children. In particular, she avoided inversions. Although only some thirty years separated her from Cather, in the interval marked changes had come about in poetics, and Church is up-to-date. Her verse is built on images; rhetoric is subordinate. These images serve, as Pound recommended, as keys to an emotional or intellectual knot of meaning, according to his definition of an image as "that which presents an intellectual and emotional complex in an instant of time." She strove for "direct treatment of the 'thing,' whether subjective or objective," and better than many other moderns avoided words that did not "contribute to the presentation." "No ideas but in things," according to William Carlos Williams's precept. Church may have profited from the example of Corbin, with whom Pound had corresponded.[33]

The conclusion is that, as Frost's work illustrates well, one does not have to be a *Modernist*—experimental, iconoclastic—to be *modern*. Thus, without self-consciousness, Church generally used free verse, but it was controlled and within the range of the comprehensible, far from shocking in design or substance. Most free-verse lines are end-stopped, the syntax allowing for at least a mild pause: "Yes, we saw the red sun go down / and the white, frost-like wafer of the moon come up…" ("No Other"). Striking enjambments are found, however, separating elements that adhere by sense: "…only a heavy-lidded / Waiting for autumn" ("Open Winter"); "…hasten the season for lovers who share no other / home than the green earth" ("No Other"); "cliffs of / sandstone" ("Enchanted Mesa"). "golden leaves or / a rosier seed plume" ("On Seeing the Wild Geese").[34]

Line length varies. At times the poet uses long, wrapped lines, reminiscent those of Walt Whitman and similar to lines of various French poets, Paul Claudel included. Some lines wrap more than once, but generally not in large blocks, so that the visual effect remains that of verse, not prose. The wrapping is done by indenting the continuing line. In "I Have Looked at the Earth," as many as four lines follow the initial one, however. On other occasions, as in "Enchanted Mesa," lines are very short. The effect then is that of quick, brief notation, excluding more developed meditations. Starting with *Familiar Journey* the capitalization style changes: capitals are used at the left margins only when ordinary usage calls for them.

Church also used traditional forms—sonnets and short poems in rhymed quatrains. The sonnets in *The Ripened Fields* are (with one exception) standard Italian sonnets in iambic pentameter, printed felicitously as one block, generally rhymed *ababcdcdefefgg*. Certain rhymed poems are among her strongest.

In her first book, *Foretaste*, themes, some recurring later, include flowers, trees, rocks, the ocean. Interpretations of how she understood the material world vary. One critic asserted that her vision was dualistic. Soul and body are separate entities, and the presence of "something spiritual and timeless in the soul," though reflected (metaphorically) in the geology of the land, providing an image of permanence, is contrasted with its organic manifestation—embodiment and bodily death—and with all material reality. The gap between man and the material world is unbridgeable. Another critic took the opposite position, finding "no dualism of self and world, of humans and earth." In numerous poems by Church, the latter reading seems more accurate. While the separateness of human bodies from each other and the rest of material reality is indisputable, the "soul," as Church felt it, is reflected in and connected to the world, animal, vegetable, and mineral, in a pantheistic vision. "We thought … with the thought of rocks" ("I Have Looked at the Earth").[35]

The landscape of northern New Mexico—mesas, canyons, valleys, mountains, pueblos—is her preferred setting, used not simply for local color but as an essential element in her outlook. T. M. Pearce observed (in the same vein in which Austin wrote of regionalism) that "poetry must have a setting, and the excellent poet is one who relates the scenes for poetic dramas to action and to characters, not for color and decoration." Other themes are the past and in particular ancestors (a theme Austin treated at length in *Earth Horizon*), as well as the body, often connected, as numerous poems mentioned here suggest, to the "world's body." Church can write embodiment out of her verse and, simultaneously, into it, and there is sexually-charged language.[36]

Nature may be "friendly," but man is in some senses an alien. The main difference between human beings and their environment is knowledge of time. Visible in the seasons and the geological past, which may stand for ancestral memory, time is a dimension of the connections between mind and matter. Primitive being "dreams" and "stirs" in everyone. Both ocean and stone express (though they cannot feel) the sense of temporality, as in this lovely synthetic image, part of a multi-line verse: "Because the tide of centuries that had swept over those rocks somehow washed over us" ("I Have Looked...") Church recalls that lava once poured from a nearby mountain, and sees the leaves turn dark in shadow. As the persona in "Alien" observes, "There is no one here who speaks my language / Nor tree, nor stone, nor time-oblivious river." In "Peach Trees," a beautiful lyric, the view of the orchard blossoming on a slope is complemented by the evocation of those who, generations before, plowed the stony earth, hoed around the young roots, and dug the irrigation ditch, designed so that water would go uphill. A woman hoeing, "ageless as the brown hills are ageless, ... dreamed, even before the slender branches had budded / of yellow fruit..."[37]

Details are well utilized, and onomastic richness contributes to the aura of poems, creating a local geography, as in "Sheep Country," where Pojoaque, Nambé, Santo Domingo, Redondo Peak, Capulin Canyon are all mentioned. The poem evokes the springtime transhumance of sheep from the canyons to the hills and sketches the herders, boys and men, some of them simple-minded, "...who do not desire anything more of living / Than to lie in the glittering shadow of an aspen / On the rim of the Valles where the sheep feed...." The poet then observes, "There are men who desire much more and find much less. / Must we all be madmen, I wonder, or innocents / To follow the sheep ... / Looking down, west, to the sea of grasses...?" "Winter Sketch" shows how, in the manner of Williams's most accessible verse ("The Red Wheelbarrow"), a few notations suffice to evoke a scene and make a poem: "Today there is snow all over the valley.... And there is a house with a blue door and a blue-framed window / Like a reminder of the sky, and a lamp lit in it / And three pigs; and a cow chewing her cud in a dooryard."[38]

In the free-verse narrative poem "Abiquiu—Thursday in Holy Week," Church sets the scene in a moonlit field, near a wall of low stone, then describes a vision of Penitentes coming out of their *morada* (private chapel), one singing, one playing the Penitente flute, and the third lashing himself with a woven whip. The speaker in the poem reflects: "I, under the cold stars, there in the cold night, watching / The greatest of remembered tragedies enacted..." The men will return to their ordinary lives, dealing with irrigation, wood, burros, sheep; but "to imitate ... / A great and tragic action, is to be lifted by it / For a moment out of commonplace living toward greatness."[39]

The motif of blood serves to connect Church's speakers to her ancestral past, especially the feminine lines. "After Looking into a Genealogy" includes apostrophes to long-dead female ancestors, whose old-fashioned names, on gravestones, are "all that is left of you, my grandmothers! All but the blood / That makes me one with you." This "blood" includes ancestral memory; it is personified as separate from the speaker, though within her—crying "like a wanderer returned when I first saw—/ I, the desert-born, this offspring of New England growing / Among New Mexico mountains /when I first saw the dogwood blossoming in Connecticut woods...." This brief vision is followed by a detailed description of a Vermont countryside, as seen in dreams (perhaps actual ones). The speaker "remembers" the first winter in America, on the shore of "the fierce grey water / Heaped between us and England"; more than one grandfather lies in the graveyard. Contrasted to contemporary women, when even the weak "live easily," are the women of the Vermont settlement and their close descendants, sturdy-limbed, going off "shoulder to shoulder with our men, and singing / Into the farther wilderness." The frontier and its challenges have disappeared. "Where can we go, we in whom your blood sings?" The Jungian vision goes back still farther than the speaker's ancestors. "...your blood leaps in me / (Obliterating time, making of me one person with my forebears, / One person who has lived since life crawled up from the waters / And became man)."[40]

Familiar Journey, Church's second collection, elicited considerable praise. Her poet-friend Long wrote that it was "a fuller picture of a Being, a Life, than any [other] I know in contemporary letters. The three aspects of our sentience—environment, personality, racial memory—are in a really wonderful balance. The triple harmony you have woven here makes a music as sane and sound as it is lyric." Elizabeth Shepley Sergeant, whose familiarity with Taos and other pueblos made her a understanding reader, reviewed the book for the *Saturday Review*. She wrote that Church was a "pristine" poet, "probably the first real New Mexican to produce a book of undeniable poetic promise out of her region and her life."[41]

Nature is again a source of themes and motifs. Rain appears as a healing element, and the ocean, which Church and her husband admired at Point Lobos, in California ("This Ocean"), contrasts well with mesas in other poems. The theme of love runs through the collection—love in its "alchemy," and "the shape of love transfixed on the face of the lover" ("Carved in Ivory"). The body of a dead artist is "atoms of dust," but his hand can "remember the shape of the body" and carve in ivory the present moment. In the title poem, full of color notations (flowers, mountains, sunset), the speaker goes "back and forth" on the familiar road "as if it were another body that contained me"—a depersonalization that distances experience and yet keeps it keen.[42]

Ultimatum for Man (1946) was favorably reviewed by William Rose Benét in the *Saturday Review*; he observed that its poetry was "distinctly of this time, the work of a fine human being, concerned with the terror of the hour." Benét's comment is similarly of its time, emphasizing the message, not the poetry as such. The title poem is an illustration of how good sentiments may make bad literature. Its sixteen lines constitute a homily, full of earnestness and pleas to abandon hatred and live in love and peace; but it is without imagery and metaphoric content, and the lines are flat statement ("There is no other way out"). "Comment on a Troubled Era" has more imagery, including moon and tides, stars and planets, making the point that nature governs man (despite the achievement of nuclear fission), and that the "proud mind" of the poet's "brethren," who spoil the world for their own greed, risks destruction thus. "The Nuclear Physicists" begins with direct statement but moves to images of fire and brimstone and the "shape of evil, towering leagues high into heaven." The final stanza, however, relies too much on biblical rhetoric (the wilderness, the last temptation, "the kingdoms of earth and all the power and the glory"), ending flatly by the statement that man must "will the world's good."[43]

Fortunately, certain poems eschew preachiness for more artistic effects. In "Omens," blood runs from a slit vein, or tastes bitter on the lips, or fills a cup in a sacrificial gesture, and an unnamed hero is carried off by two soldiers, his lips "clenched upon death," his head hung backward, his eyes staring at the dead sky. "Poem to Accompany the Gift of a Loaf of Bread" evokes those, from early Egypt onward, who cultivated grain. Using words from the Eucharistic ritual, the final stanza connects bread to the Christian sacrifice (and, by implication, older rites). Despite this connection to a masculine religious ritual, the poem strikes one as a woman's, rooted in earliest agriculture, nurturing, and giving.[44]

In "Prelude to Act IV," a fine poem in blank verse, the poet calls upon Greek models to remind readers of the "tragedy" which "unfolds before our pity-stricken hearts." Destiny weighs heavily; Cassandra's voice still cries, "doomed to speak truth and yet be unbelieved / until the fatal end." "We live as man must live, who is both wise / and blind…." In "For the Hippolytus of Euripides," the poet recalls a production of that tragedy. Euripides knew "what we must know / and what we dare not know: that life is stern / beyond our power to make it what we will."

> This is man's greatness, to behold his fate
> unswerving as a wave, strong as the sea,
> nor yet to stand aside, nor shield his eyes
> but with his whole heart and with all his mind
> to praise this beauty even though he dies.

It should be observed that Church's general predilection for Greek myth, with its powerful sense of fatality, does not exclude her use of Native American stories, as in the 1976 poem "Basalt Dike with Petroglyphs": "the hump-backed flute player / among the hidden rocks."[45]

"Vital Statistics" returns to the topic of forebears. "In 1710 my ancestor, William Cole, / died and was gathered to his fathers." His possessions consisted of land, livestock, and household goods in one small dwelling. His life is emblematic of others and other generations, joined by heritage and heredity. "What tears he wept / … my heart must guess whose blood once flowed in his / and knows the tenderness of men who march / against the world by day, who turn at night / to the strange warmth of woman by their side." He and his wife are spirits, "shaped … in the moving air." It is the woman's role that shines at the end: "She was the root that nourished the green tree / and now the tree is fallen. All its leaves / drop slowly one by one."[46]

Despite moralizing in this third collection, Church's poetic practice remains subtly modern. She draws effects from contrasts, including formal ones, as when a bold enjambment underlines elevated speech: "...inhabitants thereof who / stamped their prayers with their naked feet on the hard earth" ("Comment on a Troubled Era"). The lines of "Epitaph for Man" are rhymed, though in free verse.[47]

The previously-unpublished poems in *New & Selected Poems* (1976) include four from 1948 and others from the 1950s and early 1960s. Most are in free verse, with enjambments such as "yellow/ facsimiles" ("Even the Mountains Are Ripe"—the Navajo name for September). In that poem, berries are red, aspen golden, "as though the bright sun / were begotten a thousand times in his own image." "Master Race" (1948) is another indictment of modern science as developed by those Church calls *we*. The poem is, unfortunately, too characterized by statement. The former inhabitants of the land under the mountain, who are associated with eagle's feathers and yellow pollen, honored the earth. They have been made servile. Now, the sky is barren, the mountain no longer a source of prophecy and wisdom. The sin of the master race is, of course, hubris. "We did not fall on our knees when we rent the atom. / We could look upon God and live." Everything is for the taking, even women.[48]

"Elegy for Another Day" is in uneven meter with trochaic line endings and irregular, loose rhymes. The evening along the edge of the *loma* is serene and pastoral, the animals bedded in sheep pen or corral, the western sky still glowing like an ember. Silence reigns, but it is deceptive, "as though maternal night made all things brothers, // as though earth had not received the blood of Abel"—whereas in fact the threat of warfare remains. The free-verse poem "Still Life" is an outstanding study in quietness and latent movement. The picture is of four stones, a few sand dollars, and a water-washed root on a plate on the breakfast table. "She cannot see the stones only as stones. / She says 'If these were birds and they could fly!' / and suddenly the air is full of birds; / the colors move and sing." Likewise, "a creature ... in the root" struggles to free itself in voiceless agony. "Morning upon new morning brings no change. / The birds fly back into their stones again."[49]

The themes of age, decay, and death are central in "Alas" (1963), in which the first-person speaker begrudges "the body's slow death," thinking it would be better to be seized and eaten by an eagle or fish than by "this inward worming." In "Lament," a death is recalled by footprints. "It is the workman in you that I weep for ... / How often my own life seems past any mending." The same themes are worked into the lyrical "Elegy in Three Movements," dedicated to Alice and Haniel Long (1956), which was selected for the Best Poetry of 1957 by the Borestone Mountain Poetry Awards. The first section describes the couple's closeness ("...she had been the tree / on which the vine of his life entwined") and relates how, when the surgeon failed the husband, it was the wife who died first, going ahead as though to make "the last darkness seem familiar." Their lives were "one music," but the final chords sound. In the second section Haniel seems to keep a unicorn in a garden, or perhaps he is himself the unicorn, an extraordinary being, carefully concealing his singularity. "Love was their genius," the third section proclaims, "the cryptogram whose secret meaning / they read lifelong between them." "Love was the token they gave us, / ... ... / the curved shell left on the shore // for our hands to hold after the green wave slowly / dies back into the sea."[50]

The Ripened Fields (1978) was viewed as Church's best work to date, with only *Birds of Daybreak* garnering more praise later. The sonnets were composed between 1943 and 1953, save the last, written after Fermor's death in 1975. "What marriage," wrote Powell, "is not tested, even those rare ones called ideal, by temperamental conflict between the woman and the man?" Powell added, "Those do not survive when neither yields. The Churches' marriage transcended the testing told in these sonnets"—unlike the failed marriage depicted in George Meredith's *Modern Love*, to which he compares Church's sequence (despite differences in length and the writer's situation). According to Armitage, Peggy's sonnets were used as part of a marriage guide for the Episcopal Church. Elkins gives the series a Jungian interpretation, seeing in it "the process by which our fragmented souls are made whole."[51]

Whether or not the sequence was planned out or simply grew as Church added poems—quite likely—her choice of the sonnet form was felicitous; the short, well-tempered form affords focus and intensity within simplicity. Suggestions of fertility in the title fit well the biological reality of marriage by indicating promise fulfilled and harvest to come.

Birds of Daybreak: Landscapes and Elegies (1985) was assembled by Church the year before she died. Sarton praised it highly. The cover illustration, repeated inside, was inspired by Mimbres pottery designs (from southern New Mexico and Arizona). The collection is dedicated to the memory of Fermor, "who shared with me fifty years of clouds and stones and desert rivers." Five of the poems were previously published or read on tape. In the touching elegy "On the Putting to Death of an Old Dog" the poet foresees her own end as an old woman grasping at the end of a dream.[52]

A multi-part poem, "Black Mesa: Dream and Variations," synthesizes well landscape, body, myth, and mind. Church compares the mesa to a ship with black sails; it, too, is like a dream, from a past world. The image recalls the ship in which, having conquered the Minotaur in the Labyrinth, Theseus returns to Athens, neglecting, however, to hoist the white sails to show success; his father dies. Later in the poem, after the Turtle Dance (Peggy had seen a performance at San Ildefonso), the poet speaks of the maze of herself. Addressing the mesa, she calls it a still body, a lodestone, an essence of fire, a hand.[53]

Birds of Daybreak shows how the environment had changed in the decades since Peggy's girlhood—and how she had changed. It is not simply a matter of innocence versus experience, and not principally a matter of urbanization. In the background is the splitting of the atom, a watershed. Worn paths near a pueblo ruin have been widened and scraped (by her own feet and others'); among collapsed walls the speaker hears no echoes of time, but only silence, which is not that after music ("A Lament on Tsankawi Mesa"). "Roadside Museum" evokes a small, tawdry natural history museum, frequented by tourists who, with little concern apparently about other sentient beings, gape at animals and birds kept in unspeakable conditions. A horned owl, blinking in the daylight and tethered by one leg on ground the poet likens to Golgotha, is as miserable as King Lear on the heath. "Endangered Species" mourns a whooping crane that died of lead-shot poisoning. Not content with extinguishing birds, man takes arms against other men. An offended goddess foresees that from such violence men will produce their own annihilation.[54]

Prose Works

The House at Otowi Bridge, structured along a double narrative line, unites the story of Warner's life in New Mexico to strands of Church's biography, as a means of self-disclosure. Additional texts—paratexts, separate, though connected to the main threads of the book—are woven into the main body of the book: quotations from Oppenheimer and a New York *Times* article on Niels Bohr; passages from Warner's journal (which she kept until February 1935), a published essay by her and an unfinished manuscript dealing with her life; portions of Church's diary and a previously-published article. The appendices contain additional paratextual elements: one of Warner's recipes, samples of her celebrated Christmas letters, poems by Church, and two short letters from others. Thus main text and paratext are composed of several voices, reinforcing each other. This structure does not spring apparently from the desire to innovate; it was pragmatic, called forth by the material itself. In addition, Warner's story is interlaced with that of nearby San Ildefonso Indians, particularly Atilano Montoya, called Tilano, who came to work for Warner when he was nearly sixty, remained devoted to her as servant and friend, and outlived her. Warner had for the Tewas of San Ildefonso the cordial affection and respect that Armer had for the Navajos, reciprocated in each case.. "Because.... Edith and Tilano still live as part of my own inner world, I try now to join the broken threads of her story together and weave them with my own."[55]

Atilano Montoya of San Ildefonso Pueblo. Courtesy Kathleen D. Church.

Church and Warner had much in common. Edith, from Pennsylvania, was the eldest daughter of a Baptist minister. She taught school, then worked for the YWCA. Late in 1921 she suffered some sort of breakdown. Church attributed it partly to the burden of duty. "Like a captive bird she was torn by the instinct to seek her freedom, though her mind was for a long time unaware of what she fought for." After the Great War, "her body, unable to stand the strain, rebelled." In the fall of 1922, hoping to recover her health, she went to a guest ranch in Frijoles Canyon (part of Bandelier National Monument), after a friend described it to her. She lived thenceforth in New Mexico. Surprisingly, in 1928 she was appointed caretaker of the bridge crossing the Rio Grande at Otowi, some miles below Los Alamos. She took up residence in the house by the bridge, where she stayed until a new road made the location unattractive; scientists from the Los Alamos labs then worked beside Indian friends to build her a new house elsewhere.[56]

Her choice of New Mexico was felicitous. She reacted much like Cather's Thea, in *The Song of the Lark*. Church evokes the landscape as Warner must have discovered it initially and then sketches her later explorations, for which she gradually gathered strength. Climbing a mesa trail, Warner found "a place where she could sleep in the shelter of a sun-warmed rock." It will be recalled that "she waked feeling as though the strength of earth and sky had filled her." Warner also explored the numerous pre-Columbian ruins on the mesa top, admiring the kivas, metates (grinding-stones), shards, petroglyphs, including the Plumed Serpent (Awanyu), associated with springs, creeks, and rain, and visible in a seven-foot long horizontal petroglyph in Pajarito Canyon. "Wherever [Warner] walked fragments of boldly decorated pottery spoke of the ancient people's love of beauty." Like Armer, Church knew that material images signified spiritual reality: "Not the river, but the force embodied in the river; not the cloud but the life-giving energies of the cloud.... Rain is one of the many forms of deity."[57]

Church does not espouse explicitly Warner's quoted statements or the reflections she attributes to her. But by painting Edith's portrait, the artist does her own. Interior evidence—the parallelism in the two lives, the selection and arrangement of materials, the warmth with which Edith is described, and the poems—suggest close agreement. Church admired her simplicity and security of being, "deeply related to the feminine forces in the earth." She wrote that Edith was "the only woman with whom I would change lives." The day Edith died, Peggy "flew about frantically my little cage, like a wild bird," though she knew nothing of the death until later.[58]

A word about Church's *Wind's Trail* is pertinent, since it too was connected closely to how she saw herself. Never completed, it was contracted for as a biography of Austin for young readers, but its tone and approach evolved as Peggy worked and came to view biography as a matter less of factual accuracy than understanding. Based largely on portions of *Earth Horizon*, it also utilizes material she consulted at the Huntington Library and reprints selections from poetry written during Austin's college years. For Church, Austin's work was, it appears, both an inspiration and a burdensome legacy. "I myself was smitten with the landscape and some of her philosophical essays and felt that she expressed some of the things I was groping for." As a southwestern nature poet, Church was well placed to study her subject; she was, additionally, familiar with the conflict between objective and subjective selves. She was temperamentally different, however, not putting herself forward like Austin, who "would walk the fine line ... between humility toward the creative powers and the most outrageous identification of her own ego with them." Like Austin, Church may have felt guilt, though that is unclear; similarly, she understood the dark side of artistic creation. Seeing what she feared was misdating in Austin's account of a drought, she was gratified to find that the date was accurate; she concluded that the event had great significance for Mary, for "what she felt was a drought in her soul."[59]

Church's writing for children began with *The Burro of Angelitos*, with striking black-and-white illustrations, published in 1936; it won the Julia Ellsword Ford Foundation prize for a humorous child's book. While young children can probably follow the story line as read aloud, the vocabulary is more suited to older readers. As a child, Peggy's mother had ridden a burro named Lightfoot, hard to round up but obedient to her; she remembered him fondly in stories she told her children, and these stories may have inspired Church's text. Kathleen Church sees it as an attempt to preserve some of the isolated Pueblo and Hispanic customs that were, even at that date, threatened by social change—among them, woodcutting and burro-packing. When

Official scenic historic marker of New Mexico honoring Peggy Pond Church. Photograph by S. K. Finney. Author's collection.

Tranquilidad de Oñate, formerly known chiefly for indolence, learns the two skills almost by chance, he preserves his forefathers' traditions.[60]

The Pancake Stories, written for Church's children when they were young, and *Shoes for the Santo Niño* appeared posthumously. The latter was rediscovered by Snyder and Kathleen Church. Published as a pamphlet, with illustrations by Charles M. Carrillo, it was turned into an opera, with music by Stephen Paulus and libretto by Andrea Fellows Walters. The work had nine performances in Albuquerque and Santa Fe by the Santa Fe Opera, partly in connection with the centennial celebration of New Mexico statehood. Julia Church Hoffman, the poet's granddaughter, trained and directed the children. Kathleen Church considers, however, that the music was not suited to young singers.[61]

Willow Tree

An untitled Church poem of 1975 begins: "Poems ache / in the heart / the way stones do / in our abdominal organs." In an unpublished "Coda" to her earlier "Elegy for the Willow Tree" (the tree in question had been radically pruned, to her regret), the poet calls herself an old willow, from which the birds have fled, in which the sap no longer rises. "I leave my own vacancy on the waiting air." The lines, which can serve as a farewell, show how one can speak truly of a *body* of writing in her case—her poems and prose being close not only to her own body but also to the body of nature, the earth.[62]

CHAPTER SIX

Alice Marriott

Marriott as Ethnologist and Writer

Trained in anthropology, specializing in ethnology, and with field experience, Alice Marriott was well qualified to describe aspects of the Southwest. She published more than a score of volumes on the Kiowas of western Oklahoma, other Plains tribes, New Mexico Pueblos, and additional topics related to the region. She worked on two significant exhibits concerning Indians, the first at the Golden Gate International Exposition in San Francisco (1939, 1940), the second at the Museum of Modern Art (MOMA) in New York (1941). Her New York *Times* obituary stated that she had "helped break the stereotype of Indians as uncivilized savages." She stands out as a woman researcher in what was a man's field, where she attempted to fill lacunae left by their practice. Had she remained a scholar only, her career could still have been distinguished.[1]

Instead, she chose to write for a general public, popularizing Indian history and lore, especially in *The Ten Grandmothers* and *María: The Potter of San Ildefonso*. Her work is considered a forerunner of the method called "narrative ethnology." The two volumes just mentioned and many other pages fall into the important category of oral history (as gathered and preserved by researchers). Her literary skills, probably innate—handling of story line, pacing, levels of language—were well applied. (In high school, she won a short story prize.) Her writings constitute an "Indian world," a recognizable, though personal, landscape and society comparable to Mary Austin's California desert, Willa Cather's Blue Mesa, Laura Adams Armer's haunting Navajo land, and Peggy Pond Church's Pajarito Plateau. Legend and history, tribe and individual are interwoven. Her characters Sitting Bear, Eagle Plume, Spear Woman (all Kiowas), Annie, a white captive, and María Martínez are not easily forgotten. In memoirs, she portrayed herself, as woman and ethnologist. In 1967 Martin Shockley remarked:

"She writes with extraordinary perception and charm," adding (doubtless correctly then) that she was "one of the few Anglos who represent the Indian way of life with sympathy and humor." Her numerous publications, including essays in the *New Yorker* and the *Southwest Review*, were well received. Here she will be assessed as a literary figure, though critiques by ethnological authorities are taken into consideration. In these combined roles—writer and ethnologist—she made a significant contribution to women's history.[2]

Younger than Austin, Cather, and Armer—nearly two generations separated her from them—she still had much in common with them (and with Church, slightly older)—sharing similar interests, concerns, and feminine vision. She was acquainted with Dorothy Brett, Mabel Dodge Luhan, and Oliver La Farge; the three introduced her, she said, to work by modern artists such as Henri Matisse. She was a good friend of Mary Wheelwright, who had known Austin and who, with Hastiin Klah, a Navajo, founded the Wheelwright Museum in Santa Fe. Marriott resided for a while near San Ildefonso Pueblo (close to the Pajarito Plateau), and she did research among the Hopis, where she lived in a boarding house with White Bear and his Anglo wife. Though she had no children herself, she practiced story-telling with nieces and nephews and wrote books for young people, which constitute an important part of her production. *Sequoyah: Leader of the Cherokees*, a biography, was a selection of the Junior Book-of-the Month Club.[3]

Background; Work Among the Kiowas

Alice Lee Marriott was born to Richard Goulding Marriott, who immigrated from England as a boy, and Sydney Cunningham Marriott on 8 January 1910 in Wilmette, Illinois (north of Chicago). British English was the household standard. With her grandfather, Alice sometimes visited the Field Columbian Museum, which exhibited anthropological material from the 1893–94 Chicago World's Fair. During World War I, her parents moved to Oklahoma City. She referred to herself—doubtless feeling so—as "a native Southwesterner." Her father was with an insurance company; her mother worked as an accountant. Alice died 18 March 1992 in Oklahoma City; she had returned from New Mexico to that state and became (1968) Artist-in-Residence at what is presently the University of Central Oklahoma, teaching creative writing and folklore. The cause of death, according to her friend Margaret Lefranc, was heart failure. She had suffered also from Bell's Palsy, was blind in one eye, and had numerous falls and fractures. She had been assisted by her friend and frequent co-author, Carol Rachlin, who shared a home with her. Rachlin, who had a degree from Columbia University, was a sculptor but also a specialist in Indian textiles; she studied weaving using the "suspended warp technique" and developed great skill herself. Rachlin was younger but deaf. Marriott left a long manuscript concerning Spanish-American folk stories of New Mexico *santos*.[4]

Marriott received a B.A. magna cum laude in English and French at Oklahoma City University in 1930 but also studied library science as preparation for a practical career. (Her parents thought she was not pretty enough to attract a husband.) She was hired at the Muskogee Public Library, where her assignment included cataloguing materials relating to the Five Southern (or "Civilized") Tribes. Thus she discovered Henry Rowe Schoolcraft's volumes known by the short title *Indian Tribes of the United States*, a pioneer ethnological work. Drawn by the topic but forced by illness to resign her position, she returned home and, as soon as possible, enrolled at the University of Oklahoma to study anthropology, newly added to the curriculum at the undergraduate level. Without previous preparation, she took freshman courses. Her liking for the discipline as well as her energy and good fortune kept her in it. She was drawn to ethnology, which she defined in the standard American way as the science of living *cultures*, though she acknowledged that the peoples connected to them are always part of the study. She was thus interested in groups, that is, the general; but in fact individuals—especially women—held her attention even more, a good thing for a future creative writer.

Her first field assignment was summer work among the Modoc, a Plateau culture tribe in southern Oregon. She drew from a hat the name of her first informant there, Mary Many Feathers, who had been to the Carlisle Indian School, a Friends institution in Pennsylvania, and who had thus assimilated much white culture while remaining a tribal member (and re-adjusting better than some). Marriott seemed to know instinctively how to profit from the contacts. Then and later she displayed no little talent as an observer and particularly an interviewer.

When she was awarded the B.A. in anthropology (1935), she was the first woman to receive such a degree from an Oklahoma institution. Her advisor was Forrest Clements, who had studied under a protégé of Franz Boas. She remained for a year as a graduate assistant. She carried out field work, thanks to university support. There were fifty-seven federally-recognized tribes in Oklahoma then. Told during an interview to choose for her practical work between the Arapahoes and Kiowas, she let chance decide, according to whether her professor picked up a cigarette or his pipe. When he chose his pipe, it was the Kiowas. She was assigned to their reservation at Anadarko, southwest of Oklahoma City. They became, as she put it, *her* Indians—the tribe she knew and cared most for. (In 1983 she spoke at the dedication of the Kiowa Cultural Center there.) She did not, however, learn to speak Kiowa, a five-toned pitch language (somewhat degraded in the twentieth century); hence the importance of interpreters. She also worked with Cheyennes, Cherokees, Tewas (San Ildefonso and other pueblos), and Hopis. Some years later she wrote, in response to those real or virtual critics who would censure her and others for making Native Americans a topic of study—thus "objectifying" them—that the Indians themselves liked to have certain customs of theirs and their history, previously oral, recorded for the sake of the young people and the future.[5]

When Marriott began her field work, the terms "discrimination" (in today's sense) and "ethnocentricity" had not, she noted, been coined and circulated; nor would she have needed them. She was without racial biases. "There, but for an accident of Nature, go I" was her viewpoint, to which she added the orthodox anthropologist's conviction that "not only all men, but all cultures, had been created equal; equal in interest, equal in complexity at one point or another, equally, as our world says, high." Names such as "Indian," "Hispanic," and "Anglo" were for her means of identification, not judgments. Race was "a purely physical thing." She avoided patronizing her subjects. In New Mexico, where Hispanic blood was a marker of status and power, "thirty-odd years ago, if there was any segregation or patronization, it worked the other way [anti–Anglo]." She maintained such good relationships with the Kiowas at Anadarko that respected women, encouraged by her principal informant, Spear Woman, adopted her into the tribe, naming her Hummingbird Girl (she had red hair). The Cheyennes, whom she knew later, called her "Spirit Woman." Yet she did not gloss over past cruel behavior either toward or by Native Americans. She expressed regret at how the Indians had been treated, as well as her desire to compensate, in some sense, for what they had suffered, but noted "exceedingly hard-boiled and narrow-minded Indians" in New Mexico. Additionally, she wrote twice about the 1833 attack by Osages on a Kiowa campground while fighting men were absent. The Osages killed women and children and decapitated many of them; they also stole one medicine bundle (see below). When the men returned, they found the women's heads stuck into cooking pots.[6]

Marriott found that the lives of Indian women had been studied far less than men's—a condition resulting from the fact that nearly all the anthropologists who had investigated the Native Americans were male and were, in fact, biased toward their sex. "Anthropology is generally a man's trade." (In passing, she noted that a woman anthropologist had to work twice as hard as a man to advance similarly.) More broadly viewed, the anthropologists' custom was part of the masculine vision of the American west. She set out to remedy the defect. She could raise topics with women that she could not have broached effectively with men, marriage, for example.[7]

Indian Arts and Crafts Board

From 1938 until 1942, Marriott was a field representative for the Indian Arts and Crafts Board, created in 1935, after John Collier became Commissioner of Indian Affairs in 1933. (Collier had organized the national campaign against the Bursum Bill.) Her sense of art, of "Finished in beauty," was doubtless strengthened during this time. Her charge was to assist Indians in developing their crafts sufficiently to increase their incomes. Women could do such work at home. While there was no easel art or other European form, some types of artisans' work were very fine, and as early as the 1920s, there was recognition that native crafts should be showcased. The Indian Market in Santa Fe (originally known by a longer name), organized in 1922 by Kenneth Chapman and Edgar Lee Hewett, director of the Museum of New Mexico, featured Navajo rugs and silver work, Pueblo pottery, and other products. Nina Otero-Warren, a supporter, wrote that sales of these products could inspire the Indian to "appreciate the history and traditions of his own race and ... continue the native arts of his people." Creating markets could help Indians become self-supporting and "assume the responsibilities of citizenship."[8]

Making the native products saleable was a challenge. The market and the wares did not match well, and in many cases the products required adaptation, principally because, when directed to outsiders, they had to change from clearly functional (such as a water pot) to representational (of a design, a group) or aesthetic. Under Marriott's direction, younger people were encouraged to take up skills, and a school of easel art was created that endured until the late 1980s and beyond. Such efforts were not entirely new; Austin and others had wished for Indian arts and crafts to prosper by means of "special efforts for adapting the work of Indian artists to modern requirements." Austin had viewed federal legislation as more harmful than good, however. Her own program for Indian arts revival has been called "coercive and paternalistic."[9]

During this period Marriott was assigned to teach anthropology at the Sherman Institute, the Indian School in Riverside, California. The class was for school teachers employed by the Bureau of Indian Affairs. The potters María and Julián Martínez, whom she had met in San Francisco, were there. She drove to California with a Texas friend, Lenore Sloan. Crossing Arizona, they visited a craftsmen's show at Flagstaff; Alice found the wares mediocre. On the way back from Riverside, they stopped in New Mexico to attend the Corn Dance at Santo Domingo Pueblo, one of the greatest southwestern celebrations. This seems to have been her first significant visit to the state. It was then, it seems, that she and her friend climbed the Puyé Cliff Dwellings at Santa Clara Pueblo.[10]

In 1942, when the Indian Arts and Crafts board suspended field operations, Marriott began work for the American Red Cross, assigned to locations in the Southwest. She initially had a huge territory, from San Antonio through Trans-Pecos Texas (and, practically speaking, across the border into Mexico). Her next area was smaller but more populous: New Mexico, north to south, from the Arizona border eastward to the Rio Grande. At the end of World War II, she left the Red Cross and moved near Santa Fe, with the purpose of writing a book on the Martínez couple. She received research support from the Rockefeller Foundation through the University of Oklahoma. To live in the potters' pueblo, San Ildefonso (north of Santa Fe, east of the Pajarito Plateau), was out of the question; in practice, it was closed to Anglos. Instead, she rented, for $5 a month, a crumbling adobe "mud pie" in "The Valley," next door to Nambé Pueblo—by the old roads, some twenty miles north of the capital.

Life in New Mexico Beginning in 1945

Marriott's life in New Mexico after the war cannot be separated from that of Margaret Lefranc ("Martha" in Marriott's writing), a landscape painter, textile designer, and line-drawing artist, who illustrated a half-

Impression of Alice Marriott, 1960s. Acrylic. By Nell Norris. Author's collection.

dozen of Marriott's books. Sometimes identified as Frankel and sometimes by her married name, Schoonover (though she was divorced), Margaret (1907–1998) was born in Brooklyn and died in Santa Fe. In 2012 a blogger quoted a mutual friend as saying that Margaret was "an old closet case." In 1996 she won the New Mexico Governor's Award for Excellence in the Arts. As an adolescent she had lived both in Berlin, where she studied at the Kunstschule des Westens, and Paris. During a subsequent stay in Paris she studied with André Lhôte. Her work was exhibited there and in American cities, including Santa Fe, starting in 1946. Prior to settling in New Mexico, she lived in New York City, where she had a gallery for some years and taught at Cooper Union, and in the village of Hunter, in the Catskills, where she received artist friends.[11]

Even before the war, in 1939 Lefranc had driven to Taos, where she met Frieda Lawrence and Nicolai Fechin. She later remembered watching a ceremonial native dance. Then or later, she became acquainted with Georgia O'Keeffe and Laura Gilpin and her companion, Betsy Foster. Since Marriott dated her acquaintance with Lefranc from "several years" before they started sharing a house, it is plausible that they met that year. The two exchanged letters, and when in 1945 Marriott proposed settling in New Mexico, Lefranc made a trip west to assist her in choosing a place to lease (the crumbling adobe). Lefranc had already noticed how the area lent itself to landscape painting. She proposed staying for the winter and sharing the household to reduce expenses. She went east, sold her residence, and returned to New Mexico, while Marriott moved her things from Oklahoma.[12]

Their first year together in Nambé is evoked humorously in Marriott's memoir *The Valley Below* (1949), an important biographical source. She specified in an author's note that no character or place was invented; pseudonyms were used, presumably as authorial defense, since the models had not been consulted on the portraits. The book is also a non-technical ethnological study, treating, among other topics, life in Santa Fe as contrasted with rural life, and the different traditions and mores of Spanish, Indian, and Anglo communities. Pueblo dances are described at length.

The house Marriott rented "hugged the earth." It lacked windows, electricity, and space, having only a kitchen, a bedroom, and a bedroom-studio, which served as the living room (a room was added later). Although the *acequia hija*, or secondary irrigation ditch (public), crossed the property, their own water came from a well; the pump barely worked. Water was in any case a constant concern owing to scarcity of snow and rain. There was no indoor toilet; the women used a privy. They washed in the kitchen sink or on occasion went to a public bath house in Albuquerque. Having experience at repairing her old farmhouse and being clever mechanically (she repaired a car), Margaret was able to make numerous improvements; other work was hired out. The two got along remarkably well with their Spanish and Indian neighbors, who retained elements of Old-World courtesy though they lived as peasants (albeit land-owning); their character and customs are presented especially well. Marriott and Lefranc saw the men most, because the latter worked for them often, but it was with the women that they felt special closeness. "We were women, and our neighbors came to us for help because they knew we would understand and would give it." In due course Lefranc and Marriott purchased the house and property. They discovered they had put down roots.[13]

In time the two, who were civic-minded, became connected to the Santa Fe intellectual and arts community. By 1945, the city, swollen because of Los Alamos and other installations, had a population of some thirty-five thousand, of which a fourth or so were Anglos. The northern New Mexico of the 1920s, with Luhan, D. H. Lawrence and Frieda, the Taos painters, Witter Bynner, and, a bit later, O'Keeffe, had changed; but in the post-war period it still had tremendous intellectual and artistic vitality. Painters and writers "set the tone for the community at large." Marriott was, however, less interested in leading the artist's or connoisseur's life than in understanding the creation of art and other cultural objects through her ethnological research, and, as a side interest, collecting fine pottery. (Unfortunately, boys whom she and Lefranc befriended destroyed some of the collection. Later she was, however, able to donate pots to the Stovall Museum, now the Sam Noble Museum, at the University of Oklahoma.)[14]

When her friendship with Marriott was broken off, Lefranc built herself a house in Santa Fe; she paid for the land and the heavy construction (doing the rest of the labor herself) with her share of the royalties from the book on María Martínez, for which she did twenty-five drawings of pots and sketches of the famous potter. Lefranc's subsequent close friends included Sandra Edleman, a poet whom she met in the Miami, Florida area, where Margaret's parents had settled, and Sandra Mackenzie, a faithful companion, who traveled back and forth with her there.[15]

Questions of cultural misappropriation and patronizing, which arose earlier in this study, must be addressed in connection with Marriott's writing and Lefranc's illustrations showing Native American individuals and products. It was noted that Marriott was without prejudices, and she had learned (*invented* might be a better word) etiquette in dealings with tribal members. Neither she nor Lefranc displayed, as far as can be ascertained, condescension or aloofness toward the native peoples they presented in word and drawing. Knowledge was not, to Marriott, an expropriation of others or gesture of control. People were her subjects only in the sense of "focus of interest," and she used available means of informing others about tribes and mores. The Martínez couple and Marriott's informant Spear Woman, along with additional figures on whom she relied, clearly did not feel demeaned by her interest. One Kiowan, an old blind man, requested that she visit him so that he might speak with her. Lefranc's drawings and Marriott's or Marriott and Rachlin's photographs are invaluable in documenting individuals and tribes.[16]

Marriott, who was buried from All Souls' Episcopal Church in Oklahoma City, was sensitive to the transcendent dimensions of human existence. Throughout *María: The Potter of San Ildefonso* and elsewhere, she writes tenderly of Pueblo and Spanish beliefs, including the natives' celebratory dancing and the flagellation of the Penitentes. A Nambé acquaintance, José de la Cruz de Romero, who taught her many practical things—to clean a wood stove, plant alfalfa, visit a tribal council—also introduced her to the *santos*, those beings that were, as far as he was concerned, friends. "He taught me that men and women of whatever faith can transcend the pettiness of their surroundings and rise above them to the feet of God." In 1946 she participated in the Easter pilgrimage to the Santuario of Chimayó (northeast of Santa Fe), where healing was reported. The pilgrimage was organized initially by former prisoners of the Japanese. She drove to Española and then walked with the others. She recalled hearing a veteran say, "Who is that Anglo woman and why is she here with us?" An old man replied, "Quiet, my son; she has the right."[17]

The Ten Grandmothers

The initial draft of *The Ten Grandmothers* (1945), a specialized scholarly study of the Kiowas, so dissatisfied Marriott that she burned the manuscript. Its later version, a remarkable narrative accomplishment, received very favorable reviews and stayed in print for decades. At more than 300 pages, it is substantial. For it she devised a hybrid genre, which reads like fiction; she used literary measures throughout. Her approach to her subject is sympathetic—"feeling with." Whether the data are scientific (information credibly recorded by others, elicited in her interviews, or gained from observation) or folkloric or mythological (vetted as such by earlier scholars or herself), the resulting book fits the definition of "salvage ethnography" of the early twentieth century. Partly because "the family is the real basis of all social relations," she was convinced that ethnology should proceed not from the group (as was customary) but from the particular to the general, working outward. That may explain how later articles of hers were identified as *stories*. Marriott called them *sketches*.[18]

The specialists' reception of *The Ten Grandmothers* was mixed. Marriott's former professor, Clements, wrote that the organization "gives the book a vitality which would have been absent had you followed the orthodox ethnographic report style." An Indian reader commented that "the

Alice Marriott holding a copy of *The Ten Grandmothers*. Photograph by Richard Cobb, Oklahoma Publishing Company Collection. Courtesy Oklahoma Historical Society, image #2012.201.13382.0821.

book read like a novel." It was consulted by the Kiowas themselves—evidence of its ethnological value. Yet more than one anthropologist considered it unrepresentative and lacking authority because its informers belonged to a single (though extended) family, some educated and all Christianized. The family with which Marriott worked "could not speak for all Kiowas and thus would not be representative." Certain reviewers criticized the lack of scholarly paraphernalia. Other commentators noted Marriott's role in framing and arranging the material and thus her assumption of authority, though in the preface she indicated her attention to "tell these stories as much as possible as they were told to me."[19]

The title phrase refers to sacred tribal medicine bundles, sometimes called "Grandmother Gods," which must be honored, protected (by two guardians, a man and a woman), and, during nomadic wanderings, transported under strict conditions. They were used in the Sun Dance, a major ceremony, highly ritualistic. According to an informant, these bundles were still in existence when Marriott wrote but had not been opened since the 1890s, when the last elder authorized to inspect and pray over them died without naming a successor. Someone knowledgeable planned to explain them to her, but when his intention became known he was threatened with a curse. Use of the title phrase was viewed by some as offensive, constituting misappropriation of Kiowa religious matters for public consumption. Marriott was criticized likewise for making Kiowa names public.[20]

Marriott stated in the preface that the material was collected mostly in the summers of 1935 and 1936, though some was added subsequently. George Hunt and his daughters served as her interpreters. She had met the family on Thanksgiving weekend 1934 when, owing to a chance storm, she was stranded in an isolated area; the Hunts (renamed "Camps") took her in. Thanks to them, she was able to interview two people in their mid-nineties. The family called her "Story-Writing Woman." She became a close friend of Ioleta Hunt McElhaney ("Elizabeth"), who served as an interpreter and informant. It was she who arranged for Marriott's adoption.[21]

While the narratives are discrete, many are thematically linked—by typical Kiowa behavior, Marriott noted—and characters recur. The work "exposes the intense cultural incursions the Kiowa people faced"—federal interference, Anglo settlement, the decline of the buffalo, the pressure of Christianity, and assimilationist policies. Like a chronicle, the book is organized along a time-line, using three versions of the Kiowa year count, a pictographic mnemonic record begun in 1832–33. From that year on, each summer and each winter was identified by a specific event ("Winter the woman was stabbed," "The dry summer Sun Dance"). From 1833 until 1888 all the sites of the Sun Dance are identifiable. For the available years, the tribal counts were checked against a chronology published in 1893 by James Mooney (1861–1921), a controversial anthropologist from the Smithsonian Institution who worked in Oklahoma. Mooney's chronology and the three others are given in an appendix, collated with the standard American calendar. The chapters are organized into four parts: "The Time When There Were Plenty of Buffalo," "The Time When Buffalo Were Going," "The Time When Buffalo Were Gone," "Modern Times." Each chapter has a title and a subtitle, the latter borrowed from Mooney or the year count of George Poolaw, a Kiowa, whom Marriott interviewed at length. Drawings at chapter headings are based on Mooney's reproductions of native drawings or, for later years, on Kiowa pictographs (but not copied exactly).[22]

Insofar as the book can be viewed as fiction, it is a multi-generational, episodic historical novel, based on facts, with loose construction but a governing plot, succinctly summarized by subtitles. The ultimate direction of the plot is toward acculturation. There is resemblance to the epic, likewise, since the fate of the Kiowa people as a whole is at stake. Characters are born, marry, grow old, and die. Two principal figures, historic, called in the text Spear Woman and Eagle Plume, were still alive in the 1930s; along with Sitting Bear (Hunt's father-in-law) and his son, they are at once representative and, to some degree, individual. The action begins in 1847, when Eagle Plume is a baby.

The presentation is by authorial exposition (or summary) and scenes. The principal signs of fictionalizing are the attributed thoughts and dialogue. Whatever details Marriott's informants may have remembered, they cannot have recalled lengthy conversations and still less unspoken reflections. The Kiowa corpus of oral tradition is general, not personal. As it was noted in the Introduction, the procedure of inventing material is the stock-in-trade of historical novelists and even some historians. It assumes that historical writings should present the spirit of the period under examination and, if fitting, the "worm's-eye view," available chiefly through evidence of individual lives. Marriott had a great deal of ethnological information, but for the earliest decades she could have no corroboration other than recollections of aged informants. Her use of invented speech makes her pages lively and helps create, or re-create (in the case of events reported by others, such as the Sun Dance), "moments" in the Kiowa story. Sales of *The Ten Grandmothers* would not have been the same if her book had been merely an ethnological treatise.[23]

The narratives include background and introduction of characters, development of some incident or major event so as to create suspense, then its outcome or resolution. Characters become persuasive, or "real," as they are drawn into the developing action, and much information is conveyed. Following her awareness of the relative neglect of women by anthropologists, Marriott devotes more pages to women's lives than most others writing on Plains Indians, and her portraits of girls and women are convincing, even their inner dimensions. As she noted elsewhere, though Kiowa society was not matriarchal (unlikely among unsettled peoples, in a polygamous system), "The women frequently dominated their households."[24]

In the first sketch, the Kiowas have moved a great deal, and there is tension. "You could tell that something was going to happen, all right." Sitting Bear watches the camp, thinking. Then his second wife comes to him with her baby, Eagle Plume, in her arms. "She was a fine woman, though he didn't love her as he did his first wife…" They watch the shadows across the hill. "Something is coming across the flat," he says. "Looks like men on horseback," adds his second wife. "Looks like Comanches," says Sitting Bear. Readers are now prepared for plot development (though the clash between the two tribes is in fact a minor strain). Themes include war, hunting, religion, and medicine, all connected to the theme of power—personal and tribal strength, and also a mysterious power, given to certain males of the tribe, that can be lost or regained. This mysterious force, acknowledged and increased by dancing, is required for a successful hunt, for war, for healing. It can be used as an aphrodisiac or even magic. The Sun Dance, its celebration, is featured prominently.[25]

The primary theme of the chronicle, however, is that of change, generally brought about by whites, with its necessary correlative, adaptation or failure (enforced assimilation or tribal suicide). The Kiowas are between two cultures. As generations pass, buffalo become scarcer because of homesteading and fencing; available land shrinks and the Kiowas' nomadic life is constricted; there are fewer horses; trading with whites increases and commercial products such as sugar are introduced. A girl who has studied at the Carlisle School returns so altered that she barely fits in, but she chooses to stay, re-adopting some local ways ("going back to the blanket"), yet determined to teach others her learning, as a means for them to survive. (Marriott made clear that she admired the Carlisle training, which, when summarized, sounded harsh, civilizing Indian youth "by forcibly thrusting them into the white man's mold," and was severely criticized by some observers and participants, but was well received by others and, in its way, was beneficial in practical terms.)[26]

Marriott gives evidence of disagreement on how to deal with whites, who have "the power." There are hostile encounters between soldiers and the natives; governmental plans for the Indians to become farmers fail. Christianity, introduced by missionaries, brings enormous change. Contrasted to it is the peyote religion, introduced by the Comanche chief Quanah Parker, which quickly gains popularity. Polygamy, practiced in the past to offset the loss of men in war, raiding, and hunting, must be replaced by monogamy, according to American law. "Things changed around them," Spear Woman reflects, "but the buffalo and the Sun Dance stayed the same. Now they were both gone." Eagle Plume tells her that there will be a new dance and a new belief.[27]

Sitting Bear, who loses his son in war, becomes so grief-stricken that he defies tribal taboo and brings home the boy's remains, attempting then to live as though he were not dead. Sitting Bear is charged later with taking part in a raid on a white family's ranch, during which the husband is killed, the cattle are let out through torn fences, the house is burnt, and two children are abducted. The raid leads to a confrontation with army authorities, and ultimately the tribe is captured by an army contingent and sequestered for the winter in a horse corral at Ft. Sill, a miserable experience. Though not guilty—he had not participated—Sitting Bear dies willingly at officials' hands (in what amounts to suicide) because he sees that his age has ended; he can no longer lead his people as their life becomes radically different. His death stands for ultimate defeat by assimilation.[28]

Signs of crisis multiply in time. Eagle Plume, now leader, outlaws traditional revenge against any fellow Kiowa, seeing that tribal law, if applied strictly, will hasten ruin. The buffalo cannot be brought back by even the most solemn of ceremonies. The only choice is to change the mode of living. As the chronicle concludes (1942), Eagle Plume, now an old man himself, sees the braves off to war, singing traditional songs as they leave to join America's battles. The two cultures have been joined with some practical success; the surviving buffalo are on display in an animal park, the Kiowas drive cars. No one can assess properly the cultural loss, however.

Winter-Telling Stories *and Associated Works*

Marriott's second book, *Winter-Telling Stories* (1947), was drawn from Kiowa legends or myths, as she terms them, which appeal to both children and adults. The dedication indicated plainly that her informant Hunt was the source of the stories, but Marriott was named as author. The publication history is noteworthy. The first edition was illustrated by Roland Whitehorse, a Kiowa artist, historian, and story-teller (1920–1998). The great-grandson of the last principal Kiowa chief, he was from the Anadarko area; he attended the Indian School in Riverside and studied at the Dallas Art Institute. The pictures, in color, including tribal motifs, are striking, with elements of humor and mockery. Unfriendly viewers could have seen them, however, as somewhat unflattering. (Saynday, the main character and story-teller, is identified in the text as "a funny-looking man.") The book was reset and reprinted in 1969, with the label "compiled by Alice Marriott." The black-and-white illustrations in the later edition are by Richard Cuffari, identified as a native New Yorker and resident of Brooklyn. His illustrations are entirely without mockery; the designs have beautiful curves, and the human figures good lines and handsome features. What is more significant is that the 1969 edition omits one story, "How the White Crow Turned Black," viewed as offensive. This is clearly a case of ethnic bowdlerizing. Twenty-five years before, Marriott did not mind including this tale, nor Whitehorse illustrating the collection.[29]

As late as 1973, children in southwestern Oklahoma were familiar with the corpus of Saynday stories; since their schooling was in English, it can be assumed that the book was intended for them as well as for readers elsewhere. Saynday is a synthetic figure combining the trickster with the hero of remote times, who performed great cosmic deeds but who is no longer on earth, having gone, as the postscript recounts, to live in the eastern sky. There he has made five new, bright stars that shine only in the summer. He has authority (he speaks of "my world"). For instance, he made rules for how the stories should be told. "Always tell my stories in the winter, when the outdoors work is finished. Always tell my stories at night.... Always begin the stories the same way ... 'Saynday was coming along....'" Between a short prologue and "The End of Saynday," the tales are grouped into "The Saynday-Does-Good Stories" and "The Saynday-Makes-Trouble Stories," in which, in an age-old reversal of plot, the trickster gets himself trapped or is duped (partly because he is greedy). The other characters are generally animals.[30]

Saynday and the animals often work together for good; he is the thinker, they his helpers. In "How Saynday Got the Sun," when all the earth on their side is black, the fox, the deer, and the magpie help him take the sun from the village people on the other side; but then there is too much light. Saynday casts the sun into the sky, where it can travel around so that both sides of the world share it in turn. In another story, when all the animals except White Crow are nearly starving, Saynday, using flattery, tricks the bird into giving up his quiver for a few minutes and finds in it good buffalo meat. By further guile and disguise he learns where the buffalo are hidden—in a huge hole under a rock. He chases them to the surface, disguises himself as a cocklebur on the last buffalo, escapes from the White Crow family, and furnishes meat henceforth to the Plains people. In an associated tale, White Crow is angry and frightens off the herds; but Saynday traps him through an elaborate feint; then Spider Woman wraps White Crow in her web and smokes him until his feathers turn black. "You will always be black, to show that you tried to starve the people." A similar tale relates how Bobcat, who breaks a promise, got his spots. In the final story, clearly a modern version (the Montgomery Ward catalogue is mentioned), Saynday tricks his white counterpart.[31]

The intertextual connection among the Saynday stories, certain other books by Marriott, and especially *Plains Indian Mythology* (1975), by Marriott and Rachlin, directed toward adults, shows how Marriott shaped her materials for different audiences. The latter volume presents Kiowa stories along with material from the Pawnee, Osage, Arapaho, Cheyenne, Comanche, and other tribes. The connections among these tribes and their overlapping bodies of myth are summarized. The Kiowa emergence myth, with Saynday as the central character, is included. People are already formed, but the world is dark. Saynday leads his people out of the night through a tree trunk. The story includes a dispute among them and a division of the tribe into two bands, which have never found each other again. "How the People Caught the Sun" is the Saynday tale sketched above. "Why the Prairie Dogs' Tails Are Short" is a version of "How Saynday Ran a Footrace with Coyote" in *Winter-Telling Stories*. A modern episode called "The Traders from Mexico," told to Marriott by a participant, appears in a longer version in *The Ten Grandmothers*.

"The Winter the Stars Fell," from *Plains Indian Mythology*, recounts the great meteor shower of 1833–34, which lasted many nights, recorded in Kiowa calendars as "The Night the Stars Fell." Medicine Men brought out the "Grandmother" bundles, to which people prayed, but to no avail, until the skies returned to normal with the coming of spring. That event was followed by a solar eclipse some months later, during which the Kiowas, in the spirit of their mythology, cried, "A snake has come up from under the world and is swallowing the sun!" One Medicine Man, with power from the bobcat, performed his dance in the darkness; the sun reappeared.[32]

"Grandmother Spider" belongs to a cycle unique among Plains Indians but related perhaps to Navajo and Pueblo myths, a fact pointing (with other evidence) to contacts between Plains tribes and those to the west. This cycle is part of the Ceremonial, or summer-telling, stories and is connected to the medicine bundles. In this tale, twin boys kill in succession four bears (sacred, totemic beings, greatly feared), whose ears become trophies, kept in eight rawhide cases, which, when added to each boy's shield, become "holy things to guard the people." A cleansing ritual in a sweat lodge and rub-down with sage, along with fasting and praying, removes the threatening bear power.

Indians on Horseback (1948), directed toward older children, is a brief history of American aboriginal mores as Marriott knew them from other scholars' research and her informants. Lefranc furnished sketches, including details of Indian dress, equipment, and activities, and a map showing the probable land bridge between Asia and Alaska. The text outlines what scholars generally believe about the coming of aborigines and the progress of some down the continent to the edge of the Great Plains, described as they might have appeared then. Later come Spanish explorers and their crucial contribution to Plains life, horses ("wonderful big dogs"). The Sun Dance, healing ceremonies, foods, and clothing are summarized. As always in Marriott's books, one finds imaginative poetic descriptions, such as this evocation of dawn: "Along the edges of the plains the earth and the sky would meet and run and be stuck together with a little bit of mist."[33]

María: The Potter of San Ildefonso

María: The Potter of San Ildefonso (1948) is a mixed-genre book, consisting of art history, testimonial, ethnology, sociology, and, principally, biography—both facts and interpretation. Lefranc designed the end papers and furnished sketches and drawings, showing María, a room, the pueblo, nearby ruins, the process of firing ware, and twenty-five pieces of pottery by María and others. More than a hundred pages concern María Montoya's girlhood; the author clearly believed it was important for the whole story. María's birth date was uncertain (1881 or 1887). She is shown playing with her sisters and selling her mother's fresh cheeses or trading for them—perhaps a foreshadowing of her business acumen. She makes a pilgrimage with her parents to Chimayó in thanks for being cured of what was probably measles, and she takes home some earth, dug from a dark pit, known

María Martínez with Alice Marriott taking field notes at San Ildefonso Pueblo. Courtesy Western History Collections, University of Oklahoma.

to be healing She attends school and subsequently marries Julián Martínez. A crucial episode is the couple's discovery of an interesting potsherd among ruins. Their effort to duplicate it results in a new method of firing and, through error, the creation, around 1919, of the famous Martínez black-on-black pottery (matte on a shiny surface, generally). the wife doing the pot itself, the husband the design.

Marriott devoted enormous time and effort to her undertaking, for which the point of departure was extensive interviews (1945–46). (Julián was dead by then, from alcoholism.) Insofar as possible, the author wished to present María in her own words, "informally, as a story"; the information as given is said to be "in every regard as the people of San Ildefonso would have it presented to the reading public."[34]

The interviews were not question-and-answer exchanges or built around topics proposed by Marriott, but rather arose from subjects suggested by María, who pursued them as she wished. No tape recorder is mentioned; Marriott did not like the device and relied on notebook and pencil. (She remarked in *Greener Fields* how unsatisfactory recording was. Unlike a notebook, it could catch intonations, but it could not catch gestures and expressions; and it was a strain, even an impediment in interviews with elderly informants and sometimes others.) María was, to some degree at least, trilingual; Marriott could use both English and Spanish. Though the style is generally unadorned, imaginative phrasing appears occasionally. Marriott speaks of a warm December day, with sun and "a little wind that picked heavy thoughts from your heart and carried them away." As María leaves with her younger sister for St. Catherine's Indian School in Santa Fe and glimpses her mother, tears come into her eyes. "She turned around again quickly, and looked straight at a tree beside the road until it had gone by and her tears had stayed behind with it."[35]

The book was reviewed in the *Chicago Sunday Tribune, New York Herald Tribune,* and elsewhere and was selected by the Natural History Book Club. The anthropologist Ruth Underhill found the work unsatisfactory, perhaps too hagiographic.[36]

The third-person narrative is roughly chronological. Dates or inclusive periods are given in chapter headings, but many incidents cannot be assigned accurately to the calendar, showing, if more evidence were needed, how unreliable memory is. The reporting, whether authorial summary or scenic presentation, is thus mostly re-creation, with dialogues and thoughts, which could not have been recalled precisely. María's improper English grammar appears chiefly in passages concerning her later life, clearer in memory than earlier years and thus more frequently presented in her raw, unmediated discourse. Themes recur, and local scenes and landscapes are evoked as in fiction. Domestic scenes dominate, not highly dramatic as a rule, though there are elements of suspense, as in the pottery-firing scene, where the outcome is in doubt.

Like *The Ten Grandmothers, María* is a study in acculturation and resistance to it. Marriott stressed that in San Ildefonso, a closed Tewa pueblo, certain aspects of pueblo life, particularly religious beliefs and practices, might not be discussed with non-members, according to custom and the elders' decisions. The pueblo was small, with a plaza (later a second plaza), a church, a kiva, and one store selling manufactured products. The men were generally subsistence or small cash-crop farmers on their own land, with minor sources of income on the side.

Marriott structured into her book, through foreshadowing, the changes brought by five or six decades, up to World War II. The turn of the twentieth century saw increased confrontation of two cultures, that of outsider Anglos and the Indians.' By the time of María's wedding, heavy logging had begun in the mountains, creating erosion, water run-off, sagging stream-banks, and crop failures. Many men were obliged to find work outside of the pueblo. The male population shrank so that certain dances could not be performed. Archaeologists were at work excavating sites on the Pajarito Plateau and Puyé Canyon. Julián was among the local men hired to assist in the digging.

Changes in pueblo life were less radical, however, than those experienced by the Kiowas, because the Pueblos had for centuries been settled in villages and had means of subsistence. In addition, though the Spaniards had imposed their language and Catholic faith with some success, that European veneer had not destroyed the underlying native culture. The pueblo was thus doubly communal. Its members supported each other and the whole and did not generally face an intrusive federal government. "Human life depended as much on unity within as on rain without." The Tewa language was preserved; men still practiced their native religion, designed in part to favor the coming of rain; governance, including the regulation of water, was local; winter storytelling was practiced. Dances, important on the calendar, included Easter dances, corn dances, and the *pintito*, which featured *fours* (coming out four times, bowing four times to the four corners of the world), in which the men wore evergreen boughs on their heads and arms. Still, economic and social developments elsewhere did affect the Pueblos, and old customs, particularly the language, needed protecting. María's mother wanted her daughters dressed "like white girls"; and the white teacher in the pueblo, well-meaning but perhaps unreflective, urged María to go away to study, possibly in New York, in order to become a teacher herself. In the early 1940s, María's sons all registered for Selective Service; some were called. One was married in a Catholic ceremony only, without the customary native rite.[37]

The depiction of women *as women* and their roles is striking. These functions are not merely assignments; they are existential, felt and recognized as the very being of women. Never a wife and mother herself, Marriott nonetheless portrayed María and her mother, Reyes, with delicate and persuasive strokes, as they confronted their situation and dealt with husbands and children. No anthropological or sociobiological explanation is offered for their situation, their functions, and, most important, their understanding of the differences between men and women. Whether or not Marriott knew of sociobiology, then a young science, her concern was biography and ethnography, not social evolution. It is noteworthy, however, that María went beyond traditional feminine functions; she not only had a profitable pottery business but owned agricultural land, which she leased to tenant farmers.[38]

Marriott observes that María's method of overcoming obstacles "might have been predicted from a study of the group to which she belongs." Presumably Marriott was right; the attribution does them honor. Any number of women from other cultures could, however, recognize themselves and their attitudes in the portrait. Reyes "had taught her daughters that it was the woman's part of living to hold things together." It was not just a question of performing tasks; what was at stake was the type of strength belonging to each sex and its manner of functioning. *The Ten Grandmothers* illustrates similarly, often in detail, the positions and tasks of women (such as food preparation, tanning, and sewing). But in that volume the Kiowa women are portrayed from the outside, not inside, whereas, thanks to Marriott's closeness to her central character and María's revealing statements, readers are persuaded that she and Reyes felt themselves to be as they are shown. Crucial episodes in their lives, including the death of an infant girl, Reyes's death, and Julián's drinking bouts, offer particular windows.[39]

Unsurprisingly, houses, dress, and utensils are featured prominently—pots, obviously, the most prominent object, originally functional only but, like many other human products, susceptible of enhancement and thus going beyond instrumentality. The identification of woman with hearth is strong; a home (like hogans and Kiowa tepees) is nearly an extension of herself. Indeed, in San Ildefonso, houses normally belong to women; they may arrange and dispose of them as they wish and usually leave them to their daughters. Food, barely more fundamental, is closely identified with the house in which it is stored, prepared, and consumed. Girls play house as they get ready for their adulthood; they learn to grind meal and prepare dishes; they make pottery. When María is homesick (she and Julián lived for some years in the *palacio* in Santa Fe, by then a museum, and spent months displaying their skills at three world's fairs), she yearns to return to her house, a living part of the visible pueblo and an image of the invisible one.

Moreover, Marriott implicitly identifies woman with vessel by part titles, beginning with "The Clay Is Shaped" (childhood) and "The Bowl Is Polished" (schooling and wedding) through "The Bowl Is Fired" and "The Finished Bowl." The latter period witnesses not only the apogee of the potter's work but also, unfortunately, decline: significant breaches in the pueblo walls, a little girl's deafness, and Julián's drinking and death. Woman, individually and collectively, holds within her the people's essence. When San Ildefonso ware becomes famous, each craftswoman, emulating María and Julián, signs her bowls, jars, and vases, graphically completing the identification of herself and her work. This step, however, must be understood within the pueblo context. The economic gains made through adapting to another culture (that is, selling to a national market) are not mainly individual; they help keep their own alive.

A related book, *Indians of the Four Corners* (1952), suitable for older children and adults, is an introductory handbook. For words and names such as *metate, pueblo,* and *Hopi,* the pronunciations are given in an informal phonetic spelling. The drawings, by Lefranc, are invaluable for those who wish to picture native processes such as spinning, plaiting or "finger-weaving" and products such as basketry and neolithic tools. Several native songs and poems, considered authentic, such as "Song of the Sky Loom," are furnished. Additionally, Marriott presents verses representative of Anasazi poetry, or "pre-conquest nonmaterial culture," as it can be reconstructed from modern pueblo-dwellers' lore.[40]

Hell on Horses and Women

In 1953 Marriott published *Hell on Horses and Women*, based on oral accounts. It celebrates ranch women in the western states from the early twentieth century through the 1950s. Lefranc provided small drawings for the chapter headings. The title has irked more than a few, doubtless; one commentator found it demeaning, implying women's weakness. In a 1993 reprint, however, Margot Liberty praised the book, identifying it as "the first collection of accounts by or about ranch women."[41]

The book, which bears an ethnologist's stamp, contributes to social and economic history of the west. The alliterative title comes from an unidentified cowman's statement quoted in the front matter: "The cow business is a damn fine business for men and mules, but it's hell on horses and women." (Mules endure the heat better than horses and are calmer and surer-footed; they were not as a rule used in ranch work, however, not being suited to it, temperamentally.) Marriott had hoped to organize her book in pairs of narratives, one from pioneer days, the other from the present. Such proved impractical, but period contrasts are prominent. The scenes range from Montana and North Dakota to Nebraska, Texas, New Mexico, Nevada, and elsewhere. The list of informants, whose help Marriott acknowledges warmly, is long.[42]

The book is dedicated to members of the Pampa, Texas, "Semi-sewing

Circle," which included Marriott's friend Sloan (with whom Alice shared her recipe for avocado soup). Women of various ages, skills, and circumstances are depicted. To a few, taken westward as brides or for other reasons, the territory and modes of living were entirely unfamiliar; getting acquainted proved to be hard occasionally, if amusing. Even to a bride from Dallas who moved within her state to the Big Bend, the adjustment was enormous.

From the title onward, women are set apart. "The world of the west was from the beginning a man's world." Men had a chance to get their own way and keep the status quo. It is emphasized how traditionalist cattle country—and its men—("conservative critters") are. Chivalry (Marriott is not unaware of the pun) is central; the book "helps you to understand what is behind the life of a woman on a ranch and why her men treat her as they do." The short, selected bibliography is built around books by men, concerning mostly men. No book resembles Marriott's, but two titles are revealing: *No Dudes, Few Women: Life with a Navaho Range Rider*, by Elizabeth Ward, and Agnes Morley Cleaveland's *No Life for a Lady*.[43]

Marriott's stance is not anti-patriarchal and accusatory. The book does not "reflect a battle of the sexes; not my own—I haven't any battling feelings on the subject—nor anybody else's." Men are generally portrayed favorably. Nevertheless, being Freudian, as she said, she believed that men might have felt guilt about their women's lives. Hers is thus a corrective vision. She noted that, in her hearing, the title expression always came from male speakers; as for women, even old pioneer types she managed to track down denied that their life was hell. She conveys with skill and comprehension women's daily lives, often through their eyes. A recurring theme is schooling for the children. The importance of houses is enormous, whether the home be a sod hut, a cabin, or a modern ranch house, and the almost visceral relationship between dwelling and woman is well explored. When the men are away on ranch business, as is often the case, wives have to perform the work of two, including, frequently, the most physically demanding.[44]

Exposition is done by summary, scenic presentation, and dialogues, many invented, one surmises, with bits of recorded or remembered sentences, part of recollections that enable a skilled writer to flesh out scenes and characters. The recurrence of settings and families helps tie together the discrete chapters. "In My Own Voice," a sort of preface, provides insight on the matter. "One ranch recurs in story after story, but nothing happens there that does not also happen elsewhere. Let the JL on the

Powder River stand ... as the archetype of small-to-medium ranches, where humor, courage, and determination, more than money to hire hands, make the wheels go round." The writing is often metaphoric, with bits of farce elsewhere. Marriott uses free indirect style and indirect style (as in "Yes, ma'am, he'd been out of the state some; he'd been as far east as Denver").[45]

The author acknowledged that even as she wrote uses changed—another mode of acculturation. By 1950 there was prosperity in some areas, depending upon rainfall and other factors. One Texas ranch wife takes a tour of Europe. A girl from Arizona goes to Sweet Briar College. The longhorn cattle, descendants of Spanish stock, have nearly vanished, replaced partly by breeds from Great Britain; saddles used by British immigrants were replaced long before; herding is done chiefly by Jeep. Marriott's own attitude toward modernization and other alterations in ranch life is somewhat conservative, doubtless through nostalgia. "Yet ... as long as the Big Horns soar white-crested against the turquoise of a Wyoming August, as long as the sixty measured miles of the Big Bend south of Marfa shimmer with the blaze of ocotillo in May ... just so long certain thought patterns and words will persist among the men and women of the cattle country."[46]

One chapter, though not set in the Southwest, deserves notice because it underlines the author's sensitivity to improper treatment of Native Americans. In South Dakota, a young Indian woman has just seen her two brothers depart for the Korean War; yet she cannot get served in a white café. Nor does policy allow her to run for rodeo queen—except that the tribal elders, perhaps sensing that the moment is suitable for change, urge her to do so anyway, as a sign of respect for those going to fight. So, riding a beautiful palomino, and encouraged by her grandmother, who had attended the Carlisle Indian School, she breaks with custom and participates in the parade. Of course the story must end well, though those familiar with mores at the time can imagine undercurrents of resentment.[47]

Greener Fields *and Subsequent Works*

Greener Fields (1953) constitutes another generic blend—a handbook on certain American Indians, a memoir, and an introduction to a field ethnologist's life. It also includes narratives, intended to illustrate factual material. Three chapters appeared in the *New Yorker*. It is almost pedagogical, showing how much Marriott wanted to make herself and her work understood. The narrative chapters alternate irregularly with expository ones concerning anthropological research, terminology, concepts, and practical topics of interest to ethnologists, such as etiquette and techniques for interviewing. Her sense of natural beauty and her literary gifts are displayed, as in this evocation of the horizon in Oklahoma on summer evenings. "Daylight and dusk merge imperceptibly with one another and with dark. The sky turns by slightest degrees from turquoise to ... royal blue, and always, even on a starless night, misses being black."[48]

Early chapters recount her initial contacts with anthropology and her experiences among the Modoc in southern Oregon. Her Oklahoma field work occupies an important place. The meeting (chapter 8) of her family with Elizabeth's, notably the grandmother, who announces that she loves the white girl and wishes to adopt her, is a discreet, tender scene with which any fiction writer could be pleased; it stands as a testimony to Marriott's exceptional empathy. The following chapters are devoted to Pueblos. Whether through Lefranc's influence or not, Marriott shows skills as a colorist, speaking of their arts (murals, pottery, textiles, and others): "Above all, the Pueblo Indians were painters. Earth in their country was of many hues: chrome and gamboge yellows, the blue or green of volcanic muds, white from deposits of kaolin, reds from hematite cliffs, and black from the charcoal of their fires." "The End of a Beautiful Friendship" recounts the visit of a sand-painter to the San Francisco Exposition.

Black Stone Knife (1957) is chiefly an entertaining story, though it contains information on the Kiowas and other tribes. It concerns a lengthy journey (of nearly three years) made on foot by Kiowas—young men and a boy—as far south as Mexico. It was based on a true story, recorded by Mooney in 1892; she heard an account from very old grandchildren of the participants. Marriott re-created the characters and dramatized their adventures in an suspenseful way, appealing especially to boys, but tenderly also.[49]

A somewhat similar book, *Indian Annie: Kiowa Captive* (1965), can be enjoyed by young people or adults. Generically, it is a romance, very roughly comparable to nineteenth-century tales focused on Indian captives and noble savages. Several true cases of abduction by Kiowas provided the basis, with changes in names and telescoping of certain events. Marriott had information from interviews with eye-witnesses, secondhand narratives, and Thomas Battey's *The Life and Adventures of a Quaker Among the Indians*, presumably the inspiration for one character. She specified that the model for Annie was not her acquaintance Millie Durgan

Goombi, the mother of Hunt's second wife, though Goombi had been captured as a small child, grew up as a Kiowa, and married a Kiowa.

The author's aim was to depict Kiowa life in the last third of the nineteenth century, when the pace of change brought by whites—especially the disappearance of the buffalo—accelerated, and to show what happened to the Kiowas who took the "peace road," rather than resist. The book is thus a study in acculturation, its limits and possibilities—including acculturation from white to Indian, the unusual direction. The story is also a morality tale. Indian customs, particularly domestic life and the Sun Dance, are described. Echoes from other Marriott books are heard, especially *The Ten Grandmothers*; the two works could usefully be read together. Spear Girl becomes a friend of the white captive, a redhead, who, in the ceremony at the time of the Sun Dance, is re-named Hummingbird Girl. Marriott thus writes herself into the book.[50]

In 1865, Annie's family, in Tennessee, refuses to remain in land occupied by Northerners and leaves for Texas. During a raid on nearby property, Annie, aged ten, is captured. (The ethical grounds for such abduction are not questioned.) Her captor and his wife, who had lost a daughter to smallpox, take excellent care of her. She adapts well to Kiowa ways and learns to love her new mother. By the conclusion of the story she is eighteen, a woman; she chooses to remain with the tribe; not "back to civilization," whence she came (and with which the tribe must seek accommodation more and more), but "back to the blanket." "The Kiowas are my people."[51]

When blue-coated soldiers, whom, as a Southerner, she dreads, come in search of abducted white girls vaguely described on their list of Indian captives, Annie hides to avoid being returned by force to white life. When her true parents find her, they do not understand why she remains with the tribe; her father protests vigorously against her decision to marry Black Wolf. She does not reject all features of white life, however. She opens a school for men who can learn English and act as interpreters, and she agrees to marry in a Christian chapel and visit her white parents often. In a telling episode, she confronts a soldier (in her eyes, a "Yankee") who says he has come to protect the settlers. Reflecting that he was probably among those who helped starve the Kiowas by holding them captive in the horse corral at Ft. Sill, she challenges him.

"Did you ever think about protecting us?"

"Us? Who do you mean by us?..."

"The Kiowas. All the Indians."

Learning that he comes from Springfield, Illinois, she continues, "You know what [Lincoln] stood for. The right of all people to be free and to belong to themselves.... If you don't think one man can own another, why do you think it's right for one man to starve another?"[52]

A Double Contribution

Marriott did not live only for her writing; yet, even with her scientific approach toward knowledge, she nevertheless wrote herself into her pages. She is an outstanding example of a woman who succeeded in her professional life and cultivated a literary offshoot, attached at the trunk, flowering on its own. Her enthusiasm for making ethnology comprehensible to non-specialists, including children, is visible throughout her writing, as are her concerns for preserving what should be honored from the past (whether material or not) and making of the present a fulfilling experience both ethical and aesthetic.

Chapter Seven

Lands of Enchantment

The southwestern lands evoked in writings by the five figures examined above—Mary Austin, Willa Cather, Laura Adams Armer, Peggy Pond Church, and Alice Marriott—were to them, as to many others, exceptional, endowed by nature and history with a magnetic appeal, combining abundant beauties, exotic charm, and ineffable spiritual qualities. Despite varying degrees of isolation, aridity, rockiness, extremes of heat and cold, and other characteristic drawbacks, the areas these authors depict all deserve the New Mexico nickname, "Land of Enchantment" ("Tierra del encanto"). Even the rising plains of western Oklahoma, as described by Marriott, the least lyrical of the five writers, present unusual interest, by the interactions between the land and the traditions of the nomadic Kiowa culture.

Perhaps, however, one should say not *despite* these drawbacks, or what appear to be, but *because of*; for those who are drawn to the Southwest as visitors or settle there—or who, belonging by birth, stay and love it—though all know they cannot count generally on rich soils, gentle topography, abundant rainfall, and trees everywhere, may find greater attraction and meaning in the very difficulties presented by the region: its recalcitrant earth, dry arroyos, rough contours, great distances, mirages, and the struggles of its peoples. Beauty may be made from scarcity—a type of natural minimalism. Those who are devoted to the Southwest believe that under the harshness of the lands lies a hidden heart. Verities are not disguised nor misted over, provided that one knows how to see. "There is a nakedness about the southwest, a bald truthfulness which allows of no subterfuge, and brooks no flattery," wrote Armer. She added what she called a commonplace (which is key also to Austin's *Cactus Thorn*): "Once in the desert, men cannot rest until they return." Themselves enchanted with the region, these women writers saw in fact that it was not so barren as others believed, and from its features, history, and lore they created enchantments of their own in fresh, original prose and verse. In their way, their pages provide intimations of the spiritual forces to which native beliefs point and of the charms wrought by ritual and expressed through art.[1]

The present study has had as its aim to examine, by reference to pertinent works by these authors, aspects of the Southwest and their various literary expressions from around 1900 into the following six or so decades—and, what is more important, to draw from their respective writings a keen, detailed vision, intersecting at many points. What has been uncovered has value not only in itself, and as representative of its time, but for present and future readers in the greatly changed circumstances of the twenty-first century.

The study has likewise attempted to redress considerable imbalance in the reputations of these writers, since they have been remembered in very different ways. Austin and Cather are widely acknowledged to have been, and to remain, major figures in American literature; the stock of both is high. (This is only partly because they lived for a while and published in New York and so were part of the northeastern literary scene; their southwestern books were and remain among the most admired of their large and varied output.) Yet, though certain books by Austin were reprinted and it was acknowledged that *The Land of Little Rain* and other writings had brought a *frisson nouveau* (new shiver) to American writing, her fame was less than Cather's, and it suffered eclipse; but it has now rebounded, thanks to new studies and enlarged perspectives. While not nearly so well known as those two figures, Armer, Church, and Marriott, in their individual ways, were likewise exceptional, having taken on challenging, indeed original projects, studying both broadly and deeply the places where they lived and worked and the native residents. Armer's writing, which might be mistaken for a *violon d'Ingres*, was, rather, a deep and complementary strain of her artistic vision of the Southwest, expressed also in her painting and photography (which have received more critical attention). Marriott brought to her study of the Kiowas and New Mexico Indians and Hispanics her ethnologist's training and experience, a fact that explains why she is noted as an anthropologist, though it is her own brand of creative ethnology that makes her deserving of consideration here. For fifty years, Church wrote poems and prose about her state—its unique history, its beauty—but also took on the intimate subject of marriage and the immediate and awful topic of the bomb. All five women displayed in their careers admirable determination to pursue their undertakings and follow them to fruition; and their achievements stand out by their insight and originality.[2]

Loose personal contacts and more distant ones existed among these writers, as was noted in previous chapters. Austin and Cather, close contemporaries, were acquainted; they corresponded, and evidence indicates that each read works by the other. Their relations were not always smooth, though, and they may be viewed as sometime rivals. As a young woman, Church met Austin, wrote to her as an admirer, and took her life as a topic for a book. Church and Marriott both had the experience of living near Rio Grande pueblos and interacting closely with residents. Armer met members of the D.H. Lawrence circle that had given some of its fame to Taos, a pueblo that Cather visited (of which she wrote, also) and where Church lived later. These connections, some chance, are less significant, however, than the authors' overlapping aesthetic and cultural positions, which were made clear earlier.

While some forty years separate the birth dates of the older generation from those of Church and Marriott, all five came of age as women and artists in a period that can be seen now as an important middle one. They precede the numerous women writers born after 1950 who belong to the vastly-altered New West; they follow earlier figures whose writing contributed to forming nineteenth-century views of the territory treated in this book, such as Helen Hunt Jackson (1830–85), author of a treatise in favor of Indian welfare called *A Century of Dishonor* (1881) as well as the famous *Ramona* (1884), and Sarah Winnemucca (ca. 1844–1891), whose *Life Among the Piutes* (1883) [sic] is viewed by some as the first autobiography by a native woman.[3]

What does this chronological placement mean? Opportunities for women in literature—for the necessary leisure, for travel, publication, and cultivation of literary connections—had certainly increased by 1900. Even more important is the fact that these writers saw the Southwest before it went through the enormous changes wrought after the 1950s. That is, they were not born too late to witness and gather material from periods that, retrospectively, appear crucial. It is true that in 1893, as Austin and Cather were on the threshold of their literary careers, Frederick Jackson Turner announced that the western frontier, responsible, in his view, for American democracy as it had developed, had been closed, effectively (as he saw it) ending open-ended expansion and its cultural and political implications, along with opportunities for certain kinds of individualistic ventures. (The U.S. Census Bureau had already stated officially in 1890 that the frontier had broken up, that is, no longer existed.) A certain idea of America and the free individual facing west had lost not its power but a particular representative political and cultural value as myth. Turner's sweeping pronouncement, suggesting homogeneity, did not, of course, fit perfectly the reality of America then, and his view was not shared by all. There were inner frontiers. Enormous regional differences of many sorts remained, including radical distinctions among groups and peoples, and vast tracts of wilderness still allowed for personal confrontation with the land.

Thus even as Jackson wrote, Austin's family members, recent arrivals in California, were attempting to homestead in difficult conditions on high desert soil, in what she called the land of lost borders. The various Native American tribes that appear in the pages of all five writers—chiefly Paiutes, Navajos, Hopis, Rio Grande Pueblo Indians, and Kiowas—still maintained somewhat closed cultures; they remained connected to and heavily influenced by their distinctive past, with its religious beliefs, tribal customs, and remembered and ongoing trials. In California, Austin observed long-established ways of Indian life and learned lore of untold age. Armer and Marriott witnessed the last decades before the upheavals of the 1950s and 1960s in America and yet could speak with tribal members (Kiowas and Navajos) who recalled what life was like for their people in the 1860s. Church knew much of pioneer life, through her grandparents; her own life was rustic for years. In addition, she familiarized herself with the native traditions around her, though pueblos remained still somewhat closed and self-sufficient. She also was, however, a literary witness to enormous post-war changes in customs, schooling, work opportunities, and social institutions, as to the beginning of the atomic age, surely a historical watershed.

Moreover, these writers' interest in preservation of past and more recent cultures and conservation of the natural world around them could be voiced in ways that have become difficult, if not impossible, for following generations. That is, they could think and write apolitically, though not coldly—subtly, and without hyperbole. As outsiders, they could study and speak of Native Americans without being accused of patronizing and imperialism, or effectively silenced, and without recourse to the postcolonial categories of such thinkers as Frantz Fanon and Edward Said, according to which the Other is always a menace or a prey, someone to oppress or by whom to be oppressed. They avoided becoming part of the later hardening, even polarization of opinion on environmental matters and getting embroiled in controversies swirling around aspects of the Native American heritage and Anglo development (urban, industrial, agricultural) in the Southwest. Their moods and modes were generally marked by hope, not anger or near-despair (Church's poems in *Ultimatum for Man* are an exception). Lyricism about their region was possible. To be sure, they acknowledged the struggles of the past and historical wrongs, ancient and more recent, but could celebrate without self-consciousness the endurance of native tribes and the beauties, natural and man-made, of the Southwest. Their audiences were fresher—more ingenuous—than those for whom many southwestern women write today, particularly Native American authors such as Louise Abeita (E-Yeh-Shuré or Blue Corn) and Leslie Marmon Silko.

Thus, despite chronological separation and differences in life, career, and location, these five authors often sound alike; the factual commonplaces of the area (geographic, ethnographic, historical) and certain of their implications, while perceived through individual eyes and voices, are shared—frequent, if not constant. To say that identical or similar themes, motifs, and symbols appear over and over is not to suggest triteness or imitation, especially since the themes include some of the most fundamental to human existence. Certain features, certain images recur—bread, stones, trees, sun and moon—in age-old uses, showing how the deepest insights and strongest emotions can be expressed by modest, even trivial suggestions (King Lear's "Pray you, undo this button"). All five women touched on the topics of ancient ruins, petroglyphs, pottery and shards, textiles, animal legends, and native beliefs, especially cosmology, through all of which their eyes penetrated layers of time and meaning. Motifs circulate among their books and poems: the value of water; the importance of goodness and beauty; the fragility of the desert; the grandeur of the mountains and sky. Even place names recur: Truchas Mountains, the Enchanted Mesa, Canyon de Chelly, the Little Colorado. Stability and recurrence, in nature and human life, are emphasized frequently, from diurnal repetition—life at its most fundamental—to yearly rhythms of creation, to the cycle of life and death and the far reaches of prehistoric and geological time.

To live, in fact and in art, in the southwestern places that appealed deeply to them and to cultivate southwestern topics was, for these writers, to be themselves. As they spoke of their region, they also inscribed their personality in their texts, shaping their experiences in local terms, interweaving the personal and the geographic, and ultimately knowing themselves, at least partly, in terms of the Southwest. The desert is always a woman, Austin had observed. Their strategy—not simply literary, but a deeply personal commitment—provides the uniqueness of their voices, which are recognizable so often as feminine and yet are individual. Although certain texts—Austin's *Earth Horizon*, Armer's *In Navajo Land*, Church's *The Ripened Fields*, and Marriott's *Greener Fields*—are explicitly or at least plainly autobiographical, elsewhere one does not usually find direct presentation of the self. The person is inscribed subtly in the colors, shapes, and voices of other figures and even in the landscape and other inanimate features, all treated with cultural sensitivity and a refined style. Is Cather the same as her character Thea, resting on blankets in a small chamber of the ruins among the cliffs? Certainly not, but the author is not a stranger to the character either.

Against a dramatic southwestern background characterized by both grandiose proportions and epic enterprises—topics preferred frequently by male writers—these authors undertook characteristically to write of small-scale achievements on the level of houses, villages, individual lives—speaking of experiences they had undergone themselves, and typically feminine ones. It will be recalled that one of Austin's characters proclaims women to be closer to "earth's moulding realities." This familiarity with earth was paralleled by their interest in the arts and crafts of the quotidian and small-scale use of the land (for sheep-raising, and farming in valleys and canyon-bottoms). Like her mother and brother, Austin and her husband attempted to cultivate the California desert soil; she camped out; she characteristically chose small topics, such as a single tree, a small fire, or modest figures: neighboring miners, sheepmen, Indians, a wandering woman, and animals for whom that desert was home and sustenance. Cather similarly went camping, in the Anasazi ruins of Colorado, and set scenes among the stones; she wrote of hogans built from willows, of peach trees, of homesteads made of sun-baked earth, against sun-baked adobe walls. Armer, kneeling on the ground, learned the art of sand-painting; she too slept sometimes outdoors or in a small tent, as did Church. Marriott collected native pottery, wrote of its most famous artisan then, and lived in a dilapidated "mud-pie" (the cramped adobe house she shared with Margaret Lefranc).[4]

Perhaps, of all the thematic threads that can be followed in the writings of these artists, the two most recurrent and important are belief in the unique, and precious, qualities of the Southwest, both human and geographic, and hence the conviction that it, and those who dwell there, must be protected and preserved. It is easy to imagine what these writers would have thought of the disasters that have befallen the Southwest in the twenty-first century: droughts such that entire bodies of water shrivel up, the Gold King Mine spill and indifference to the sufferings of the nearby Navajos, and looming water wars. Comprehensive understandings of the past and present, as seen in fine writing about the Southwest, lead to recognizing that by proper stewardship of land and human resources the natural world and local cultures must be honored and protected against predation. "It is the duty of all living men to maintain the harmony they are aware of in the world around them," wrote Church. Again and again in her pages and those by the others one finds expressions of admiration for the southwestern landscape and other features, even awe, devotion, and concern, going far beyond the ordinary. Though connected to these women's experience of local life and their close associations with residents (Native Americans, Spanish Americans), this concern had nothing to do with their own ethnic interests and everything to do with others, their culture, and the imperative to preserve the earth.[5]

To envisage a place so ardently is an act of espousal. Of course it is mental, or psychic; but it can be viewed almost as somatic. Certainly, physical sensations are emphasized in the writings studied here. The three least intellectual senses, the most proximate, receive full importance. Textures, in weavings, pots (glazed, unglazed, or decorated in relief), leaves, grains of sand, rocks, cliffs have an important place. Similarly, tastes and aromas play their role (of goats' ribs, fry bread, honey, peaches, conifers, smoke from cooking or ceremonial fires, rain). Hearing obviously has its place too in the physical encounter with the Southwest: wind, thunder, the sound of melting snow-water dripping or of raindrops in trees or on dry soil, a wild animal's call, drums, chanting, and pounding feet at festivals.

The greatest means of knowing the Southwest displayed in works examined above is obviously vision, a sympathetic grasping, focusing closely on a flower or cactus or animal tracks in the sand, but also reaching far over the landscape, taking in the sky in its grandeur. If one looks carefully and wisely, vision then contributes to synthesizing perceptions, creating rich mental images and going beyond them to penetrating insights. One may then see life clearly and see it whole. As Austin wrote, speaking of earlier peoples and their intellection of their environment: "The plant world begins to stand to man not for itself but for ideas." In a poem addressed to her friend Tilano, from San Ildefonso Pueblo, and dedicated to Laura Gilpin, who photographed him, Church sees that

> There is a cloud behind you
> in which the corn is mirrored.

> The narrow stalks have the shape of holy beings
> drawn on a sacred stone.
> ....
> The corn is an image of your inner being...⁶

The wonders that these women identified and experienced in the Southwest led to the enchanting qualities of their work—images, style, characters, word-pictures. Their writing may be viewed as kin to incantations practiced by Native Americans in dances, sand-painting ceremonies, and secret rites. Not that literary art is true sorcery (neither is Indian ritual, of course); but it does more than charm in the ordinary sense. It uses imagination to comprehend the deeper realities of experience; it draws readers and listeners into sensing mystery in natural phenomena and honoring spirit everywhere. At its best, it creates from the region living myth and thus may provide what Austin described as "a way of seeing things that is native to the deepest self of man." Thus the vision displayed by these writers is moral, and their writing appeals to the moral imagination as well as the aesthetic sense, carrying out what Samuel Johnson considered as the aim of literature: leading readers properly to enjoy life more or be able to endure it better.⁷

Chapter Notes

Preface

1. Numerous critics rightly consider Cather's works set in Plains states as "western"—that is, frontier stories. The history, physical conditions, and means of human development there are very different, however, from those in the Southwest. See Susan J. Rosowski, *Birthing a Nation: Gender, Creativity, and the West in American Literature* (Lincoln: University of Nebraska Press, 1999), chapter 3.

2. Vera Norwood, "Women's Place: Continuity and Change in Response to Western Landscapes," in Lillian Schlissel, Vicki L. Ruiz, and Janice Monk, eds., *Western Women: Their Land, Their Lives* (Albuquerque: University of New Mexico Press, 1988), 174.

3. Young, "Literary Tradition, Lionel Trilling, and the Transmission of the Literary Work," *Explorations: The Twentieth Century*, xi (2009), 91–105; White, *The Content of Form: Narrative Discourse and Historical Representation* (Baltimore: Johns Hopkins University Press, 1987). Certain thinkers go farther than White, asserting that the aims and notions of historical accuracy and truth are fundamentally fictions of power. On presentism, see also Richard Weaver, *Ideas Have Consequences* (Chicago: University of Chicago Press, 1964), 67. Despite being denounced repeatedly in recent decades, chronological examination of an author's work remains an accepted model. See, e.g., James Booth, *Philip Larkin: Life, Art and Love* (London: Bloomsbury, 2014).

4. On indigenous writing, see, for example, Michael Castro, *Interpreting the Indian: Twentieth-Century Poets and the Native American* (Albuquerque: University of New Mexico Press, 1983).

5. Janis P. Stout, *Through the Window, Out the Door: Women's Narratives of Departure, from Austin and Cather to Tyler, Morrison, and Didion* (Tuscaloosa: University of Alabama Press, 1998), xiv; C. S. Brosman, interview with Grau, *Louisiana English Journal*, n.s. 5,2 (1998), 32–33; de la Torre, quoted by Alec Wilkinson, "Something Borrowed," *New Yorker*, 5 October 2015, 32; Willa Cather, *Selected Letters*, ed. Andrew Jewell and Janis Stout (New York: Knopf, 2013), 226.

6. The Porter statement is quoted in Sylvia Ann Grider and Lou Halsell Rodenberger, *Texas Women Writers: A Tradition of Their Own* (College Station: Texas A&M University Pres, 1997), 22.

7. Unlike the Iowa writer Jay Sigmund, in *Pinions* (New York: James T. White, 1923), they would not, presumably, have praised "manifest destiny" insofar as it caused the displacement of the Indians, the destruction and disappearance of the buffalo herds.

Chapter One

1. Alan Axelrod, *Art of the Golden West* (New York: Abbeville Publishers, 1990), 11; Krutch, *Grand Canyon: Today and All Its Yesterdays* (New York: Sloane, 1958), 16; *Perpetual Mirage: Photographic Narratives of the Desert West*, organized by May Castleberry (New York: Whitney Museum of Art, 1996).

2. A useful example of altered critical views and new lines of argument is provided by Krista Comer, *Landscapes of the New West: Gender and Geography in Contemporary Women's Writing* (Chapel Hill: University of North Carolina Press, 1999). Another study

emphasizing new critical approaches and a "hemispheric context" is Reginald Dyck and Cheli Reutter, eds., *Crisscrossing Borders in Literature of the American West* (New York: Palgrave Macmillan, 2009). None of the authors under examination in the present study belongs by date to the new generation of women writers (whose works appear beginning around 1970), and most of the latter's concerns are expressed entirely differently.

3. Morgan is quoted in Anne Tucker, ed., *The Woman's Eye* (New York: Knopf, 1973), 93 (henceforth Morgan). It has been argued that the word "region" refers not to geography but to a geopolitical entity controlled by outside powers. Janis P. Stout believes that geographical terminology for the American west "is inherently ethnicized, radicalized, and certainly politicized." See her *Picturing a Different West: Vision, Illustration, and the Tradition of Austin and Cather* (Lubbock: Texas Tech University Press, 2007), 241 n1. See also Heike Schaefer, *Mary Austin's Regionalism: Reflections on Gender, Genre, and Geography* (Charlottesville: University of Virginia Press, 2004). Among other Southwest women writers of the period who could have been included in the present study, Alice Corbin (1881–1949) and Mabel Dodge Luhan (1879–1962) deserve particular notice. Both are mentioned here from time to time.

4. Krutch, in *The Desert Year* (New York: Sloane, 1951), 13, cites Bernard de Voto: the west begins where the annual rainfall drops below twenty inches a year—that is, the hundredth meridian. Western species of birds begin to predominate there. For a narrow definition of *Southwest*, see Martin Shockley, *Southwest Writers Anthology* (Austin: Steck-Vaughn, 1967), introduction. A wider definition appears in Mabel Major, Rebecca W. Smith, and T. M. Pearce, *Southwest Heritage*, rev. ed. (Albuquerque: University of New Mexico Press, 1948), 1.

5. Kloss and Hewett are quoted in Marta Weigle and Kyle Fiore, *Santa Fe and Taos: The Writer's Era, 1916–1941* (Santa Fe: Ancient City Press, 1982), 49, 67. See also La Farge, *Laughing Boy* (1929; rpt. Franklin City, PA: Franklin Mint, 1977), 36; Corbin, *Red Earth* (1920; new ed., compiled and ed. by Lois Rudnick and Ellen Zieselman, introduction. by Rudnick, Santa Fe: Museum of New Mexico Press, 2003), 7, 37, 51–53; Hillerman, *The Spell of New Mexico* (Albuquerque: University of New Mexico Press, 1976), vii; Andrew Elkins, *An-other Place: An Ecocritical Study of Selected Western American Poets* (Fort Worth: Texas Christian University Press, 2002), 2. Mabel's husband Tony Lujan spelled his name with a J, generally. See Luhan, *Intimate Memories*, condensed and edited by Rudnick (Albuquerque: University of New Mexico Press, 1999), xx n6.

6. The contentions in this paragraph are a product of older understandings of the American Southwest as explored through the authors treated here. Various more recent observers have undertaken to remap the west, culturally and topographically, and thus have blurred the distinctions offered by the present author. See n. 1, viz. Comer, 62.

7. Alice Roberts, introduction to Colin Renfrew, *Prehistory: The Making of the Human Mind* (2007; rpt. London: Folio Society, 2013), xvii (henceforth Roberts); Peggy Pond Church, *The House at Otowi Bridge: The Story of Edith Warner and Los Alamos* (Albuquerque: University of New Mexico Press, 1959), 5 (henceforth *Otowi*); Marriott, *Greener Fields* ((New York: Crowell, 1953), 9. According to a basic anthropological understanding of the term, culture is an integrated system of socially-acquired values, beliefs, and rules of conduct that define behavior in a given society. Marriott's definition is both wider and more specific: "The sum-total of the habits, beliefs, arts, skills, speech, customs, traditions, mores, and knowledge *of man as a member of society*" (41) (Marriott's italics). T.S. Eliot's brief definition remains serviceable: "All the characteristic activities and interests of a people." See his *Notes towards the Definition of Culture* (New York: Harcourt Brace Jovanovich, 1949), 30.

8. Bandelier, *The Delight Makers*, introduction Charles F. Lummis (New York: Dodd, Mead, 1916), preface. Audrey Goodman, in her *Translating Southwestern Landscapes: The Making of an Anglo Literary Region* (Tucson: University of Arizona Press, 2002), uses the phrase "Mary Austin and the Modernist Southwest" as a running footer for chapter four. Cather was "neither a rebel nor an innovator," wrote Susan J. Rosowski, *Birthing a Nation: Gender, Creativity, and the West in American Literature* (Lincoln: University of Nebraska Press, 1999), 67. The judgment applies to other authors in the present study with respect to rebellion, but not to all innovation. What is meant by *desire* here is not connected to the frequently-cited use of the term by Patricia Meyer Spacks, who applies it to narrative and "the emotional force implicit in the acts of

reading and writing fiction ... to latent as well as overt erotic elements in fiction." See her *Desire and Truth: Functions of Plot in Eighteenth-Century English Novels* (Chicago: University of Chicago Press, 1990), 1.

9. Lincoln, *Native American Renaissance* (Berkeley: University of California Press, 1983), 45; Kirkpatrick Sale, *The Conquest of Paradise: Christopher Columbus and the Columbian Legacy* (New York: Knopf, 1990), 368; Charles Montgomery, *The Spanish Redemption* (Berkeley: University of California Press, 2002), 2–3 (see also 13–15 on traditions and heritage in New Mexico).

10. Morgan, 93.

11. Vera Norwood and Janice Monk, *The Desert Is No Lady* (New Haven: Yale University Press, 1987), 8. On early photography in the west, see Goodman, chapter three. Curtis was among photographers who arranged their shots to maximize the attractiveness of the landscape. The ideal of the noble savage, dating from Michel de Montaigne, subsequently reinforced by John Dryden, Voltaire, and others, became part of the American wilderness-as-garden myth. The idealizing of natives remains a staple of film and literature today; it is encouraged by some Native Americans, mocked by others.

12. Marriott, *Greener Fields*, 248. In her diary Church wrote of being "thrust suddenly into the midst of a prehistoric world," of shards "like the unsorted pieces of a giant picture puzzle ... or like letters from an undeciphered alphabet." See Shelley Armitage, ed., *Bones Incandescent: The Pajarito Journals of Peggy Pond Church* (Lubbock: Texas Tech Press, 2001), 206 (henceforth *Bones*). Armitage uses the term "androgynized creative identity" (*Bones*, 212). It should be specified that the five present authors remained attached to Occidental cultural traditions (including logic) and, like the ancient Greeks, acknowledged and honored nature as order. Their positions were opposed to those of later, radical feminists. The latter include Monique Wittig (1935–2003), who wrote that "one is not born a woman" and wished to overturn not only gender roles but reason, and Shulamith Firestone, who went so far as to assert that "feminists have to question, not just all of *Western* culture, but the organization of culture itself, and, further, even the very organization of nature" (italics in the text). See Firestone, *The Dialectic of Sex: The Case for Feminist Revolution* (New York: Morrow, 1970), 2, 11–12.

13. On the end of the pastoral dream, see Annette Kolodny, *The Lay of the Land: Metaphor as Experience and History in American Life and Letters* (Chapel Hill: University of North Carolina Press, 1975); Leo Marx, *The Machine in the Garden* (New York: Oxford University Press, 1964). The quoted phrase is from Professor Donald Pizer, private communication, 24 October 2013.

14. The phrases "Finished in beauty," and "In beauty it is finished," sometimes "In beauty it is begun," are common throughout Navajo chants and ceremonies. They are quoted in La Farge, 62, 88, 164, 291; N. Scott Momaday, *House Made of Dawn* (1968; rpt. Harper Perennial Classics, 1999), 130; Austin, *One-Smoke Stories* (1934; new ed., critical introduction by Noreen Groover Lape (Athens: Swallow Press / Ohio University Press, 2003), 110. Momaday is of Kiowa and Cherokee extraction. His title comes from a Navajo song that appears in Armer's *Waterless Mountain*. "Finished in beauty" was the original title of Church's *The House at Otowi Bridge*. See Sharon Snyder, *At Home on the Slopes of Mountains: The Story of Peggy Pond Church* (Los Alamos: Los Alamos Historical Society, 2011), 205.

15. Slavitt, cover 4 of C. S. Brosman, *On the Old Plaza* (Macon: Mercer University Press, 2014). Cather fought with Houghton Mifflin to retain the illustrations in *My Ántonia* when the publisher protested against the cost. Stout (xviii) emphasizes Cather's concern for graphic work in her books.

16. Marriott, *The Valley Below*, with drawings by Margaret Lefranc (Norman: University of Oklahoma Press, 1949), 134; Swift, "A Voyage to the Houyhnhnms" in *Gulliver's Travels* (1726), quoted in John Darwin, *Unfinished Empire: The Global Expansion of Britain* (London: Allen Lane, 2012), 30. Marriott adds (135) that "every anthropologist of note in the United States has at some time or the other worked in the Southwest." There are Tiwa and Tewa pueblos; the latter include Taos, Picuris, and, farther south, Isleta and Sandía. Whether all writers on the subject respect the Tiwa/ Tewa distinction is uncertain.

17. Armer, *In Navajo Land* (New York: David McKay, 1962), 22. The Mesa Verde structures were not entirely unknown to whites but had remained unexplored. According to his brother Clayton, Wetherill swam the Mancos River on, or with, his horse and rode into the mesa complex. See Phyllis C.

Robinson, *Willa: The Life of Willa Cather* (Garden City, NY: Doubleday, 1987), 198. On the Wetherils see Frances Gillmor and Louisa Wade Wetherill, *Traders to the Navajo: The Wetherills of Kayenta* (Albuquerque; University of New Mexico Press, 1979).

18. *In Navajo Land*, 71. The Paiutes and Shoshone, about whom Austin wrote, were scattered, not on tribal lands. Armer pointed out that "strength, power, and beauty" were attributed to long hair (*In Navajo Land*, 53). Austin, who fought the Bureau of Indian Affairs over dancing restrictions, broached the topic in "White Wisdom," in *One-Smoke Stories*. The phrase on stereotypes is quoted in Charlotte Whaley, *Nina Otero-Warren of Santa Fe* (Albuquerque: University of New Mexico Press, 1994), 119. See 117 on Otero-Warren's assessment, reported by La Farge. Burke's voice was not the only one; Indian dancing and long hair for men were viewed by many other whites as particularly primitive. Charles Lummis, Austin's mentor, accused the Indian agent Charles Burton of imposing a "reign of terror" on the Hopis at Oraibi by requiring that men cut their hair. (Burton's demand was ultimately overturned.)

19. Quoted in Whaley, 51, 89.

20. *In Navajo Land*, 18 (a short summary of early ethnological research on the Navajos); Sarah Deutsch, *No Separate Refuge* (New York: Oxford University Press, 1987), 37. A collection of Navajo legends, collected and prepared by Washington Matthews, was brought out by the American Folklore Society in 1887.

21. Although the Antiquities Act of 1906 forbade mishandling of ancient artifacts and potsherds and removal except by authorities, gathering of such was widely practiced in the early decades of the twentieth century, both by those wishing to resell them and by locals collecting for themselves. Around 1919, the potter of San Ildefonso, María Martínez, and her husband created their famous ware on the basis of an unusual shard they found in nearby ruins.

22. Lon Tinkle, quoted in Margaret Hartley, ed., *The Southwest Review Reader* (Dallas: SMU Press, 1974), xiii; Susan Goodman and Carl Dawson, *Mary Austin and the American West* (Berkeley: University of California Press, 2008), 272 (Williams quotation); Corbin, 53; Rudnick, introduction to Corbin, 18; Montgomery, xiii; Goldman, *Continental Divides: Revisioning American Literature* (New York: Palgrave, 2000), 5. The phrase on "hundreds ..." is from the Sunstone Press publisher's note to books in its Southwest Heritage Series.

23. Austin, "Regional Culture in the Southwest," *Southwest Review*, 14 (July 1929), 474; Austin, "New York: Dictator of American Criticism," *Nation*, 111 (31 July 1920), 129–30; Austin, "Regionalism in American Fiction," *English Journal*, 21 (Feb. 1932), 97–107; Stout, 138. The Bierce phrase is quoted in Esther Lanigan Stineman, *Mary Austin: Song of a Maverick* (New Haven: Yale University Press, 1989), 90. See also 131.

24. "Regional Culture," 474.

25. Comer, 31–32, 248 n24; Fetterley and Pryce, *Writing Out of Place: Regionalism, Women, and American Literary Criticism* (Urbana: University of Illinois Press, 2003), 2.

26. *Greener Fields*, viz. 254; Armer, *The Trader's Children* (New York: Longmans, Green, 1937), 58, 238.

27. White, *The Content of Form: Narrative Discourse and Historical Representation* (Baltimore: Johns Hopkins University Press, 1987); Lukacs, *A Short History of the Twentieth Century* (Cambridge: The Belknap Press of Harvard University, 2013), 1–2.

28. MacKinnon, *Toward a Feminist Theory of the State*, quoted in Fetterley and Pryce, 251; Roberts, xiv, xvi-xvii. On "feminine art," see Tucker, introduction.

29. Stout, passim; Kolodny, 136–37; Patricia Limerick, *The Legacy of Conquest: The Unbroken Past of the American West*, quoted in Martha Blue, *Indian Trader* (Walnut, CA: Kiva, 2000), xxv; she cites Larry McMurtry's phrase on the "Triumphalists."

30. Shelley Armitage, *Women's Work: Essays in Cultural Studies* (West Cornwall, CT: Locust Hill Press, 1995), 58; Austin, *Cactus Thorn*, foreword and afterword by Melody Graulich (Reno: University of Nevada Press, 1988), 10; Kolodny, 139 (Ransom quotation); Snyder, 29.

31. Sale, 141. Georgi-Findlay is quoted in Patricia Loughlin, *Hidden Treasures of the American West* (Albuquerque: University of New Mexico Press, 2005), 162.. For a statement on how conquest and settlement by force were, as late as the mid-twentieth century, viewed as nearly inevitable, see Walter F. McCaleb, *The Conquest of the West* (New York: Prentice-Hall, 1947): "If force shall come in time to be displaced as the dominant factor in the affairs of men, it will be accomplished through revolt ... against barbarities and bloodshed.... Until this revolt shall bring enlightenment to

mankind, history will continue to report that force, in one guise or another, is continuing its march through the world" (xii). Carolyn Heilbrun claimed that women's experience was nearly absent from western writing; numerous critics have followed suit. See "The Masculine Wilderness of the American Novel," *Saturday Review*, 55 (January 1972).

32. *Women's Work*, 62.

33. Armer, *Southwest* (New York: Longmans, Green, 1935), 91.

34. Paglia, *Sexual Personae: Art and Decadence from Nefertiti to Emily Dickinson* (New Haven: Yale University Pres, 1990), 287; Sherry Ortner, "Is Female to Male As Nature Is to Culture?" in Michele Zimbalist Rosaldo and Louise Lamphere, eds., *Women, Culture, and Society* (Stanford: Stanford University Press, 1974), 67–87; "The Correspondence of May Sarton and Peggy Pond Church," in *Women's Work*, 305–306; *Bones*, 77; Austin, *The Ford* (1917; rpt., foreword by John Walton, Berkeley: University of California Press, 1997) 61; Peggy Pond Church, *The Wind's Trail: The Early Life of Mary Austin*, ed. Shelley Armitage (Santa Fe: Museum of New Mexico Press, 1990), 4; Cynthia Taylor, "Claiming Female Space: Mary Austin's Western Landscape," in Leonard Engel, ed., *The Big Empty: Essays on Western Landscapes as Narrative* (Albuquerque: University of New Mexico Press, 1994), 126; Austin, *Lost Borders* (New York: Harper, 1909). While the "big empty," as Taylor says, may not "be exploitable," the evocation is erotic, and the terrain takes its place in the literary history of cold, dangerous beauties whom men do seek to conquer. See also "Feminist Anthropology: The Legacy of Elsie Clews Parsons," in Ruth Behar and Deborah A. Gordon, eds., *Women Writing Culture* (Berkeley: University of California Press, 1995). Lest the assertions and viewpoints expressed in this section appear so out-of-date as to be invalid, it may be noted that in 2015 the winner of the Nobel Prize for Literature, Svetlana Alexievich, stated that she had interviewed many women and that in writing she "wanted to know how a woman feels.... Women tell things in more interesting ways. They live with more feeling. They observe themselves and their lives. Men are more impressed with action." Masha Gessen, "The Memory Keeper," *New Yorker*, 26 October 2015, 37.

35. *Bones*, 77. Armitage asserts that Austin and Church challenged assumptions about women's weakness and their identification with culture rather than nature (*Bones*, xiv).

36. Austin, *Earth Horizon* (New York: Literary Guild, 1932),15.

37. *Cactus Thorn*, 42; Austin, *The American Rhythm* (1923; new and enlarged ed., New York: Cooper Square, 1970), 90; *Trader's Children*, 30; *Southwest*, 107; *Bones*, 206; Montgomery, 17.

38. Sale, 368; Lesley Poling-Kempes, *Ladies of the Canyons* (Tucson: University of Arizona Press, 2015), 16.

39. Austin, *Starry Adventure* (Boston: Houghton Mifflin, 1931), 277–78; *Southwest*, 108; Matthews, *The Night Chant, A Navaho Ceremonial. Memoirs of the American Museum of Natural History*, vi: Publications of the Hyde Southwestern Expedition (New York, 1902), 6; *Otowi*, 13, 16. Warner was referring to the mesa and the Sangre de Cristo range, partly forested but entirely different from eastern mountains. Warner added, "I think I could not bear again great masses of growing things." Gilpin's photographs come from her *The Enduring Navaho* (Austin: University of Texas Press, 1968), 236–37. "He-Rain" is reproduced in Corbin, 80.

40. *Bones*, 71, 205.

41. *The Ford*, 8–9; Snyder, 225; Marriott, *María: The Potter of San Ildefonso* (Norman: University of Oklahoma Press, 1948), 7. Fergusson is quoted in Lawrence Powell, *Southwest Classics* (Los Angeles: Ward Ritchie Press, 1974), The phrase "the strange mothering of stones" comes from Brosman, "Tres Hermanas," in *Journeying from Canyon de Chelly* (Baton Rouge: LSU Press, 1990). Church kept a journal devoted to poems about stones. See *Bones*, 219 n1. In Corbin's work, Church saw examples of stone imagery and the closeness of stony landscape to the feminine element. E.g.: "An old, old woman who mumbles her beads / And crumbles to stone" (Corbin, 27).

42. Austin, *Land of Little Rain* (Boston: Houghton Mifflin, 1904), 168–69; Cather, *Willa Cather on Writing*, foreword by Stephen Tennant (Lincoln: University of Nebraska Press, 1976), 19; Elkins, 12; *Bones*, 207; *Trader's Children*, 238.

43. *Cather on Writing*, 16.

44. Willa Cather, *Selected Letters*, ed. Andrew Jewell and Janis Stout (New York: Knopf, 2013), 226; Stineman, 129. The rest of Cather's statement is quoted in chapter three below.

45. On the golden age of children's litera-

ture, see Sara Maitland, introduction to Andrew Lang, ed., *The Orange Fairy Book* (1906; illustrated ed., London: The Folio Society, 2013), viz. xii. Charles Kingsley's *The Water-Babies*, Lewis Carroll's *Alice's Adventures in Wonderland*, Rudyard Kipling's *Just So Stories*, Kenneth Grahame's *The Wind in the Willows*, and writings by Louisa May Alcott and Mark Twain illustrate this development, which was connected to what has been called "the invention of childhood" in the Victorian period, itself related to social concerns of the century. Several of these books cultivate fantasy and the exotic. "Children's books after Carroll were less serious, more entertaining, and sounded less like sermons and more like the voices of friends ..." Morton N. Cohen, *Lewis Carroll: A Biography* (New York: Knopf, 1995), xxii.

46. This observation does not mean that such products are "collaborative exercises rather than the objectifications of the identity of a coherent authorial ego," as one critic wishes to think about books. See Martha Schoolman, *Abolitionist Geographies* (Minneapolis: University of Minnesota Press, 2014), 9.

47. Lukács, *Realism in Our Time*. Preface by George Steiner. Trans. John Mander and Necke Mande (New York: Harper & Row, 1964).

48. *Otowi*, 5; *Cather on Writing*, 54.

Chapter Two

1. John Walton, foreword to Austin, *The Ford* (1917; rpt. Berkeley: University of California Press, 1997), ix; Lawrence Powell, *Southwest Classics* (Los Angeles: Ward Ritchie Press, 1974), 103; Austin, *Literary America, 1903-1934: The Mary Austin Letters*, selected and ed. by T. M. Pearce (Westport, CT: Greenwood Press, 1979), 24, 83. For a bibliography of pertinent Austin works, see Joy W. Lyday, *Mary Austin: The Southwest Works* (Austin: Steck-Vaughn, 1968).

2. Hazard Adams and Leroy Searle, *Critical Theory Since 1965* (Tallahassee: Florida State University Press, 1986), 163; Ruth Amossy and Dominique Maingueneau, eds., *L'Analyse du discours dans les études littéraires* (Toulouse: Presses Universitaires du Mirail, 2003) (my translation); M. M. Bakhtin, *The Dialogic Imagination*, ed. Michael Holquist, trans. Holquist and Caryl Emerson (Austin: University of Texas Press, 1981). The obvious validity of these points does not justify interpretations that ignore the author and original context. A famous professor insisted once to his seminar that the word *screw* in an Emily Dickinson poem should be taken in today's coarse sexual sense; to objections, he said that how Dickinson understood the word was not pertinent.

3. Fletcher, "Alice Corbin and Imagism," *New Mexico Quarterly Review*, 19 (Spring 1949), 49; Austin, *Earth Horizon* (Boston: Houghton Mifflin, 1932), 194; Austin, *Mother of Felipe and Other Stories*, ed. Franklin Walker (n.p.: Book Club of California, 1950), 7, 8; Powell, 113; Susan Goodman and Carl Dawson, *Mary Austin and the American West* (Berkeley: University of California Press, 2008), review by Karen S. Langlois, *Western American Literature*, 46, 1 (Spring 2011), 104–105 (henceforth Goodman and Dawson); Austin, *The Children Sing in the Far West* (New York: Houghton Mifflin, 1928), vii; Austin, "The Walking Woman," *Lost Borders* (New York: Harper, 1909), 208; Bynner, "Desert Harvest," *Southwest Review*, 14,2 (July 1929), 493.

4. Austin and John Muir, *Writing the Western Landscape*, ed. Ann H. Zwinger (Boston: Beacon Press, 1994), x; Powell, 332; Cathryn Halverson, *Playing House in the American West: Western Women's Life Narratives* (Tuscaloosa: University of Alabama Press, 2013),117; Barney Nelson, *The Wild and the Domestic: Animal Representation, Ecocriticism, and Western American Literature* (Reno: University of Nevada Press, 2000), 24; Austin, *The Flock* (Boston: Houghton Mifflin, 1906), chapter 11. Nelson's book is excessively personal. Muir, Aldo Leopold, and, later, Joseph Wood Krutch and Edward Abbey are among outstanding ecological spokesmen of the twentieth century. E.g. Krutch, "Conservation Is Not Enough," *The Voice of the Desert* (New York: Sloane, 1954). Rousseau's views were set out in his work known as *Discours sur les sciences et les arts* (1750) and elsewhere.

5. George W. Cronyn, ed., *The Path on the Rainbow* (New York: Boni and Liveright, 1918), republished as *Native American Poetry* (Mineola, NY: Dover, 2006), xxii; Austin, *Indian Poetry* (New York: Exposition of Indian Tribal Arts, © 1931); *Earth Horizon*, 266–67 (on Indian sufferings). In the second decade of the twentieth century numerous collectors and critics began taking interest in aboriginal

poetry and music, notably Natalie Curtis (Burlin), who lived in New Mexico, a tenacious gatherer of southwestern Indian songs. In 1917 *Poetry* published an issue devoted to Indian chant and song. Sergeant and Cassidy are quoted in Austin, *One-Smoke Stories* (1934; new ed., critical introduction by Noreen Groover Lape (Athens: Swallow Press / Ohio University Press, 2003), xxiii, lxiii n124 (henceforth *One-Smoke*). On Austin's acquaintance with Sergeant, who went to Taos for her health in 1920, see Pearce, "Mary Hunter Austin," in Fred Erisman and Richard W. Etulain, eds., *Fifty Western Writers: A Bio-Bibliographic Sourcebook* (Westport, CT: Greenwood Press, 1982), 28. Alice Corbin contributed to *Path on the Rainbow*. On Armer's pamphlet, see chapter four. See also Michael Castro, *Interpreting the Indian: Twentieth-Century Poets and the Native American* (Albuquerque: University of New Mexico Press, 1983), 5, 19–22. On Owens Valley Paiutes, see Mark T. Hoyer, *Dancing Ghosts: Native American and Christian Syncretism in Mary Austin's Work* (Reno: University of Nevada Press, 1998); Dolan H. Eargle, Jr., *The Earth Is Our Mother: A Guide to the Indians of California* ... (San Francisco: Trees Co. Press, 1986), 199–22.

6. Goodman and Dawson, 36; *Earth Horizon*, 128–29; Esther Stineman, *Mary Austin: Song of a Maverick* (New Haven: Yale University Press, 1989), 46. The Church phrase comes from "Meditation," among her unpublished papers.

7. Moers, *Literary Women* (Garden City: Doubleday, 1976), viz. xv. Austin's feminism is of an older strain than contemporary feminist thought; hers is what Nina Baym identified as freedom from male domination— "*from* sex"—rather than "freedom *through* sex" (erotic experience). From Baym's introduction to the Modern Library Edition of Kate Chopin's *The Awakening*, quoted in Morris Dickstein, "*The Awakening*: Between Feminism and the Fin-de-siècle," *Explorations: The Twentieth Century*, xi (2009), 11. (Dickstein does not agree entirely with Baym.) Yet in its connection to conservation, Austin's feminist imagination is closer to contemporary forms.

8. Stout, *Picturing a Different West: Vision, Illustration, and the Tradition of Austin and Cather* (Lubbock: Texas Tech University Press, 2007), xix; Vera Norwood, "Women's Place: Continuity and Change in Response to West-

ern Landscapes," in Lillian Schlissel, Vicki L. Ruiz, and Janice Monk, eds., *Western Women: Their Land, Their Lives* (Albuquerque: University of New Mexico Press, 1988), 159; Halverson, 116; Austin, *Beyond Borders: The Selected Essays of Mary Austin*, ed. Reuben J. Ellis (Carbondale: Southern Illinois University Press, 1996), 115; Shelley Armitage, ed., *Bones Incandescent: The Pajarito Journals of Peggy Pond Church* (Lubbock: Texas Tech Press, 2001), xiv, xxiv, 147. Armitage's use of the word *nature* differs from Shulamith Firestone's radical use (see chapter one). On Austin generally, see Graulich and Elizabeth Klimasmith, eds., *Exploring Lost Borders: Critical Essays on Mary Austin* (Reno: University of Nevada Press, 1999).

9. Pearce in Erisman and Etulain, 20; Goodman and Dawson, 5, 36.

10. Concerning populist tastes, it should be noted that among poets Austin favored, to judge by her *The American Rhythm* (1923, 1930; new and enlarged ed., New York: Cooper Square, 1970), were Walt Whitman, Vachel Lindsay, and Carl Sandburg, all populists. Yet, denying that a native "imagistic" art was impossible, Austin compared Indian verse to the Imagists,' a modernist and elitist movement. See Castro, 22. One critic labels certain narratives of Austin's "modernist." See Elizabeth Jane Harrison, "Zora Neale Hurston and Mary Hunter Austin's Ethnographic Fiction: New Modernist Narratives," in Harrison and Shirley Peterson, eds., *Unmanning Modernism: Gendered Re-Readings* (Knoxville: University of Tennessee Press, 1997).

11. Austin, *Cactus Thorn*, foreword and afterword by Melody Graulich (Reno: University of Nevada Press, 1988), 8, 32; *One-Smoke*, 134.

12. Austin, *Experiences Facing Death* (Indianapolis: Bobbs-Merrill, 1931), 273.

13. Austin, "The Friend in the Wood," in Peggy Pond Church, *Wind's Trail*, ed. Shelley Armitage (Albuquerque: University of New Mexico Press, 1990), 196; Austin, *The Land of Little Rain* (1903; facsimile rpt., foreword by Marcia Muth, Santa Fe: Sunstone, 2007), 247 (henceforth *Little Rain*); Austin, *The Basket Woman* (Boston: Houghton Mifflin, 1904,1910), iii; *Earth Horizon*, 371. On Friend-of-the-Soul-of-Man (with or without hyphens) and Wakonda (= strength of spirit), see *One-Smoke*, 26, 81. Sergeant described Austin as a "mystic" who knew more than she could express and yet was "tied down to the mud and the granite and the sandhills." Quoted in Marta Weigle and Kyle Fiore, *Santa Fe and*

Taos: The Writer's Era, 1916–1941 (Santa Fe: Ancient City Press, 1982), 43. Castro wrote that Austin had a "somewhat mystical attitude toward the land" (15). See chapter one for a working definition of *mysticism*. Austin's understanding did not include the occult, the esoteric, or magic.

14. Greeley, *The Catholic Imagination* (Berkeley: University of California Press, 1988), 1; Gioia, "The Catholic Writer Today," *First Things*, 238 (Dec. 2013).

15. *Literary America*, 124; Stineman, 37. Austin recognized that Indian science had limitations. Meadowlarks' tongues, used by Paiutes, could not, for instance, improve her daughter's speech. See *Earth Horizon*, 246.

16. *American Rhythm*, 39; Augusta Fink, *I-Mary: A Biography of Mary Austin* (Tucson: University of Arizona Press, 1983), 85, 128.

17. *Lost Borders*, 132, 183. An early biography is Helen McKnight Doyle, *Mary Austin: Woman of Genius* (New York: Gotham House, 1939; rpt. with afterword, 1985).

18. Goodman and Dawson, 5, 33.

19. Goodman and Dawson, 13; *Wind's Trail*, 120, 121, 157.

20. Austin, *Can Prayer Be Answered?* (New York: Farrar and Rinehart, 1934); *Experiences Facing Death*, 25; Goodman and Dawson, 41. On prayer, see below also.

21. *Wind's Trail*, 104. Austin used the title phrase previously, e.g., *American Rhythm*, 67. For additional commentary on her childhood as represented in the autobiography, see Halverson, 117–20.

22. Church found that Jim corresponded frequently, alluding to his homestead and plans for Mary and Susanna to file claims (*Wind's Trail*, 172).

23. *Earth Horizon*, 309. Halverson asserts that the work is narrated in the third person throughout (115).

24. See *Earth Horizon*, viii; *Wind's Trail*, 162–65. The journalist was probably J. E. McClure, co-editor.

25. Austin recounts the camel expedition in *The Land of Journeys' Ending* (New York: Century, 1924), 225–26 (henceforth *Journeys' Ending*). See also *The Flock*, 226–27.

26. *Earth Horizon*, 350.

27. *Earth Horizon*, 231.

28. *Literary America*, 25; Nina Baym, *Women Writers of the American West, 1833–1927* (Urbana: University of Illinois Press, 2011), 267. Asthma or malnutrition may have contributed to Ruth's death.

29. See *Mother of Felipe*, 29–93. On Lummis, see Audrey Goodman, *Translating Southwestern Landscapes: The Making of an Anglo Literary Region* (Tucson: University of Arizona Press, 2002), chapter one.

30. Walton credits Austin with helping to organize the arts community in Carmel (*The Ford*, ix), but Gertrude Atherton and others had settled earlier (*Literary America*, 61). On Lummis's "generic christening," see Goodman and Dawson, 44.

31. *Earth Horizon*, 310. A Paiute healer contributed to her understanding of prayer; see Goodman and Dawson, 40.

32. Graulich confirms the affairs (*Cactus Thorn*, 113, 116); Armitage, 205–206. MacDougal was the author of *The Nature and Work of Plants* (New York: Macmillan, 1900). How close Austin was to Luhan is unclear. Stineman believes Austin and Luhan were not lovers (170–71). Alice Marriott reports that one participant in a Luhan "salon" ca. 1912 at which peyote was used committed suicide. See Mariott and Carol K. Rachlin, *Peyote* (New York: Crowell, 1971), ix.

33. *Earth Horizon*, 330, 349; Stineman, 60; Armitage, xli.

34. Quoted in Charlotte Whaley, *Nina Otero-Warren of Santa Fe* (Albuquerque: University of New Mexico Press, 1994), 130. The assessment of Austin's paintings is by Nell Norris (interview, 1 December 2013).

35. Quoted in Fink, 235.

36. Graulich, afterword to *Earth Horizon* (Albuquerque: University of New Mexico Press, 1991); Cynthia Taylor, "Claiming Female Space: Mary Austin's Western Landscape," in Leonard Engel, ed., *The Big Empty: Essays on Western Landscapes as Narrative* (Albuquerque: University of New Mexico Press, 1994), 120 (Taylor applies this assessment likewise to *Lost Borders*); Krista Comer, *Landscapes of the New West: Gender and Geography in Contemporary Women's Writing* (Chapel Hill: University of North Carolina Press, 1999), 125.

37. *Little Rain*, viii-ix. Abbey's phrase, from the Penguin Books republication (New York, 1988), is quoted in Goodman and Dawson, 268; the phrase on "mystical nature sketches" comes from *Dictionary of Literary Biography* 78 (Detroit: Gale, 1988), 14.

38. *Little Rain*, 3, 16, 144.

39. *Little Rain*, 40.

40. *Little Rain*, 139.

41. *Basket Woman*, vii-viii.

42. *Basket Woman*, 157. Bighorn mountain sheep cannot move through heavy snow.
43. Austin, *Isidro* (Boston: Houghton Mifflin, 1905), 171.
44. Goodman and Dawson, 87.
45. *Isidro*, 399. For an example of medieval use of the stag, see *The Hours of Catherine of Cleves*, introduction and commentaries by John Plummer (New York, Braziller, n.d.), image no. 124, in which the animal, rearing up, has his forelegs crossed and a crucifix between his antlers. The MS., from Utrecht, dates from about 1440. Austin was acquainted with a "lone buck" antelope on the Tejon Range; once in a windy rainstorm they took shelter together in a half-ruined settler's shack. See *Earth Horizon*, 194. The animal appears in "The Last Antelope," *One-Smoke*.
46. *The Flock*, 193–94. Goodman and Dawson assert that Austin's book had "neither forerunner nor follower" (270). Kupper quotes Austin (*The Golden Hoof* [New York: Knopf, 1945], 78).
47. The history of the establishment and development of the park is complicated. Muir is credited with an important role (1890), but there had been earlier government grants of land and concessions in the valley.
48. *The Flock*, 71, 72.
49. *Lost Borders*, 3, 4, 10–11. Might Austin have thought of Thoreau's statement (in which the term *border* has a slightly different sense from hers) that he sought "a border life"? In his essay "Walking" he wrote that he would not have "every part of man cultivated," any more than "every acre of earth." Austin surely wished, as he did, "to regard man as an inhabitant, or a part and parcel of Nature, rather than a member of society." (This essay is widely available in Thoreau literature, e.g., *The Portable Thoreau* [New York: Viking Press, 1964].)
50. *Lost Borders*, 74, 191.
51. *American Rhythm*, 43; Stineman, 113–14. For a study of native myths in the play, see Hoyer, 101–17. He believes that the two topics, women (with feminist subtext) and Indians, are well blended.
52. Stineman, 114–16, notes very harsh judgments. See also Castro, 13, 37; *Literary America*, 39; Pearce, "Mary Austin and the Pattern of New Mexico," in "Southwesterners Write," *Southwest Review* 22 (Jan. 1937), 307. Castro reports that anthropologists "regard devices like archaisms, vocables, and word distortions in a tribal context as elements of magic language."

53. *The Ford*, cover 4 (Graulich comment); Welty, *The Eye of the Story: Selected Essays and Reviews* (New York: Random House, 1978), 148; Didion, *Where I Was From* (New York: Knopf, 2003).
54. *The Ford*, xiv (Bierce), 61.
55. *The Ford*, 19, 21, 68, 166, 290, 384.
56. Graulich, afterword to Austin, *The Trail Book* (Reno: University of Nevada Press, 2003), 211, 226; *Earth Horizon*, 331. Austin's vision anticipates elements of the College Board's revised Advanced Placement U.S. History Standards (2014)
57. Austin, "The Folk Story in America," *South Atlantic Quarterly*, 33 (Jan. 1934), 19; *Trail Book*, 150. "Iron Shirts" might appear anachronistic, since the pre–Columbians did not have iron; the term is doubtless intended to suggest Spanish words for *steel* and *armor*.
58. Stineman, 172; Spinden, introduction to his *Songs of the Tewa* (New York: Exposition of Indian Tribal Arts, 1933; republished, co-ordinating editor Margaret Lefranc, preface by Marriott, Santa Fe: Sunstone Press, 1976), 63. Spinden included Washington Matthews for his "lasting monuments," *The Mountain Chant* and the *Night Chant* (see Armer chapter).
59. See Stineman, 172–73; *American Rhythm*, 19, 38; *One-Smoke*, xxxii, xlix. The translations, most composed by 1910 and published by 1914 (65), are often good poetry, perhaps thanks to Austin's skill. The striking poem "The Eagle's Song" (92–93), on death, is included in Alice Corbin Henderson's *The Turquoise Trail* (Boston: Houghton Mifflin, 1928). Unfortunately, inversions, second-person singular verbs, and other earlier uses ("perchance," 97) detract from certain poems in Austin's collection. She wrote that "Amerind dance drama" was "recognizably of the same type as the pre–Aristotelian mysteries of fertility." Cf. *American Rhythm*, 46–47. Austin was willing to oppose scholars such as Franz Boas, in replying to his criticisms concerning her review of Ruth Bunzel's *The Pueblo Potter*. See excerpt in *One-Smoke*, xlvii. Frank Hamilton Cushing had translated Zuni material by 1901; Austin later did an introduction to his *Zuñi Folk Tales* (© 1901; rpt New York: Knopf, 1931).
60. Stineman, 65; Powell, 95, 103.
61. *Journeys' Ending*, 5.
62. *Journeys' Ending*, 37–38.
63. *Journeys' Ending*, 46.
64. *Journeys' Ending*, 418–19. The lift of the plateau is factual.
65. Comer, 158; *Cactus Thorn*, 98, 118. The

name Dulcie ("Sweet") recalls Agua Dulce, a place name from *Lost Borders* (85).

66. *Cactus Thorn*, 9, 47, 56, 57, 81, 87,93, 98; afterword, 118.

67. *Children Sing*, vii, 37. In "The Golden Fortune" (*Basket Woman*), Austin speaks of "sheep of the mountains that God shepherds on the high battlements of the hills" (154).

68. Austin and Ansel Easton Adams, *Taos Pueblo* (San Francisco: Grabhorn Press, 1930; facsimile ed., Boston: New York Graphic Society, 1977). Unpaginated. Adams's judgment on Austin's stature is quoted in Goodman and Dawson, 269. He later provided photographs for an edition of *The Land of Little Rain*, introduction by Carl Van Doren (Boston: Houghton Mifflin, 1950).

69. For Ranchos church, see "The Early Work of Laura Gilpin," *Center for Creative Photography, Research Series* (University of Arizona), 13 (April 1981), plate 18.

70. Austin, *Starry Adventure* (Boston, Houghton Mifflin, 1931), dust cover; Goodman and Dawson, 252; Rebecca W. Smith, "The Southwest in Fiction," *Saturday Review*, 25 (16 May 1942), quoted in Pearce and A. W. Thomason, *Southwesterners Write* (Albuquerque: University of New Mexico Press, 1946), 344. Unfortunately, errors in Spanish, particularly in accent marks, abound in the novel.

71. *Starry*, 340.

72. *One-Smoke*, 82. "The Last Antelope" is borrowed, emended, from *Lost Borders*. On shaping the ms., see *One-Smoke*, xxvi. The *Times* review appeared on 18 March 1934. Sergeant reviewed this volume for *Books*, 8 April 1934. The quotation has echoes of Ralph Waldo Emerson's poem "Brahma."

73. *One-Smoke*, 120. The situation recalls similar plots in Louisiana Creole writing in which a *Créole de couleur*, man or woman, cannot marry the chosen one and consequently dies.

74. Powell, 95; Stineman, 78.

Chapter Three

1. Stephen Miller, "Elizabeth Hardwick: The Mystique of Manhattan," *Sewanee Review*, 121, 4 (Fall 2013), 600. Pittsburgh, in western Pennsylvania, may be classed as "industrial Midwest," but the state is "east" to someone from Nebraska. Certain fiction sometimes erroneously called "southwestern" ("A Wagner Matinee," "The Sculptor's Funeral," and "A Death in the Desert," set in Wyoming) is not treated here. On the book project, see Cather, *Selected Letters*, ed. Andrew Jewell and Janis Stout (New York: Knopf, 2013), 208 (hereafter *Letters*). Cather published a piece on the "Mesa Verde Wonderland" in the Denver *Times* (31 January 1916). See Stout, *Picturing a Different West: Vision, Illustration, and the Tradition of Austin and Cather* (Lubbock" Texas Tech University Press, 2007), 140 (henceforth *Picturing*). For some years the Santa Fe railroad, for advertising purposes, commissioned works of art featuring southwestern landscapes and native inhabitants, sometimes on horseback, who looked proud and rugged, yet afforded exotic contrast to the passing trains.

2. On the extant correspondence, see *Letters*, Introduction, vii. The greatest gaps are letters Cather wrote to Lewis and Isabelle McClung Hambourg. The Willa Cather Trust oversaw the publication of these letters, drawn from seventy-five different archives. The authorities contend that the author herself would understand the decision to publish them, now that figures named in the letters are deceased; they believe additionally that it is better for her reputation and readers that the actual text of the missives be made public, not merely allusions and paraphrases, as in *A Calendar of the Letters of Willa Cather*, ed. Stout (Lincoln: University of Nebraska Press, 2002).

3. Welty, *The Eye of the Story: Selected Essays and Reviews* (New York: Random House, 1978), 47. Biographical details in this and the following paragraphs come from *Letters* and the following additional sources: Cather, *Early Novels and Stories*, with notes and chronology by Sharon O'Brien (New York: Library of America/ Literary Classics, 1987), 1299–1318 (hereafter O'Brien 1987); Cather, *Stories, Poems, and Other Writings*, with notes and emended chronology by O'Brien (New York: Library of America/ Literary Classics, 1992) (hereafter O'Brien 1992); David Harrell, *From Mesa Verde to "The Professor's House"* (Albuquerque: University of New Mexico Press, 1992); Edith Lewis, *Willa Cather Living: A Personal Record* (New York: Knopf, 1953); Phyllis C. Robinson, *Willa: The Life of Willa Cather* (Garden City, NY: Doubleday, 1983); James Woodress, *Willa Cather: Her Life and Art* (New York: Pegasus, 1970); Woodress, *Willa Cather: A Literary Life* (Lincoln: University of Nebraska Press, 1987); Wyatt-Brown, *Hearts*

of Darkness: Wellsprings of a Southern Literary Tradition (Baton Rouge: LSU Press, 2003). On Cather's identification as a Virginian, see *Letters*, Introduction, xi.

4. O'Brien 1992, 634. Details of Vickie's portrait include sturdy build, dark blue eyes, vitality, and features of manner and character that fit Cather well. Another character is based on her father, and many further details justify Robinson's judgment that the story is Cather's most autobiographical (259).

5. *Letters*, 561 (see also 226 on Cather's distaste for Hambourg); Woodress, 91; Stout, *Willa Cather: The Writer and Her World* (Charlottesville: University Press of Virginia, 2000), 89 (henceforth Stout 2000). In *Picturing*, Stout calls Cather an "ambiguous lesbian" (37). See also Stout, *Willa Cather and Material Culture: Real-World Writing, Writing the Real World* (Tuscaloosa: University of Alabama Press, 2005). In "Celibate Friendship in Willa Cather's *Death Comes for the Archbishop*," *St. Austin Review*, 14, 6 (Nov.-Dec. 2014), Edward Mulholland, a Catholic commentator, acknowledges that she probably felt "same sex attraction" but "does not appear to have built her life around it." See additionally Marilee Lindemann, *Willa Cather: Queering America* (New York: Columbia University Press, 1999), and Lindemann, ed., *The Cambridge Companion to Willa Cather* (Cambridge: Cambridge University Press, 2005). On Cather, Jews, and Jewish characters, see Lisa Marcus, "Willa Cather and the Geography of Jewishness," in *Cambridge Companion*, 66–85.

6. Cather, *Willa Cather on Writing*, foreword by Stephen Tennant (Lincoln: University of Nebraska Press, 1988), 23; Milton Meltzer, *Willa Cather: A Biography* (Minneapolis: Twenty-First Century Books, 2008), 64. Since Sergeant, a journalist, was Carl Jung's first American patient at the Burghölzli (in Zurich) in 1904 and returned frequently for analysis and to gather material, it is likely that she spoke of Jung to Cather, who would have had thus direct information about his non-physical understanding of nature. See Deirdre Bair, *Jung: A Biography* (Boston: Little, Brown, 2003), 254, 338.

7. The *Press* statement is quoted in *Willa Cather in Person*, ed. L. Brent Bohlke (Lincoln: University of Nebraska Press, 1986), 2–3. The *Century Magazine* statement is quoted in Charlotte Whaley, *Nina Otero-Warren of Santa Fe* (Albuquerque: University of New Mexico Press, 1994). See also O'Brien 1987, 1302–03.

8. O'Brien 1987, 1303; *Letters*, 501. Robinson, 56. Margaret Fuller might have been another feminine beacon. Cather wrote of Kate Chopin's Edna Pontellier, in *The Awakening*, as an Emma Bovary; see Susan J. Rosowski, *Birthing a Nation: Gender, Creativity, and the West in American Literature* (Lincoln: University of Nebraska Press, 1999), 71. Cather may have known of Flaubert's intimate friend Louise Colet, a talented poet who led a high-class bohemian life. In August 1930 Cather met Flaubert's niece (and heir), Caroline Franklin-Grout, in Aix-les-Bains, France. See "A Chance Meeting," O'Brien 1992, 815–33. The principle of "making others feel" was carried farther by Paul Valéry in his contention that the artist must make others "sentir bellement."

9. *Letters*, 224. In 1897 the top of Enchanted Mesa was investigated by William Libbey, of Princeton, who used an unusual method to get up, and, independently, by archeologist Frederick Webb Hodge.; it was climbed by C. W. Douglas in 1913. See Charles F. Lummis, *The Land of Poco Tiempo* (1895; rpt. Albuquerque: University of New Mexico Press, 1952), 43–44; Lesley Poling-Kempes, *Ladies of the Canyons* (Tucson: University of Arizona Press, 2015), 144.

10. *Letters*, 561. The phrase on the tragic necessity of life is quoted in Robinson, 27.

11. O'Brien, 1987, 468 (part 2, chapter 5). Stout sees a modernist strain in Cather's reconceptualizing of the west (*Picturing*, 37,41). Certainly, unneeded generalizations such as the following, concerning aching feet, would be excised by later writers: "Nobody did anything about broken arches in those days, and the common endurance test of old age was to keep going after every step cost something" ("Old Mrs. Harris," O'Brien 1992, 647).

12. *Letters*, 226, 561. The work she had in mind may be *My Ántonia* (1918), told from the viewpoint of a boy and a man, or "Blue Mesa," which became the central section in *The Professor's House*. Its principal characters are men, as in *Death Comes for the Archbishop*. Jewett's phrase is quoted in Robinson, 157.

13. *Letters*, 149, 154, 166; "My First Novels (There Were Two)," *Colophon*, June 1931; republished in *Cather on Writing* and O'Brien 1992, 963–65. The commentator is E. K. Brown, quoted in Lawrence Powell, *Southwest Classics* (Los Angeles: Ward Ritchie Press, 1974), 122. The Balzac quotation is from "Une

Passion dans le désert" (1830), collected in *Etudes de moeurs; Scènes de la vie militaire* (Paris: Conard, 1912), 403. Certain critics do, however, apply to Cather the term *mystic*, e.g., Ellen Moers, *Literary Women* (Garden City, NY: Doubleday, 1976), 260.

14. Quoted in Harrell, 8.

15. *Letters*, 151, 207, 209, 226; Harrell, 44–45.

16. *Letters*, 382, 566. Cather did pass through the area by train in 1940. The connection between Cather and Austin is broached frequently, e.g., Austin, *Earth Horizon* (New York: Literary Guild, 1932), 359; Esther Lanigan Stineman, *Mary Austin: Song of a Maverick* (New Haven: Yale University Press, 1989), viz. 12; *Picturing*. Might Cather have borrowed for her character's name in *The Professor's House* Austin's title *Outland* (1910, published in the U.S. in 1919)? Stout is among those who believe so, noting the parallels between Austin's fantasy novel and Cather's work. See Stout, *Through the Window, Out the Door: Women's Narratives of Departure, from Austin and Cather to Tyler, Morrison, and Didion* (Tuscaloosa: University of Alabama Press, 1998), 77. Stout stresses how Austin's writing was a model for Cather. In a letter to Sergeant, 23 June 1917, Cather asked whether her correspondent had read Austin's *The Ford*, published that year. See *Letters*, 242; Stineman, 250.

17. O'Brien 1992; Cather, *Death Comes for the Archbishop*, in *Later Novels*, ed. O'Brien (New York: Library of America, 1990), 418–19 (henceforth O'Brien 1990). The term "wider range" comes from *The Song of the Lark*, in O'Brien 1987, 485. Cf. Peggy Pond Church's praise of the air. Cather wrote similarly about desert light, e.g., O'Brien 1990, 334. See comment, Stout 2000, 164. The Harvard psychiatrist and omni-author Robert Coles wrote that the light of northern New Mexico, "translucent," rather than transparent, is "so sharp, so clean, so light that one feels in a new world or possessed of new eyes." From his *Eskimos, Chicanos, and Indians*, quoted by Shelley Armitage, *Women's Work: Essays in Cultural Studies* (West Cornwall, CT: Locust Hill Press, 1995), 66, 136.

18. Rosowski, 66. Robert Louis Stevenson's *Treasure Island* is one sort of counter-example: Jim Hawkins is truly involved in the adventure but it leads to nothing for the future. Another counterexample is Alain-Fournier's *Le Grand Meaulnes (The Wanderer)*, in which one youthful character is successful in his quest but cannot live with the prize, and his double shares in the adventure only vicariously.

19. O'Brien 1992, 69–72. Also in Cather, *Five Stories* (New York: Vintage, 1956). Critics were slow in identifying the connection between the story and later novels.

20. *Cather on Writing*, 96; "On the Art of Fiction," O'Brien 1992, 939.

21. Quoted in *Letters*, Introduction, xi. See Cather's preface to the 1937 revised edition in O'Brien 1987, 1328–29.

22. The phrase on messiness comes from Cather's article "Mesa Verde Wonderland." For a lyrical treatment of this southwestern landscape, see Judith Fryer, "Desert, Rock, Shelter, Legend: Willa Cather," in Vera Norwood and Janice Monk, eds., *The Desert Is No Lady: Southwestern Landscapes in Women's Writing and Art* (New Haven: Yale University Press, 1987), 27–47. Cather had gone to Colorado and Wyoming in 1914. Landscape details in *The Song of the Lark* may reflect that travel. Cather speaks of San Francisco Mountain (O'Brien 1987, 544) (not to be confused with the San Francisco Mountains on the New Mexico-Arizona border). The peak she thus describes is also known as Humphreys Peak, the highest in Arizona.

23. Krista Comer, *Landscapes of the New West: Gender and Geography in Contemporary Women's Writing* (Chapel Hill: University of North Carolina Press, 1999), 158; Fryer, 34; *Letters*, 205; O'Brien 1987, 552. Why Comer uses the term *frustrated* is unclear, given that Cather lived with Edith Lewis. Stout 2000 (37) accepts Moers's view (258–59) that Cather's depiction of the canyon country topography—hollows, folds, ravines, twisting configurations—suggests "unguarded sexuality"; it has kinship with the "folded slopes" of Georgia O'Keeffe's New Mexico paintings, "like female genitalia." It is certain that Cather speaks, e.g., of "clefts" in close proximity to "desire" (O'Brien 1987, 544). This contemporary gynecomorphic response should not prevent readers from seeing the domestic impulse to create a private but homey refuge, on the model of the old cliff-dwellers.

24. O'Brien 1987, 685.

25. *Letters*, 366, 372. Lewis's opinion is quoted in Robinson, 241.

26. Quoted in Stineman, 128; Welty, 58; Susan Goodman and Carl Dawson, *Mary Austin and the American West* (Berkeley: University of California Press, 2008), 209.

27. *Letters*, 229; Harrell, 95. The story has

been reprinted separately; see Cather, *Five Stories* (New York: Vintage, 1956). Cather's projected "Blue Mesa" must be one of the earliest efforts to write up Mesa Verde imaginatively. In 1917 a fanciful Mesa Verde drama had been put on in Colorado by Virginia McClung, and there were other aesthetic responses, including the account of an apparition that came to Fewkes and photographs that served as documentation but were artificially dramatic. See Evan S. Connell, "Mesa Verde," in *Perpetual Mirage: Photographic Narratives of the Desert West* (New York: Whitney Museum of American Art, 1996), 77.

28. *Letters*, 362; *Cather on Writing*, 30. Might Cather have known also Gide's *La Symphonie pastorale* (1919), constructed subtly along two lines, the order of the story and the order of telling, in such a way that they join?

29. *Letters*, 567. Elsewhere Cather justified the structure as "an experiment." See Cather, "On *The Professor's House*," in *Cather on Writing*, 31–32.

30. Gérard Genette, *Figures III* (Paris: Seuil, 1972), partially translated by Jane E. Lewin as *Narrative Discourse: An Essay in Method* (Ithaca: Cornell University Press, 1980).

31. *Cather on Writing*, 32.

32. Wetherill and his colleagues tried futilely to interest people in Durango, Pueblo, and Denver in their collection of tools and pottery. Mesa Verde, now a World Heritage Site, became a national park in 1906, under the Theodore Roosevelt administration. On removal of artifacts, see Deric Nusbaum, *Deric in Mesa Verde* (New York: Putnam, 1926). Nusbaum was the stepson of the archaeologist Jesse Nusbaum, who married a friend of Church's named Aileen; he was subsequently appointed director of the fledgling Museum of Anthropology in Santa Fe. See Sharon Snyder, *At Home on the Slopes of Mountains: The Story of Peggy Pond Church* (Los Alamos: Los Alamos Historical Society, 2011), 75, 85, 98.

33. Cather, *The Professor's House*, in O'Brien 1990, 255.

34. Cather herself spoke of the overcrowded, stuffy house and the fresh air of part two. See *Cather on Writing*, 31. Cather read Anatole France in 1934 but must have known his writings earlier. See *Letters*, 501.

35. O'Brien 1990, 253.

36. Robinson, 254; *Letters*, 383, 399; *Earth Horizon*, 359; Goodman and Dawson, 209.

37. See Bohlke, 109; Robinson, 248; "On 'Death Comes for the Archbishop,'" *Cather on Writing*, 3–13; also in O'Brien 1992, 958–62, viz. 961.

38. Cather, *Death Comes for the Archbishop* (1927; rpt., intro. A. J. Byatt, London: Folio Society, 2008), xii (henceforth Byatt); *Letters*, 375, 399, 457; "On 'Death Comes …,'" O'Brien 1992, viz. 960. The Library of America Edition notes numerous "mistakes" in the book; but Cather was not concerned with historical accuracy. See also Nina Baym, *Women Writers of the American West, 1833–1927* (Urbana: University of Illinois Press, 2011), 244.

39. Howlett, *The Life of the Right Reverend Joseph P. Machebeuf…. First Bishop of Denver* (Pueblo, 1908), 300; *Letters*, 371, 379, 417; "'On Death Comes …,'" O'Brien 1992, 960. The terms "episodic, nearly plotless" come from Cliff's Notes. While such a popular commentary may be disdained, it is revealing.

40. This open letter became "On 'Death Comes …'" See also *Letters*, 417. Howlett noted that she had not acknowledged her borrowings (Byatt, x). See Michael McNierney, *Taos 1847* (Boulder: Johnson, 1980).

41. *Letters*, 398.

42. O'Brien 1990, 293. Some devout New Mexicans today remain unmoved by the priests' portraits and scenes, even hostile to the book; one, interviewed by the present author said, without further explanation, that Cather had "betrayed" the archbishop.

43. The reasons for the quarrel between Bishop Lamy and the historical Martínez are multiple and more complicated than Cather's text suggests. The priest, an adversary of Bent, came from the family who owned the Martínez ranch. The priest's participation in the murder is not proven, but, as one historian writes, "in spite of lack of evidence it is difficult to believe that Padre Martínez was not cognizant of the clandestine rumblings." Carson and his friend the explorer Ceran St. Vrain believed that the priest had been a co-conspirator. See David Lavender, *Bent's Fort* (Lincoln: University of Nebraska Press, 1954; rpt. 1972), 296, 301.

44. O'Brien 1990, 420. The bishop's apricot trees were renowned; Gustave Baumann (see chapter five) did a woodcut of them. It is unfortunate that Cather's publishers (like Austin's) did not insist upon accuracy in Spanish and French diacritical markings. On Noel, see Howlett, 240.

45. O'Brien 1990, 332, 358.

46. On the Bosque Redondo exile, see chapter four below.

47. Cecilia Tichi, "Commentary," in Lillian Schlissel, Vicki L. Ruiz, and Janice Monk, eds,. *Western Women: Their Land, Their Lives* (Albuquerque: University of New Mexico Press, 1988), 184; O'Brien 1990, 419. One of the villages is Oraibi, where Armer lived. Lewis believed that Eusabio was based on Tony Lujan. See *Cather Living*, 143.

Chapter Four

1. Laverne M. Dicker, "Laura Adams Armer: California Photographer," *California Historical Quarterly*, 56, 2 (Summer 1977), 139.

2. Armer, *The Trader's Children* (New York: Longmans, Green, 1937), 181; André, quoted by Calvin Tompkins, *New Yorker*, 5 December 2011, 66. *The Forest Pool* concerns two small Mexican boys, an iguana, hummingbirds (in a dream), and a wise parrot, whose sole words are "I have been here before." There are suggestions of ancient wisdom and ethnic traditions. The full-page illustrations are in color; there are no ornamental initials, but small two-toned drawings show related motifs.

3. Armer, *In Navajo Land*, with photographs by the author and Sidney and Austin Armer (New York: David McKay, 1962), 93.

4. Austin, *Earth Horizon* (Boston: Houghton Mifflin, 1932), 194; Armer, *Southwest* (New York: Longmans, Green, 1935), viii, 114; *Navajo Land*, 11,18; Peter E. Palmquist, "Waterless Mountain," in *Perpetual Mirage: Photographic Narratives of the Desert West*. Organized by May Castleberry (New York: Whitney Museum of Art, 1996), 119 (henceforth Palmquist); also on "Women Artists of the American West/ Women in Photography Archive," www.cla.purdue.edu/waaw/palmquist/photographs. Palmquist's essay is based considerably on Alberta Armer, *Working Hands* (privately printed 1981; henceforth *Working*). Alberta married the Armers' son, Austin, a versatile engineer, on Christmas Day 1928. Alberta's portrait of Laura is unflattering. See also Palmquist, "100 Years of California Photography: Women Innovators and Their Contributions..." in Susan R. Ressler, ed., *Women Artists of the American West* (Jefferson, NC: McFarland, 2003), 213–14.

5. "Laura Adams Armer," *Newbery Medal Books: 1922–1955*, ed. Bertha Mahony Miller and Elinor Whitney Field (Boston: Horn Book, 1955), biographical note by Bertha L. Gunterman, 101–104 (henceforth Gunterman).

A note on the book and Armer's short acceptance statement are on 99–100, 105–06. See also *Southwest*, 73, 82, 92; *Navajo Land*, 11. Certain Adams family papers, including diaries, belong to the California Historical Society. See also *Contemporary Authors*, 13 (1978, 2007), and Mabel Major, Rebecca W. Smith, and T. M. Pearce, *Southwest Heritage*, rev. ed. (Albuquerque: University of New Mexico Press, 1948), which notes Armer's "turn for mysticism" and discernment of a southwestern "pattern of life"; her first two books showed "how Navajo boys are taught dignity and reverence" (102, 158). She appears also in the broadly-defined "Directory of New Mexico Writers" in Marta Weigle and Kyle Fiore, *Santa Fe and Taos: The Writer's Era, 1916-1941* (Santa Fe: Ancient City Press, 1982), 197. She is not mentioned in Lesley Poling-Kempes, *Ladies of the Canyons* (Tucson: University of Arizona Press, 2015).

6. *Working*, 6, 20, 53; Palmquist, 119.

7. Dicker, 129. The Tahiti photographs were not utilized because the Oceanic Steamship Company official who commissioned them did not have the proper authority. Armer's Chinatown photographs and others are held by the California Historical Society.

8. Dicker, 135. On Pictorialism, see, e.g., "New York et l'art moderne: Alfred Stieglitz et son cercle 1905–1930," *Le Petit Journal des Grandes Expositions* 371 (October 2004). On Adams's rejection, see Afterword by Weston J. Naef to Mary Austin and Ansel Adams, *Taos Pueblo*, facsimile ed. (Boston: New York Graphic Society, 1977). Armer was among the Pictorialists Adams knew. See also Christian A. Peterson, *After the Photo-Secession: American Pictorial Photography, 1910–1955* (Minneapolis: Minneapolis Institute of Arts, in association with W. W. Norton, 1997). Additional samples of Armer's photography are in the Phoebe A. Hearst Museum of Anthropology (University of California, Berkeley) and the Wheelwright Museum of American Indian Art (see note 11). How many others are extant is unclear. As Therese Heyman, photography curator at the Oakland Museum, observed, "Women [photographers] were not encouraged to keep their work."

9. *Working*, 8; *Trader's Children*, 104.

10. The word "tyrannical" appears in *Working*, 75.

11. *Desert Magazine* began publication in 1937. See Palmquist, 122 n3; a date given there may be erroneous. Armer's southwestern pho-

tographs may have been inspired and shaped partly by what she knew of earlier southwestern photography (and landscape and genre painting). One predecessor was Kate T. Cory, who lived among the Hopi for seven years. On early southwestern photography and art, see Janice P. Stout, *Picturing a Different West: Vision, Illustration, and the Tradition of Austin and Cather* (Lubbock: Texas Tech University Press, 2007), 11–25. The Wheelwright Museum, founded in 1937, was called (after two other names were abandoned) the Museum of Navajo Ceremonial Art. The architect for the building was William Penhallow Henderson; its first curator was Alice Corbin. When some holdings were de-accessioned and returned to the Navajos in the 1970s, its name was changed.

12. *Working*, 53, 55; Armer, *Cactus*, with fifty illustrations in line by Sidney Armer (New York: Fred A. Stokes, 1934).

13. *Working*, 7. The subjects in the drawings are described here as "strange intrauterine creatures which, interpreted, might have implied her deep dissatisfaction with her role as a woman." The Jungian was a doctor Pfister.

14. *Southwest*, 102–103, 105; *Trader's Children*, 129–30. The hogan is shown in *Southwest*, facing 112. Why a longer lease could not have been arranged is unclear.

15. *Navajo Land*, facing 107; Palmquist, 123, n19.

16. *Working*, 48–49; *Navajo Land*, 51–53.

17. *Southwest*, viii,146, 166–67, 194.

18. *Southwest*, 11; *Navajo Land*, 19.

19. *Navajo Land*, 31, 41, 71; *Trader's Children*, 198; *Southwest*, 224. See Palmquist, 119, 123 n9; Dicker 136. The epithet "Hard-Working" was first bestowed by Ashi (see below).

20. See Poling-Kempes, 30, and Martha Blue, *Indian Trader: The Life and Times of J. L. Hubbell* (Walnut, CA: Kiva, 2000), 211. The artist Malvina Hoffman (*Southwest*, 143) visited while Armer was there.

21. *Navajo Land*, 22. The elder Hubbell was the son of an Anglo and a New Mexican woman of Spanish descent. The Ganado post is now a National Historic Site. See *Southwest*, 142, 206–07; *Navajo Land*, 35, 45; Blue, passim, 94, 282; http://rubifamilygen.com/hubbell-connection; www.friendsofhubbell.org; "Don Lorenzo Hubbell" in Wikipedia. Blue does not mention Armer's close connections to the Hubbells; her name appears only as an artist whose work hung on J. L.'s walls. See, by Paul Frank, an acquaintance of Lorenzo, "How I Came to Santa Fe to Die," in John Pen La Farge, *Turn Left at Sleeping Dog* (Albuquerque: University of New Mexico Press, 2001), 260. Thomas V. Keam founded the post that bears his name..

22. See *Navajo Land* for these photographs. Armer's desert experience was not radical compared to certain others,' e.g., Jane Digby, Isabelle Eberhardt, and Freya Stark.

23. *Southwest*, 103; Palmquist, 120–21. See *Southwest*, chapter 10, for the trip to St. John's.

24. On guilt and innocence in connection with photography, as Walter Benjamin argued, see Audrey Goodman, *Translating Southwestern Landscapes: The Making of an Anglo Literary Region* (Tuscon: University of Arizona Press, 2002), 67.

25. Michael Castro, *Interpreting the Indian: Twentieth-Century Poets and the Native American* (Albuquerque: University of New Mexico Press, 1983), 34. Armer's portraits are to be contrasted with those by Ben Wittick, taken before the end of the nineteenth century, some with faux-Victorian backdrops, most showing Anglo expectations and the natives' cooperation with those. See Goodman, chapter three.

26. See Washington Matthews, *The Mountain Chant, A Navaho Ceremony*, Bureau of Ethnology, 5th annual report (Washington, D.C.,1887), 379–467; Matthews, *The Night Chant, [sic] a Navaho Ceremony*. Memoirs of the American Museum of Natural History, vi: Publications of the Hyde Southwestern Exhibition (New York, 1902). The Night Chant poem is reprinted in *Signature of the Sun*, ed. Mabel Major and T. M. Pearce (Albuquerque: University of New Mexico Press, 1950), 7–8. See *Navajo Land*, 18, 101. Mary Austin likewise translated the text of "Invocation" under the title "Prayer to the Mountain Spirit"; both versions, quite different, are in George William Cronyn, ed., *The Path on the Rainbow: An Anthology of Songs and Chants from the Indians of North America* (New York: Liveright,1918); republished as *Native American Poetry* (Mineola, NY: Dover, 2006).

27. *Southwest*, 186.

28. See Matthews, *Mountain Chant* and *Night Chant*; see also Rose V. S. Berry, "The Navajo Shaman and His Sacred Sand-Paintings," *Art and Archaeology*, 27, 1 (Jan. 1929), 5–7 and 7–11.

29. See *Southwest*, 161; Dicker, 136 (shown in the Wheelwright Museum); Gunterman, 102–103. Mary Cabot Wheelwright, an arts pa-

tron and connoisseur and the chief resource behind the museum, was acquainted with Hostiin (or Hosteen) Klah, an eminent Medicine Man, highly respected, and with his designs and Navajo ceremonies, which she witnessed, but it is not recorded that a sand-painting was made for her. Armer's experience can be compared to an episode in Alice Marriott's *Greener Fields* (New York: Crowell, 1953), 218–22, in which a local Indian superintendent tries to persuade Todas Cosas, a Navajo Medicine Man, decked in turquoise and silver, to demonstrate sand-painting at the San Francisco Indian Exposition of Tribal Arts. Symbolism was not consciously introduced into rugs until the twentieth century. Even then, it was partly disguised. While sand-paintings had been copied in weavings before Armer wrote, and the Harvey House hotel in Gallup displayed copies by 1926, in some communities at least the paintings remained guarded by Medicine Men. Klah was the first to weave sacred Yeibichai sand-paintings, starting with the Whirling Logs, into a tapestry. His weaving was controversial among his own people. See Poling-Kempes, 264; Armer, *Waterless Mountain* (1931; rpt., New York: David McKay, 75); Armer, *Sand-Painting of the Navaho Indians* (NY: The Exposition of Indian Tribal Arts, Inc., © 1931). 5. This pamphlet (the copy of which consulted for the present study, in the Latin American Collection, Tulane University, was given by Oliver La Farge) describes the process, its connection to healing, and color symbolism. Two designs, reproduced, came from the collection of Mary Overholt, Fayetteville, Arkansas; a third was done after a drawing by Frances L. Newcomb, who, with Gladys Reichard, published *Sandpaintings of the Navajo Shooting Chant* (1937). Photographs of their drawings, based on sand-paintings, are in the Smithsonian Institution. Arthur Newcomb and his brother Charles were traders on the Navajo reservation; Frances, called "Franc," was Arthur's wife. Under the name F. J. Newcomb she published books on the Navajos. See Laura Gilpin, *The Enduring Navaho* (Austin: University of Texas Press, 1968), 80, 255. While Gilpin's photos were taken in the 1950s and 1960s, the landscapes and figures have much in common with Armer's.

30. Preface to *Waterless Mountain*, viii.

31. Church likewise attended a Hopi Bean Dance. See *Bones Incandescent: The Pajarito Journals of Peggy Pond Church*, ed. Shelley Armitage (Lubbock: Texas Tech Press, 2001), xli.

32. *Navajo Land*, 65. In *Laughing Boy*, 115, La Farge's young hero explains to his wife the design and meaning of a sand-painting (of corn) because she is "not like ordinary people."

33. *Southwest*, 154–56; Gilpin, 88. John Wetherill had located parts of what is now Navajo National Monument (on the Shonto Plateau, west of Kayenta, overlooking Tsiegi Canyon): Kiet Seel in 1895 and Betatkin in 1909. According to Goodman (77), Wittick's photographs had, well before the twentieth century, begun to transform the dance from a sacred rite into a theatrical performance. See also Alice Marriott and Carol K. Rachlin, *American Epic: The Story of the American Indian* (1969; rpt. New York: New American Library, 1970), photograph portfolio (snake dance of 1890); Jesse Walter Fewkes, *Hopi Snake Dance Ceremonies* (Albuquerque: Avanyu, 1986); Lawrence, "The Hopi Snake Dance" in his *Mornings in Mexico* (London: Secker, 1927);, "D. H. Lawrence in the Hopi Lands," in C. S. Brosman, *Breakwater* (Macon: Mercer University Press, 2009), 50–51. Dorothy Brett confirmed that the spectacle had been a tonic for Lawrence; see her *Lawrence and Brett* (Philadelphia: Lippincott, 1933), 148–49. Hamlin Garland wrote up the ceremony in 1896, defending it against missionaries and government officials (Blue, 198). Cather likewise was able to observe a snake dance. See Chronology, *Willa Cather, Early Novels and Stories*, notes by Sharon O'Brien (New York: Library of America / Literary Classics, 1987), 1308. Theodore Roosevelt witnessed one at Walpi on First Mesa in 1913.

34. *Navajo Land*, 77–83; *Working*, 63–64 (the statement that the film was made near Oraibi seems erroneous). See also Palmquist. A copy of the film is reportedly in the Wheelwright Museum, but that has not been confirmed by this writer. (The museum was closed for some years for expansion.) Reduced-sized copies were given to museums in Flagstaff and Albuquerque. The original disappeared after the sale of a processing laboratory.

35. *Laughing Boy*, 62; *Southwest*, 157; *Navajo Land*, 52, 62–63. Austin Armer's statement, from a letter, is quoted in Palmquist.

36. *Southwest*, ix, 155, 157; *Navajo Land*, 101. Jung's name does not appear in available written material by Armer. Might she have read James G. Frazier's *The Golden Bough* (1922)? Navajos are mentioned there in connection with primitive beliefs in the "external soul." Armer mentions (Bronislaw) Mali-

nowski and (C. R.) Aldrich, two students of animism, taboos, and other aspects of the primitive mind (*Southwest*, 183). Aldrich published *The Primitive Mind and Modern Civilization*, with a foreword by Jung.

37. *Navajo Land*, 95; *Southwest*, facing 36. Armer speaks of paleontologists in *Southwest* (198), and fossil bones appear in *Trader's Children*.

38. See *Southwest*, frontispiece; Matthews, *Night Chant*, 3.

39. Lubbock, *The Art of Fiction* (1921; New York: Viking Press, 1957), 40. The phrase pushes back the question but is still useful.

40. The anthropologist is A. L. Kroeber. His and other comments are quoted on cover 4.

41. Palmquist, 119, 122 (sales figure). Daniel Defoe's novel was published by Longman, the ancestor of the firm.

42. *Waterless Mountain*, 18, 206; *Navajo Land*, 93; See also *Southwest*, 30–31; www.azcapitoltimes.com. The Kaibab Plateau is mostly forested (montane species), whereas Armer writes that Navajo herders following their flocks below Waterless Mountain are among dry gramma grass and hunger cactus and that the hills are "sun-burnt." She does, nevertheless, state that the mountain is on the northern Arizona border. Her hogan, it was noted, was close to Chinle, in the east, near a mountain, called "Waterless," and Black Mountain (*Navajo Land*, 105). La Farge changed names of places or else shifted them "a hundred miles or so." See his introductory note to *Laughing Boy*, xv.

43. *Waterless Mountain*, 18, 206. *Navajo Land*, 93.

44. *Navajo Land*, 50. For additional background information, see Marriott, *Indians of the Four Corners: A Book About the Anasazi Indians and Their Modern Descendants* (New York: Crowell, 1952).

45. The frontispiece of *Waterless Mountain* is captioned with a phrase from the text: "When they came to the prehistoric cliff dwelling high in the rocks, they hurried by." The text continues, "For the holy people live there and it is not well ... to disturb them" (6).

46. On Na Nai, see *Navajo Land*, 77–84. The Wharton phrase is quoted in Susan Goodman and Carl Dawson, *Mary Austin and the American West* (Berkeley: University of California Press, 2008), 161.

47. See also *Navajo Land*, 70–71. Mary Austin mentioned the Dark Circle of Boughs and dance of the Yebitchi (or Yebitsai or Yeibichai) in "Hosteen Hatsanaí Recants," *One-Smoke Stories* (1934), ed. Noreen Groover Lape (Athens: Swallow Press / Ohio University Press, 2003). Church wrote of evergreens used in dances (*Bones*, 43). The ancient import of circle imagery was stressed by Black Elk, a Lakota, in 1931: "...the Power of the World always works in circles." See Kenneth Lincoln, *Native American Renaissance* (Berkeley: University of California Press, 1983), 45.

48. *Trader's Children*, 224; *Dark Circle of Branches* (New York: Longmans, Green, 1933), 137. Marriott noted that shells traveled eastward from the Pacific via various tribes and were regarded as treasures, probably having magical powers, including the gift of rain (since they came from the great waters). They were used for necklaces until the twentieth century. See her *Indians of the Four Corners* (New York: Crowell, 1952), 104–105.

49. *Southwest*, 211.

50. See chapter five below concerning an Anasazi petroglyph of the Plumed Serpent.

51. *Southwest*, 186–87, 194. The "border of earth" resembles Austin's "earth horizon."

52. *Trader's Children*, 74. Hubbell sold the Black Mountain post in 1922 (Blue, 252).

53. *Trader's Children*, 67. Swastikas were frequently stamped into silver before the design acquired Nazi associations. Readers will recall Armer's memory of her childhood quilt.

54. See *Working*, 110–11. Akako resents the whites' disregard for Navajo taboos. After a child who had fallen into a well was saved, government men cleaned the well and retrieved a turquoise mountain lion fetish, which he had dropped. But Akako believes the well must not be disturbed; it belongs to other powers, who should keep what they own, including the child victim. Similarly, dinosaur bones, which are *chindee* (ghosts), should not have been moved (*The Trader's Children*, 63).

55. Armer, *Farthest West* (New York: Longmans, Green 1939), 61.

56. *Navajo Land*, 99. "Old Age River" was a term for the San Juan River, a tributary of the Colorado. Cf. Mary Austin's "trail to old age" in "Hosteen Hatsanaí Recants,"143.

Chapter Five

1. Powell, introduction to *The Ripened Fields: Fifteen Sonnets of a Marriage* (Santa Fe: The Lightning Tree, 1978) (henceforth *Ripened*); Noyes, comment on cover 4 of *Birds*

of *Daybreak: Landscapes and Elegies* (Santa Fe: William Gannon, 1985) (henceforth *Daybreak*); Andrew Elkins, "Peggy Pond Church," *Twentieth Century American Western Writers* (*Dictionary of Literary Biography*, 212), 21–28 (henceforth Elkins *DLB*). The Laid assessment, from a review in *Books of the Southwest*, is quoted by Shelley Armitage, ed., *Bones Incandescent: The Pajarito Journals of Peggy Pond Church* (Lubbock: Texas Tech University Press, 2001), ix (henceforth *Bones*; see note 6 below). The publications of Bynner, a cosmopolitan figure, range more widely than Church's. In addition to the late Elkins, those few who have worked on Church include Sarah Daw, of the University of Exeter, who is preparing a thesis on her.

2. *Bones*, 27, 162; Church, *This Dancing Ground of Sky: The Selected Poetry of Peggy Pond Church*, introduction by Armitage (Santa Fe: Red Crane, 1993), cover 4 (henceforth *Dancing Ground*). *Dancing Ground* was prepared by Kathleen D. Church, Peggy's daughter-in-law and literary executrix, and Renée Gregorio. The author is grateful to Kathleen Church for communicating with her via email, telephone, and face-to-face. "Blue Heron" is included in *Dancing Ground* and in Church, *New & Selected Poems* (Boise: Ahsahta Press, 1976), with an introduction T. M. Pearce, 47 (henceforth *New & Selected*). There is overlap between these collections. *Dancing Ground* includes unpublished work, some grouped under an italicized title that does not, however, represent a published volume.

3. Elkins, *Another Place: An Ecocritical Study of Selected Western American Poets* (Fort Worth: Texas Christian University Press, 2002) (henceforth Elkins 2002), xii (Haines quotation), 3 ("It's the land ..."), 40; Sharon Snyder, *At Home on the Slopes of Mountains: The Story of Peggy Pond Church* (Los Alamos: Los Alamos Historical Society Publications, 2011), xiii (Luhan quotation) (henceforth *Slopes*). See also Armitage, *Women's Work: Essays in Cultural Studies* (West Cornwall, CT: Locust Hill Press, 1995), 309 (henceforth *Women's Work*), in which Armitage's introduction to *Bones* is reprinted. Snyder's study includes passages from unpublished correspondence and journals and is, according to the Church family, accurate. Snyder has a contract from the University of New Mexico Press to edit and publish the *Selected Journals of Peggy Pond Church*.

4. Elkins 2002, 16. The Church phrase comes from "Meditation," among her unpublished papers.

5. Long's short prose narrative, based on historical accounts, is presented as a first-person letter to the Spanish monarch. In her Afterword, Church was interested in the way Long made "the matter-of-fact Spanish soldier's journey an adventure of inner transformation, an adventure in the invisible realm of the human soul." She saw it as Long's self-revelation; he had experienced "his own shipwreck." See Long, *Interlinear to Cabeza de Vaca: His Relation of the Journey from Florida to the Pacific 1529–36* (Santa Fe: Writers' Editions, 1936; rpt., afterword by Peggy Pond Church, Tucson: Peccary Press, 1985), 36–37. "Wind's Trail I Am Seeking," Austin's second essay in *The Land of Journeys' Ending* (New York: Century, 1924), furnished the title for Church's book.

6. *Bones*, ix, xviii, 21–22, 94–95, 98–99. This volume, though useful for information and for appreciation of Church's prose, does not meet scholarly standards. What Armitage calls "essays," a sort of introduction to Church's journals, are without annotation and are subjective; certain interpretations are questionable; the documentation elsewhere is unsatisfactory; there are numerous errors; material is repeated from other sources and within the text, e.g., a passage 94–95 is reproduced 209–10. The title was chosen by Armitage.

7. Church, *The House at Otowi Bridge: The Story of Edith Warner and Los Alamos* (New Mexico: University of New Mexico Press, 1959), 18 (henceforth *Otowi*); *Bones*, 39, 42, 51, 74, 149. *Otowi* first appeared in *New Mexico Quarterly*, vols. 28 and 29. Church wrote a short essay concerning its composition, "On Building a Bridge," in *New America*, issue on "The Southwest, a Regional View," 3, 3 (Spring 1979), to which Wallace Stegner contributed a short essay. Warner similarly stated that in New Mexico the great powers were "much closer, much more available." See Sharon Snyder, Toni Michnovicz, and Los Alamos Historical Society, *Los Alamos and the Pajarito Plateau* (Charleston: Arcadia Publishing, 2011), 121 (henceforth Snyder and Michnovicz). Church was probably aware of the pre–Columbian Pajarito Plateau natives' custom of driving wildlife to a tongue, or peninsula, of the plateau, setting fire to the brush, and forcing the animals off the cliff. See John Brinkerhoff Jackson, "Man and the Land," in

John Pen La Farge, ed. *Turn Left at Sleeping Dog* (Albuquerque: University of New Mexico Press, 2001), 133.

8. *Bones*, 127–29; *Slopes*, 32. Peggy herself wrote that her father had graduated from Yale (*Bones*, 171). The flood is reflected in the multi-part poem "In Terms of Water," *Dancing*, 147–55. See also *Bones*, chronology; Armitage, *Peggy Pond Church* (Boise: Boise State University Press, 1993) (henceforth Armitage 1993), which says (6) that Ashley Pond, Jr., attended Harvard. Church was named a "living treasure" in March 1984; see www.sflivingtreasures.org

9. *Otowi*, 3; *Bones*, 150; Lesley Poling-Kempes, *Ladies of the Canyons* (Tucson: University of Arizona Press, 2015), 181. On the general ignorance of the Detroit partners concerning the conditions in Pajarito Canyon—three of them had not seen it—see Poling-Kempes, 336 n30. Under different management the Pajarito Club remained in the partners' hands and endured, as a guest ranch, until a terrible drought in 1918.

10. Paul Frank, "How I Came to Santa Fe to Die," in La Farge, 226; Marriott, *Alice Marriott Remembered*, ed. Charlotte Whaley (Santa Fe: Sunstone Press, 2009), 83. See also *Ranch School*, 9–10. Ed Fuller died at the school.

11. *Slopes*, 45; *Bones*, 74, 76, 81.

12. *Bones*, 71–72, 73, 75.

13. *New & Selected*, 57; *Slopes*, 57, 68; *Bones*, 132, 155. On arrowheads, see "Morning on Tshirege" in *Daybreak*. Tshirege meant 'bird' or 'place of birds'; hence the Spanish *Pajarito*.

14. *Bones*, 24, 91; *Slopes*, 73. Even if incomplete or inaccurate, the record is instructive. It seems to include a convent school in Albuquerque (for six months, at age eight); a convent in Los Angeles; the Francis W. Parker School, San Diego (seventh and eighth grades); a Detroit boarding school; Santa Fe High School (1917–18); the Marlborough School, Los Angeles (1919–20); two boarding schools in Connecticut (the Wabanaki School, Greenwich, and the Hillside School, Norwalk). The Parker School was run by the Templeton Johnson family, who had visited the Pajarito Club.

15. *Bones*, 137, 160, 174; *New & Selected*, 57; Church, *Accidental Magic* (Albuquerque: Wildflower Press, 2004), 6; Ruth Laughlin, "Santa Fe in the Twenties," *New Mexico Quarterly Review*, 19, 1 (1949), 61.

16. *Bones*, 118, 210; *Otowi*, 8; Lois Rudnick, introduction to Corbin, *Red Earth* (1920; rpt. Santa Fe: Museum of New Mexico, 2003), 27; Corbin, 57, 71. Monroe traveled to Arizona in 1901and 1915, seeing the Grand Canyon, the Snake Dance, and other sights, and visited Santa Fe in 1920. See Michael Castro, *Interpreting the Indian: Twentieth-Century Poets and the Native American* (Albuquerque: University of New Mexico Press, 1983), 18; Marta Weigle and Kyle Fiore, *Santa Fe and Taos: The Writer's Era, 1916–1941* (Santa Fe: Ancient City Press, 1982), 14.

17. *Ranch School*, 23; *Otowi*, 8.

18. *Slopes*, 86, 97; *Bones*, 137. The author is grateful to Corina A. Santistevan, a Taos friend of Church's from the early 1940s on, for granting her an interview (23 July 2014) and offering information and assessments on the marriage and other matters. At least one woodblock print called "El Santo" by Baumann is held in a Taos gallery.

19. Kai Bird and Martin J. Sherwin, *American Prometheus: The Triumph and Tragedy of J. Robert Oppenheimer* (New York: Knopf, 2005), 214; interview with Santistevan. When the couple settled later in Santa Fe, Peggy had, it appears, a writing studio, perhaps back of the house.

20. *Slopes*, xiii; *New & Selected*, 61.

21. *Slopes*, 118–19. Long wrote to her that he loved her and that she was "beautiful." Long had studied at Harvard and then taught in Pittsburgh but settled in Santa Fe starting in 1929. He had briefly been a lover of Bynner, an older Harvard graduate. According to Richard Bradford, Bynner was congenitally unable to have relationships with women (La Farge, 294). Long had married, and Church knew his wife, Alice. (See below on her poem concerning them.)

22. *Dancing*, 34. See *Bones*, 29–41, for various dreams. Peggy and Fermor read together *The Secret of the Golden Flower*, a classic Chinese Taoist work about meditation, translated into German by Richard Wilhelm and retranslated into English (Armitage, 29).

23. *Otowi*, 24; *Dancing*, xxviii; *Wind's Trail*, 12; Deirdre Bair, *Jung: A Biography* (Boston: Little, Brown, 2003), 335; Snyder, 128, 266 n 13; *Bones*, chronology; 23.

24. *Slopes*, 23; *Bones*, xvii, xxxv. See "The Correspondence of May Sarton and Peggy Pond Church," in *Women's Work*. Sarton published a novel, *Anger* (1982), portraying the unhappy marriage of a cold, ungiving husband and his emotional wife, a musician; Church's

confessions to Sarton may have contributed to the portrait. See Snyder, 187, for Peggy's letter to a future daughter-in-law on anger.

25. Church had contributed also to the December 1933 issue of *Poetry*, featuring southwestern verse. She also published work in *They Know New Mexico: Intimate Sketches by Western Writers* (1928), underwritten by the Santa Fe railroad, and in the annual *Folksay: A Regional Miscellany*. See Weigle and Fiore, 28. The distance between Los Alamos and the capital at the time is given variously as twelve, twenty, thirty-five miles. Frank recalled that in the 20s the drive took about four hours (228). The Writers' Editions comprised fourteen volumes, published between 1933 and 1939. The founders included Corbin and Long; he was executive director for four years. Authors paid for their publications, retaining 90% of profits. The series was, according to a news release, an explicit "revolt against the dictates of the Eastern publishing clique that determines what shall or shall not be published." Quoted in Weigle and Fiore, 40. Weigle and Fiore state that Church had been "active" in founding the Poets' Round-Ups (39).

26. From a letter to Austin, quoted in *Wind's Trail*, xi; Snyder, 98. Such a judgment might have paralyzed Church, since her self-confidence was already shaky; but she persisted. Church added that she did not have her heart set on a literary career. See also Powell, "California Classics Reread," *Westways*, 50 (April 1968), 2, quoted in Esther Stineman, *Mary Austin: Song of a Maverick* (New Haven: Yale University Press, 1989), 80; *Dancing*, ix; Snyder 2011, 99, 155; *Bones*, xiv; *Women's Work*, 303, 304. Armitage asserts that Church reappropriated what Armitage considered "devalued creative forms" (autobiographical writing) and reconstructed gender "in regard to nature and culture." She and Austin were "women writing nature—that is, rewriting the assumptions about female nature by inscribing nature as positively feminine" (*Bones*, xiv, 216).

27. Nelson, "The Necessity of Love," *Anvil* (Winter 1979), 36–37, quoted in Elkins *DLB*, 299.

28. Interview with Santistevan; Bird and Sherwin, 81; see also 25–28, 39, 73, 265–67.

29. Bird and Sherwin, 206. The Spanish reads: "Es por eso que estoy triste, morena, / por eso me pongo, me pongo a llorar / recordando las horas felices / que juntos pasamos en aquel lugar." See *When Los Alamos was a Ranch School*, with "historical profile" by Fermor and Peggy Pond Church (Los Alamos: Los Alamos Historical Society, 1974), 9–10 (henceforth *Ranch School*). See also Los Alamos Historical Association www.losalamoshistory.org and John D. Wirth and Linda Harvey Aldrich, *Los Alamos: The Ranch School Years, 1917–1943* (Albuquerque: University of New Mexico Press, 2003).

30. A 1944 poem, "Of the Dust of the Ground," concerns earthen floors.

31. *New & Selected*, 23–24. See *Slopes* and www.losalamoshistory.org "Enchanted Mesa" (*Familiar Journey*), is reprinted in *Dancing*, 105–106. See the chapter on Cather, above. Church drank scotch whisky and took Seconal, to produce unawareness, then bound her head in an airtight bag (*Bones*, 218 n12). Armitage gives the erroneous date of 1985 for the reading (*Bones*, 162; see also x).

32. Santa Fe Living Treasures site.

33. Pound, "A Retrospect," in *Literary Essays of Ezra Pound*, ed. T. S. Eliot (Norfolk, CT: New Directions, n.d.), 3–4; *The Letters of Ezra Pound to Alice Corbin Henderson*, ed. Ira B. Nadel (Austin: University of Texas Press, 1993); *Bones*, 6. Church recorded (*Bones*, 33) a dream about D.H. Lawrence and Frieda (she knew the latter in Taos); she may have read his verse composed in New Mexico and learned from it.

34. *New & Selected*, 5, 21, 23.

35. Elkins 2002, 2, 39; Nelson, quoted in Elkins *DLB*, 300 n13.

36. Pearce, iii. Pearce's assertion lies close to the spirit of Austin's defense of regionalism not as exotica but as the sine qua non of character and drama. The phrase "the world's body" is from John Crowe Ransom's book of that title (New York: Scribner's, 1938).

37. *New & Selected*, 6, 8, 13. There is a recent reissue of *Foretaste* (1933; facsimile rpt. with new foreword by Peter Deckert, Santa Fe: Sunstone Press, 2014).

38. *New & Selected*, 3–4, 7.

39. *New & Selected*, 10. On the Penitentes, see Marriott, *María: The Potter of San Ildefonso* (Norman: University of Oklahoma Press, 1948), chapter 5, and *The Valley Below* (Norman: University of Oklahoma Press, 1949), chapter 23—a gruesome account. See also Austin, *Land of Journeys' Ending*, 349–72; Alice Corbin Henderson, *Brothers of Light* (New York: Harcourt, Brace 1937). In *Starry Adventure* (Boston: Houghton Mifflin, 1931), 117, Austin uses *morada* to mean a group of Penitentes. Among other graphic portrayals

of the Penitentes is a painting by Ward Lockwood (1894–1963), who lived in Taos from 1926 until 1939.

40. *New & Selected*, 11–12.

41. *New & Selected*, iii; Sergeant, "The Santa Fe Group," *Saturday Review of Literature*, 8 Dec. 1934, 354.

42. *New & Selected*, 17.

43. *New & Selected*, iii. It was André Gide who said that "c'est avec les bons sentiments qu'on fait de la mauvaise littérature."

44. *New & Selected*, 33.

45. *New & Selected*, 36, 37.

46. *New & Selected*, 38, 39.

47. *New & Selected*, 30.

48. *New & Selected*, 44, 45.

49. *New & Selected*, 46, 52.

50. *New & Selected*, 48–50, 55, 58; Snyder, 194.

51. With one exception, the sonnets were first published by a Quaker quarterly called *Inward Light* (1954). See *New & Selected*, iii; *Dancing Ground*, xxiii; *Ripened*, introduction; Armitage 1993, 28; Elkins 2002, 32.. Meredith's marriage ended when his wife left him for painter Henry Wallis.

52. *Daybreak*, 47; *Women's Work*, 309; *Bones*, 161–62.

53. *Dancing Ground*,112–14. Peggy's interest in native dancing is attested often. In 1950 she went to Santo Domingo Pueblo to see dances, and in 1960 she witnessed Shalako dances (*Bones*, xli, 43–44).

54. In letters to Sarton, Church lamented the "Aspenizing" of Santa Fe. See *Women's Work*, 306.

55. *Otowi*, 5. Church had a photograph of Tilano by Laura Gilpin, one of a series now in the Amon Carter Museum in Fort Worth, Texas. It was inscribed, "To Peggy; she knows why …" (Information provided by Kathleen Church, who has a copy.) The picture of Tilano appearing in this chapter is by an unknown photographer. In Michael Mauldin's composition *Enchanted Land: Suite for Narrator and Orchestra*, performed by the New Mexico Symphony Orchestra (on Enchanted Land CD) (2001), Kathleen Church read passages from *The House at Otowi Bridge*.

56. *Otowi*, 13.

57. *Otowi*, 16,17, 23; Snyder and Michnovicz, 11.

58. *Bones*, 30, 36.

59. Church consulted a vineyardist concerning drought years. See *Wind's Trail*, xvi, 163; *Bones*, 105–106. See also *Wind's Trail*, x, xiv, xv. This volume contains Austin's "The Friend in the Wood." Through her parents, Church knew of Austin's first visits to Santa Fe and met Austin's niece at the Marlborough School (x-xi). By 1972 Church had finished the first section of her Austin book. In 1973, after meeting Augusta Fink, likewise at work on an Austin biography, she nearly abandoned the undertaking. Church typed up dreams of Austin and, in a book inscription to Armitage, used the phrase "To propitiate the ghost of Mary Austin" (*Bones*, xvi, xlii).

60. Church, *The Burro of Angelitos*, iIllustrations by Gigi Shaule Johnson (Los Angeles: Suttonhouse, 1936; facsimile rpt., with a publisher's note and preface by Kathleen Church, Santa Fe: Sunstone Press, 2013). The name *Tranquilidad* is, of course, sarcastic. In 1936 Church could make fun of a villager's fondness for siestas without being accused of demeaning Hispanics. The name Oñate goes back to Juan de Oñate (1550–1626), an explorer and governor. It was observed in Chapter One that his cruelty to the Indians was unusual even by standards of the time; Church would not have intended to remind readers of it. It is unfortunate that diacritics are omitted in the text, a choice, presumably, of the original publisher.

61. Email letter from Kathleen Church, 1 Feb. 2014; personal interview, 14 August 2014. Carrillo is a noted *santero* (painter of *santos*). Another musical composition, by Michael Mauldin, titled "Enchanted Land: Suite for Narrator and Orchestra," incorporated passages from *The House at Otowi Bridge* (Snyder, 241–42).

62. *Bones*, x, 107; *Dancing Ground*, xiv, 165.

Chapter Six

1. On Marriott as an ethnologist, see Patricia Loughlin, "Alice Marriott's *The Ten Grandmothers* and the Pursuit of Ethnographic Authenticity," in her *Hidden Treasures of the American West* (Albuquerque: University of New Mexico Press, 2005), 127–57, and a shorter version, "Alice Marriott: Recording the Lives of American Indian Women," in Shirley A. Leckie and Nancy J. Parezo, eds., *Their Own Frontier: Women Intellectuals Re-Visioning the American West* (Lincoln: University of Nebraska Press, 2008), 211–41. Henceforth Loughlin 2005 and 2008.

2. Loughlin 2008, 211; Shockley, *Southwest Writers Anthology* (Austin: Steck-Vaughn,

1967), 258. "Spoonbread on a Woodstove," an essay, appeared in Margaret Hartley, ed., *The Southwest Review Reader* (Dallas: SMU Press, 1974). Marriott sometimes used the term *story*. See Marriott and Carol K. Rachlin, *Peyote* (New York: Crowell, 1971), 88.

3. Many biographical details come from Marriott's *The Valley Below*, with drawings by Margaret Lefranc (Norman: University of Oklahoma Press, 1949) and *Greener Fields: Experiences Among the American Indians* (Crowell, 1953), others from Marriott, *Alice Marriott Remembered*, ed. with an introduction by Charlotte Whaley (Santa Fe: Sunstone Press, 2009) (henceforth Whaley 2009). This memoir was partly typewritten by Marriott, then, when she was ill, dictated on tape (11–16). Whaley annotated it. One portion came from an earlier interview. Chronological markers in the book are sometimes unclear. There is no other book-length source of information on Marriott. Additional sources include an interview (1 December 2013) of the present author with Nell Norris, formerly of Albuquerque, who knew Marriott and Margaret Lefranc very well; obituaries from the New York *Times* (21 March 1992), the Associated Press, and *The Oklahoman*; "Western U.S. History," Online Encyclopedia (www.encyclopedia.jrankorg/articles); and Turner S. Kobler's pamphlet, *Alice Marriott* (Austin: Steck-Vaughn, 1969). Kobler obtained information from Marriott and Carol Rachlin. Ceratin Internet summaries of Marriott's career have errors, e.g., the web site www.Taos.org The site gives numerous details but is to be distrusted, in view of its poor exposition and departures from reasonable chronology. On the Wheelwright Museum, see chapter 4 above.

4. *The Valley Below*, 9.

5. *The Valley Below*, 9. Marriott's ignorance of Kiowa was, of course, a drawback and scholarly weakness. Her case differs from that of Frank Cushing, for whose *Zuñi Folk Tales* she wrote an introduction; he spent years with the tribe and learned the language well.

6. *The Valley Below*, 129; *Greener Fields*, 9, 18, 45, 111; Whaley 2009, 10, 30, 38, 39, 87, 105. Marriott identified three great races, distinguished by bone structure, proportions, skin, hair, and minor characteristics (45). The Osage massacre appears in *The Ten Grandmothers* and *Indian Annie: Kiowa Captive* (see below).

7. *Greener Fields*, 178.

8. Whaley, *Nina Otero-Warren of Santa Fe* (Albuquerque: University of New Mexico Press, 1994), 115, 121. The state Museum of Indian Arts and Culture /Laboratory of Anthropology, which opened in 1987, is a merger of the Museum of New Mexico, founded by Hewett in 1909, and the Laboratory of Anthropology, founded by John D. Rockefeller in 1927.

9. Esther Lanigan Stineman, *Mary Austin: Song of a Maverick* (New Haven: Yale University Press, 1989), 176.

10. Sloan was a native of Oklahoma and knew Marriott there. She moved with her husband to Pampa, in the Texas Panhandle, and for years Marriott stopped at her house during her drives between Oklahoma and New Mexico. Sloan introduced her to friends in Pampa. Sloan may have helped Marriott cultivate her artistic sense; she had studied sculpture and painting and was also a ceramicist. (This information was provided by Norris.)

11. Http://edwardgarrenmft.blogspot.com/2012/12/fourth-day-of-christmas-margaret.html

This site has a fine photograph of Lefranc and a picture of her Santa Fe house.

12. One source says that, having suffered from the cold and pollution, and being advised by a doctor she should leave New York, Lefranc was happy to make the move. See *The Valley Below*, 10–12, 157.

13. *The Valley Below*, 14, 242. Marriott's and Lefranc's trying experiences anticipate Peter Mayle's *A Year in Provence*.

14. *The Valley Below*, 132.

15. According to Norris, Marriott broke up the friendship. After surgery at an Española clinic to remove a breast tumor, Marriott left the clinic early without waiting for Lefranc, though by arrangement the latter was to pick her up; instead, she went with Maria Chabot to Los Luceros, in Alcalde, the home of Mary Wheelwright, where Chabot worked as Wheelwright's companion. Yet as late as 1987 Marriott's tone concerning Lefranc was friendly (Whaley 2009, 14); relations between them were reportedly courteous.

16. The blind man, who calls to mind Tiresias, was a Grandmother god guardian (see below and *Greener Fields*, 118). See Marriott and Rachlin, *American Epic: The Story of the American Indian* (New York: Putnam, 1969) and *Plains Indian Mythology* (New York: Crowell, 1975) for photographs, from the Marriott-Rachlin collection, of Hopi, San

Ildefonso, and Kiowa subjects as well as tribal paraphernalia (henceforth *Mythology*).

17. Whaley 2009, 86–89. The Spanish word, often misspelled *sanctuario*, is indeed *santuario*.

18. Marriott, letter to her family, quoted in Loughlin 2005, 146. On "salvage ethnography," see Loughlin 2008, 217.

19. Loughlin 2005, 133, 138–39, 153–54; Luke S. Lassiter, quoted by Loughlin 2008, 222.

20. Marriott, *The Ten Grandmothers* (Norman: University of Oklahoma Press, 1945),viii, 251; *Greener Fields*, 119–20; Loughlin 2005, 139, 152.

21. *Ten Grandmothers*, xi; *Mythology*, 39. On Hunt and his family, see Loughlin 2005, 131–34; Loughlin 2008, 214–15. With "Grandma Biatonna," Ioleta's aged grandmother, and others, Marriott followed the technique of suggesting topics for the informant, a type of "stream of consciousness method." See Loughlin 2005, 141; see also below, on María Martínez.

22. Loughlin, 213. On Marriott's acquaintance with Mooney, see *Greener Fields*, 190–92. She pointed out various errors of his.

23. A bold example of historical fictionalizing is by Paul Horgan, who invented dialogues and thoughts (in free indirect style, that is, thought process or interior monologue) for peoples centuries ago. "(Was it the same river? It might be. And yet it was very far away. Rivers came from many places. Who could be sure?)" He also used poetic style and anthropomorphized landscape features. "On a flat stone up on the plain, hand. I, long ago, hand now, and forever, said the rocks, without saying who, exactly." Arguments against the technique include challenges to accuracy and plausibility and criticize increased subjectivity (see chapter one). See Horgan's *Great River: The Rio Grande in North American History*, 2: *Mexico and the United States* (New York: Rinehart, 1954).

24. *Mythology*, 57.

25. *Ten Grandmothers*, 4.

26. *Greener Fields*, 14. The phrase "Back to the blanket" was used frequently, e.g., by Oliver La Farge in *Laughing Boy* (1929; Franklin Center, PA: Franklin Mint, 1977), 60. Many Pueblo students who went away to school, especially to California, had similar difficulties, according to testimony in John Pen La Farge, *Turn Left at Sleeping Dog* (Albuquerque: University of New Mexico Press, 2001), 172–73. For Austin's excellent treatment of the topic, see "White Wisdom," *One-Smoke*

Stories (1934; ed. Noreen Groover Lape, Athens: Swallow Press / Ohio University Press, 2003).

27. *Greener Fields*, 14, 18–20 (on Christian influence), 110–11; *Ten Grandmothers*, 144. Austin treats the issue of Navajo polygamy in "Hosteen Hatsaní Recants," *One-Smoke Stories*.

28. Marriott acknowledges (*Ten Grandmothers*, 114n) that her version of the raid and the arrest of Sitting Bear, White Bear, and Big Tree differs somewhat from other accounts but is based on an informant's report.

29. Marriott, *Winter-Telling Stories*. Illustrated by Roland Whitehorse (New York: Crowell, 1947), 7; republished as "compiled by Alice Marriott," illustrated by Richard Cuffari (New York: Crowell, 1969).

30. *Winter-Telling Stories* 1947, 37. See also *Mythology*, 35, 75, 82. The names of most informants who shared the tales are given here.

31. *Winter-Telling Stories* 1947, 33.

32. *Mythology*, 131.

33. Marriott, *Indians on Horseback*. Drawings by Margaret Lefranc (New York: Crowell, 1948), 8, 30.

34. Marriott, *María: The Potter of San Ildefonso* (Norman: University of Oklahoma Press, 1948), xii, xiii.

35. *María,*, 87; Whaley 2009, 11–12; *Greener Fields*, 71, 80. St. Catherine's was founded by Katharine Drexel of Philadelphia (1886) and blessed by Archbishop Jean-Baptiste Lamy; the first edifice was constructed in part of stone ordered for the Santa Fe cathedral. This is not the same as the Indian School of Santa Fe, established by the federal government.

36. Underhill is quoted in Loughlin 2008, 230.

37. *María*, 7, 85. Readers will recall Armer's *Dark Circle of Branches*.

38. See *The Valley Below*, 152. While the term *sociobiology* dates from the 1940s, the development of that science, drawing on evolutionary theory, sociology, anthropology, and other disciplines, did not become well known until Edward O. Wilson's study of 1975, *Sociobiology: The New Synthesis*.

39. *María*, xi, 182.

40. Marriott, *Indians of the Four Corners: A Book About the Anasazi Indians and Their Modern Descendants* (New York: Crowell, 1952), preface. A drawing by Lefranc depicts an "ancestress of the whole clan," purportedly prehistoric, but attired in modern garb, with a sleeved dress and a squash-blossom necklace. Silversmithing by Pueblo Indians and others was begun only in the nineteenth cen-

tury. See Larry Frank, *Indian Silver Jewelry of the Southwest, 1868–1930* (Boston: New York Graphic Society, 1978), 4–6. Certain other depictions, including an Anasazi naming ceremony, likewise show anachronisms.

41. Marriott, *Hell on Horses and Women* (Norman: University of Oklahoma Press, 1953); rpt., foreword by Margot Liberty (Okla, 1993) (henceforth Liberty). Shelley Armitage asserted that the phrase implied "conventional assessments of women's western experiences" (viewed as disparaging) (*Bones Incandescent: The Pajarito Journals of Peggy Pond Church* [Lubbock: Texas Tech Press, 2001], xviii). Although Cathryn Halverson's *Playing House in the American West: Western Women's Life Narratives* (Tuscaloosa: University of Alabama Press, 2013), is concerned with those who wrote (letter-writers, memoirists, those who cultivated fiction), not western women in general, similar types appear—the homesteader in particular. Authors treated include Austin and Cather. Halverson's title could be viewed as demeaning as much as Marriott's.

42. One setting is the Sandhills, which appear in Cather's work, including *The Song of the Lark*.

43. *Hell on Horses*, 6, 7, 9; Liberty, x.

44. *Hell on Horses*, 10. Liberty observes that Marriott "focuses on ranch women in traditional feminine roles," leading "rewarding and satisfying lives" (ix.)

45. *Hell on Horses*, 14, 28.

46. *Hell on Horses*, 11. The present author has, however, recently seen *vaqueros* on horseback.

47. *Greener Fields*, 108.

48. *Greener Fields*, 105, 162.

49. Marriott, *Black Stone Knife* (New York: Crowell, 1957), postscript.

50. Marriott, *Indian Annie: Kiowa Captive* (New York: McKay, 1965), viz. 1–2.

51. *Indian Annie*, 153.

52. *Indian Annie*, 152–53. Annie's family owned three slaves, who, after the war, chose to stay with their former masters and accompany them to Oklahoma. Annie is fiercely southern but sees the wrongs of slavery.

Chapter Seven

1. Armer, *Southwest* (New York: Longmans, Green, 1935), viii.

2. Evidence of their presence in New York literary circles is offered, for instance, by their both being in attendance at the 1912 dinner honoring William Dean Howells. See above chapter 3.

3. Like many other westerners and would-be westerners, Austin read *Ramona* but drew more, as she endeavored to start writing, from local writers and, primarily, from her own notes. Austin owned a copy of *Life Among the Paiutes*. The accuracy of the latter work has been questioned by historians. See Susan Goodman and Carl Dawson, *Mary Austin and the American West* (Berkeley: University of California Press, 2008), 12, 65. The diary of Susan Shelby Magoffin (1827–1855), *Down the Santa Fe Trail and into Mexico*, a rich source of information, was not published until 1926 but deserves notice as one vein of pioneer writing earlier in the nineteenth century.

4. Austin, *The Ford* (1917; rpt., foreword by John Walton (Berkeley: University of California Press, 1997) 61.

5. Church, *The House at Otowi Bridge: The Story of Edith Warner and Los Alamos* (New Mexico: University of New Mexico Press, 1959), 18.

6. Austin, *The Land of Journeys' Ending* (New York: Century, 1924), 46; Church, *This Dancing Ground of Sky: The Selected Poetry of Peggy Pond Church* (Santa Fe: Red Crane Books, 1993), 22.

7. Austin and John Muir, *Writing the Western Landscape*. Edited, introduced, and illustrated by Ann H. Zwinger (Boston: Beacon Press, 1994), 80.

Bibliography

The primary sources include many original editions but also, for readers' convenience, numerous reprints and volumes of collected works, some of which are the source of citations in the chapter notes. Illustrators' names are furnished frequently. The secondary sources include background and general works—useful for readers seeking more information on the Southwest and its arts. In addition, anthologies, studies concerning more than one figure, and all volumes consulted for this book are listed. For material pertinent to a single author investigated here, readers should consult the respective chapter notes.

Primary Sources

Armer, Laura Adams. *Cactus*. With fifty illustrations by Sidney Armer. New York: Fred A. Stokes, 1934.
_____. *Dark Circle of Branches*. Illustrated by Sidney Armer. New York: Longmans, Green, 1933.
_____. *Farthest West*. Illustrated by Sidney Armer. New York: Longmans, Green 1939.
_____. *The Forest Pool*. Illustrated by the author. New York: Longmans, Green, 1938.
_____. *In Navajo Land*. Illustrated with photographs by the author and Sidney and Austin Armer. New York: David McKay, 1962.
_____. *The Mountain Chant*. 1928. Silent film.
_____. "Navajoland in 1923." *Desert Magazine of the Outdoor Southwest*, March 1960.
_____. *Sand-paintings of the Navaho Indians*. Illustrated by the author. New York: The Exposition of Indian Tribal Arts, 1931.
_____. *Southwest*. Illustrated from paintings by the author. New York: Longmans, Green, 1935.
_____. *The Trader's Children*. With illustrations from photographs by the author. Decorations by Sidney Armer. New York: Longmans, Green, 1937.
_____. *Waterless Mountain*. Illustrated by Sidney Armer and Laura Adams Armer. Foreword by Oliver La Farge. New York: Longmans, Green, 1931; rpt. New York: David McKay, 1986.

Austin, Mary. *The Arrow-Maker*. New York: Duffield, 1911; rev. ed. Boston: Houghton Mifflin, 1915.
_____. *The American Rhythm*. New York: Harcourt, Brace, 1923. Revised and enlarged as *The American Rhythm: Studies and Reëxpressions of Amerindian Songs*. Boston: Houghton Mifflin, 1930. Rpt. new and enlarged, New York: Cooper Square, 1970.
_____. *The Basket Woman: A Book of Indian Tales for Children*. 1904. School ed. Boston: Houghton Mifflin, 1910. Rpt., foreword by Mark Schlenz. Reno: University of Nevada Press, 1999.
_____. *Beyond Borders: The Selected Essays of Mary Austin*. Ed. with an introduction by Reuben J. Ellis. Carbondale: Southern Illinois University Press, 1996.
_____. *Cactus Thorn*. Foreword and afterword by Melody Graulich. Reno: University of Nevada Press, 1988.
_____. *The Children Sing in the Far West*.

Drawings by Gerald Cassidy. New York: Houghton Mifflin, 1928.

———. *Earth Horizon: An Autobiography*. Boston: Houghton Mifflin, 1932. Rpt., afterword by Melody Graulich. Albuquerque: University of New Mexico Press, 1991.

———. *Experiences Facing Death*. Indianapolis: Bobbs-Merrill, 1931.

———. *The Flock*. Illustrated by E. Boyd Smith. Boston: Houghton Mifflin, 1906.

———. *The Ford*. Boston: Houghton Mifflin. 1917. Rpt., foreword by John Walton, Berkeley: University of California Press, 1997.

———. *Indian Poetry*. New York: The Exposition of Indian Tribal Arts, 1931.

———. *Indian Pottery of the Rio Grande*. Pasadena, CA: Esto, 1934.

———. Introduction to George William Cronyn, ed. *The Path on the Rainbow: An Anthology of Songs and Chants from the Indians of North America*. New York: Liveright, 1918. New and enlarged ed.

———. Introduction to Frank Hamilton Cushing. *Zuñi Folk Tales*. 1901; new ed., foreword/ Introduction by J. W. Powell. New York: Knopf, 1931.

———. *Isidro*. Illustrated by Eric Pape. Boston: Houghton Mifflin, 1904.

———. *The Land of Journeys' Ending*. Illustrated by John Edwin Jackson. New York: Century, 1924. Rpt. Tucson: University of Arizona, 1985.

———. *The Land of Little Rain*. Illustrated by E. Boyd Smith. Boston: Houghton Mifflin, 1904. Facsimile rpt., Bedford, MA: Applewood, n.d. Rpt., foreword by Marcia Muth. Santa Fe: Sunstone, 2007.

———. *Literary America 1903–1934: The Mary Austin Letters*. Selected and ed. T. M. Pearce. Westport, CT: Greenwood Press, 1979.

———. *Lost Borders*. Illustrated. New York: Harper, 1909.

———. *A Mary Austin Reader*. Ed. Esther F. Lanigan. Tucson: University of Arizona Press, 1996.

———. *Mary Austin's Southwest: An Anthology of Her Literary Criticism*. Ed. Chelsea Blackbird and Barney Nelson. Salt Lake City: University of Utah Press, 2005.

———. *Mother of Felipe and Other Early Stories*. Ed. Franklin Walker. Los Angeles: Book Club of California, 1950.

———. *One Hundred Miles on Horseback*. Ed. Donald P. Ringler. Los Angeles: Dawson's Bookshop, 1963.

———. *One-Smoke Stories*. Boston: Houghton, Mifflin, 1934. Rpt., critical introduction by Noreen Groover Lape. Athens: Swallow Press / Ohio University Press, 2003.

——— (as Gordon Stairs). *Outland*. London: John Murray, 1910; New York: Boni & Liveright, 1919.

———. *Starry Adventure*. Boston: Houghton Mifflin, 1931.

———. *Stories from the Country of Lost Borders*. Ed. Marjorie Pryce. New Brunswick: Rutgers University Press, 1987.

———. *The Trail Book*. Illustrations by Milo Winter. 1918. Rpt., afterword by Melody Graulich. Reno: University of Nevada Press, 2004.

———. *Western Trails: A Collection of Short Stories by Mary Austin*. Ed. Melody Graulich. Reno: University of Nevada Press, 1987.

———, and Ansel Adams. *Taos Pueblo*. San Francisco: Grabhorn Press, 1930. Facsimile ed. Boston: New York Graphic Society, 1977.

———, and John Muir. *Writing the Western Landscape*. Edited, introduced, and illustrated by Ann H. Zwinger. Boston: Beacon Press, 1994.

Cather, Willa. *April Twilights and Other Poems*. 1903. Rev. as *April Twilights (1903)*. Ed. with introduction by Bernice Slote. Lincoln: University of Nebraska Press, 1962.

———. *Death Comes for the Archbishop*. New York: Knopf, 1927. Rpt., introduction by A. S. Byatt. London: The Folio Society, 2008.

———. *Early Novels and Stories*. Notes by Sharon O'Brien. New York: Library of America / Literary Classics, 1987.

———. *Later Novels*. Notes by O'Brien. New York: Library of America, 1990.

———. *The Professor's House*. New York: Knopf, 1925.

———. *Selected Letters*. New York: Knopf, 2013.

———. *The Song of the Lark*. Boston: Houghton Mifflin, 1915.
———. *Stories, Poems, and Other Writings*. Notes by O'Brien. New York: Library of America/ Literary Classics, 1992.
———. *Willa Cather on Writing*. Foreword by Stephen Tennant. Lincoln: University of Nebraska Press, 1976.
———. *Willa Cather's Collected Short Fiction*. Ed. by Virginia Faulkner. Lincoln: University of Nebraska Press, 1965.
Church, Peggy Pond. *Accidental Magic*. Introduction by Phyllis Hoge Thompson; foreword by Kathleen D. Church. Albuquerque: Wildflower Press, 2004.
———. Afterword to Haniel Long. *Interlinear to Cabeza de Vaca*. Santa Fe: Writers' Editions, 1936. Rpt., with the cooperation of Anton Long; linoleum illustrations by Mark Sanders, Tucson: Peccary Press, 1985.
———. *Birds of Daybreak: Landscapes and Elegies*. Santa Fe: William Gannon, 1985.
———. *Bones Incandescent: The Pajarito Journals of Peggy Pond Church*. Ed. with essays by Shelley Armitage. Lubbock: Texas Tech Press, 2001.
———. *The Burro of Angelitos*. Illustrations by Gigi Shaule Johnson. Los Angeles: Suttonhouse, 1936. Facsimile rpt., with a publisher's note and preface by Kathleen Church. Santa Fe: Sunstone Press, 2013.
———. *Familiar Journey*. Santa Fe: Writers' Editions, 1936.
———. *Foretaste*. Santa Fe: Writers' Editions, 1936. Rpt., foreword by Peter Deckert. Santa Fe: Sunstone Press, 2014.
———. *The House at Otowi Bridge: The Story of Edith Warner and Los Alamos*. Drawings by Connie Fox Boyd. Albuquerque: University of New Mexico Press, 1959, 1974.
———. *A Lament on Tsankawi Mesa*. Santa Fe: Thistle Press, 1980.
———. *New and Selected Poems*. Boise: Ahsahta Press, 1976; rpt. 1984.
———. *The Pancake Stories / Cuentos del Panqueque*. Drawings by Elizabeth Comfort Church; trans. into Spanish by Noël Chilton. Albuquerque: University of New Mexico Press, 2013.
———. *The Ripened Fields: Fifteen Sonnets of a Marriage*. Santa Fe: Lightning Tree Press, © 1978.
———. *A Rustle of Angels*. Drawings by Jeannie Pear. Denver: Peartree Press, 1981.
———. *Selected Poems 1930–1982*. Cassette tape recorded in 1982.
———. *This Dancing Ground of Sky: The Selected Poetry of Peggy Pond Church*. Introduction by Shelley Armitage. Santa Fe: Red Crane Books, 1993.
———. *Ultimatum for Man*. Stanford, CA: James Ladd Delkin, 1946.
———. *Wind's Trail: The Early Life of Mary Austin*. Ed. with an introduction by Shelley Armitage. Santa Fe: Museum of New Mexico Press, 1990. [Contains considerable material by Church.]
———, and Charles Carrillo. *Shoes for the Santo Niño/ Zapatos para el Santo Niño*. Los Ranchos de Albuquerque: Rio Grande Books, 2010.
Marriott, Alice. *Alice Marriott Remembered: An Edited Memoir*. Ed. Charlotte Whaley. Santa Fe: Sunstone, Press, 2009.
———. *The Black Stone Knife*. Illustrated by Harvey Weiss. New York: Crowell, 1957.
———. *The First Comers*. New York: McKay, 1960.
———. Foreword to *Teepee Neighbors* by Grace Coolidge. Norman: University of Oklahoma Press, 1984.
———. Foreword to *Indian Rawhide: An American Folk Art* by Mabel Morrow. Norman: University of Oklahoma Press, 1975.
———. *Greener Fields: Experiences Among the American Indians*. New York: Crowell, 1953.
———. *Hell on Horses and Women*. With drawings by Margaret Lefranc. Norman: University of Oklahoma Press, 1953. Rpt. with foreword by Margot Liberty. Norman: University of Oklahoma Press, 1993.
———. *Indian Annie: Kiowa Captive*. New York: McKay, 1965.
———. *Indians of the Four Corners: A Book About the Anasazi Indians and Their Modern Descendants*. New York: Crowell, 1952.
———. *Indians on Horseback*. New York: Crowell, 1948.

_____. *Kiowa Years: A Study in Culture Impact.* New York: Macmillan, 1968
_____. *María, the Potter of San Ildefonso.* With drawings by Margaret Lefranc. Norman: University of Oklahoma Press, 1948.
_____.Preface to *Songs of the Tewa* by Herbert Joseph Spinden, trans. New York: The Exposition of Indian Tribal Arts, 1933. Republished; co-ordinating editor Margaret Lefranc. Santa Fe: Sunstone Press, 1976.
_____. *Saynday's People: The Kiowa Indians and the Stories They Told.* Lincoln: University of Nebraska Press, 1963. (Combines in abridged versions *Winter-Telling Stories* and *Indians on Horseback*.)
_____. *Sequoyah: Leader of the Cherokees.* New York: Random House, 1956.
_____. *The Ten Grandmothers.* Norman: University of Oklahoma Press, 1945.
_____. *These Are the People: Some Notes on Southwestern Indians.* Santa Fe: Laboratory of Anthropology, 1949.
_____. *The Valley Below.* Norman: University of Oklahoma Press, 1949.
_____. *Winter-Telling Stories.* Illustrated by Roland Whitehorse. New York: Crowell, 1947. Rpt., "compiled by Alice Marriott," with one story omitted; illustrated by Richard Cuffari. New York: Crowell, 1969.
_____, and Carol K. Rachlin. *American Epic: The Story of the American Indian.* New York: Putman's, 1969; New York: New American Library, 1970.
_____, and Carol K. Rachlin. *American Indian Mythology.* Illustrated with photographs. New York: Crowell, 1968.
_____, and Carol K. Rachlin. *Peyote.* New York: Crowell, 1971.
_____, and Carol K. Rachlin. *Plains Indian Mythology.* New York: Crowell, 1975.
_____, McReynolds, Edwin C., and Estelle Faulconer. *Oklahoma: The Story of Its Past and Present.* Norman: University of Oklahoma Press, 1961.

Secondary Sources

Abbey, Edward. *Desert Solitaire: A Season in the Wilderness.* New York: McGraw-Hill, 1968.
Adams, Ansel. *Ansel Adams: An Autobiography.* Boston: Little, Brown, 1985.
The Ahsahta Anthology: Modern and Contemporary Poetry of the American West. Boise: Ahsahta Press / Boise State University, 1996.
Armitage, Shelley. *Women's Work: Essays in Cultural Studies.* West Cornwall, CT: Locust Hill Press, 1995.
_____, and Elizabeth Jameson, eds. *The Women's West.* Norman: University of Oklahoma Press, 1987.
Axelrod, Alan. *Art of the Golden West.* New York: Abbeville Publishers, 1990.
Ballantine, Betty, and Ian Ballantine, eds. *The Native Americans: An Illustrated History.* Atlanta: Turner Publishing, 1993.
Barnes, F. A., and Michaelene Pendleton. *Canyon Country Prehistoric Indians.* Salt Lake City: Wasatch Publishers, 1995.
Baym, Nina. *Women Writers of the American West, 1833–1927.* Urbana: University of Illinois Press, 2011.
Beauvoir, Simone de. *Le Deuxième Sexe.* Paris: Gallimard, 1947.
Blue, Martha. *Indian Trader: The Life and Times of J. L. Hubbell.* Walnut, CA: Kiva, 2000.
Brett, Dorothy E. *Lawrence and Brett—a Friendship.* Introduction by John Manchester. Santa Fe: Sunstone Press, 1974.
Castro, Michael. *Interpreting the Indian: Twentieth-Century Poets and the Native American.* Albuquerque: University of New Mexico Press, 1983.
Comer, Krista. *Landscapes of the New West: Gender and Geography in Contemporary Women's Writing.* Chapel Hill: University of North Carolina Press, 1999.
Corbin, Alice. *Red Earth.* Chicago: Seymour, 1920. New ed., compiled by Lois Rudnick and Ellen Zieselman; introduction by Rudnick. Santa Fe: Museum of New Mexico Press, 2003.
_____ (as *Henderson*), ed. *The Turquoise Trail: An Anthology of New Mexico Poetry.* Boston: Houghton Mifflin, 1928.
Coulter, John M. *Manual of the Botany of the Rocky Mountain Region.* New York: American Book Co., 1885.
Deutsch, Sarah. *No Separate Refuge: Culture, Class, and Gender on an Anglo-Hispanic Frontier in the American Southwest, 1880–1940.* New York: Oxford, 1987.

Dictionary of Literary Biography, vols. 9, 54, 78, 206, 212, 221, 256, 275 (on Austin, Cather, and Church; also, Bynner, Corbin, Monroe).

Dyck, Reginald, and Cheli Reutter, eds. *Crisscrossing Borders in Literature of the American West*. New York: Palgrave Macmillan, 2009.

Engel, Leonard. *The Big Empty: Essays on Western Landscapes as Narratives*. Albuquerque: University of New Mexico Press, 1994.

Erisman, Fred, and Richard W. Etulain, eds. *Fifty Western Writers: A Bio-Bibliographic Sourcebook*. Westport, CT: Greenwood Press, 1982.

Faris, James C. *The Nightway: A History and a History of Documentation of a Navajo Ceremonial*. Albuquerque: University of New Mexico Press, 1990.

Fetterley, Judith, and Marjorie Pryce. *Writing Out of Place: Regionalism, Women, and American Literary Criticism*. Urbana: University of Illinois Press, 2003.

Fontana, Bernard L. *A Guide to Contemporary Southwest Indians*. Tucson: Southwest Parks and Monuments Association, 1999.

Frank, Larry. *Indian Silver Jewelry of the Southwest, 1868-1930*. Boston: New York Graphic Society, 1978.

Gibson, Arrell M. *The Santa Fe and Taos Colonies: Age of the Muses, 1900-1942*. Norman: University of Oklahoma Press, 1983.

Gillmor, Frances, and Louisa Wade Wetherill. *Traders to the Navajo: The Wetherills of Kayenta*. Albuquerque: University of New Mexico Press, 1979.

Gilpin, Laura. *The Enduring Navaho*. Austin: University of Texas Press, 1968.

Goldman, Anne E. *Continental Divides: Revisioning American Literature*. New York: Palgrave, 2000.

Goodman, Audrey. *Translating Southwestern Landscapes: The Making of an Anglo Literary Region*. Tucson: University of Arizona Press, 2002.

Gurian, Jay. *Western American Writing: Tradition and Promise*. Deland, FL: Everett/Edwards, 1975.

Halverson, Cathryn. *Playing House in the American West: Western Women's Life Narratives*. Tuscaloosa: University of Alabama Press, 2013.

Hartley, Margaret, ed. *The Southwest Review Reader*. Dallas: SMU Press, 1974.

Hewett, Edgar L. *Pajarito Plateau and Its Ancient People*. Albuquerque: University of New Mexico Press, 1938.

Horgan, Paul. *The Centuries of Santa Fe*. New York: Dutton, 1956; Albuquerque: University of New Mexico Press, 1994.

_____. *Great River: The Rio Grande in North American History*, 2 vols. 1: *Indians and Spain*; 2: *Mexico and the United States*. New York: Rinehart, 1954.

Houk, Rose. *The Four Corners Anasazi: A Guide to Archeological Sites*. Durango, CO: San Juan National Forest Association, 1994.

Jensen, Joan, and Darlis Miller, eds. *New Mexico Women: Intercultural Perspectives*. Albuquerque: University of New Mexico Press, 1986.

Kolodny, Annette. *The Lay of the Land: Metaphor as Experience and History in American Life and Letters*. Chapel Hill: University of North Carolina Press, 1975.

Krutch, Joseph Wood. *The Desert Year*. New York: Sloane, 1951.

_____. *Grand Canyon: Today and All Its Yesterdays*. New York: Sloane, 1959.

_____. *The Voice of the Desert*. New York: Sloane, 1954.

Kupper, Winifred. *The Golden Hoof: The Story of the Sheep of the Southwest*. New York: Knopf, 1945.

La Farge, John Pen, ed. *Turn Left at Sleeping Dog: Scripting the Santa Fe Legend, 1920-1955*. Albuquerque: University of New Mexico Press, 2001.

La Farge, Oliver. *Behind the Mountains*. Boston: Houghton Mifflin, 1956.

_____. *Laughing Boy*. 1929. Rpt. Franklin Center, PA: Franklin Mint, 1977.

_____. *Santa Fe: The Autobiography of a Southwestern Town*. Norman: University of Oklahoma Press, 1959.

Lawrence, D. H. *Birds, Beasts and Flowers*. New York: Seltzer, 1923.

_____. *Mornings in Mexico*. New York: Knopf, 1927.

Leopold, Aldo. *Round River: From the Journals of Aldo Leopold*. New York: Oxford University Press, 1953.

———. *Sand County Almanac*. New York: Oxford University Press, 1949.
Limerick, Patricia Nelson. *Desert Passages: Encounters with the American Deserts*. Albuquerque: University of New Mexico Press, 1985.
Lincoln, Kenneth. *Native American Renaissance*. Berkeley: University of California Press, 1983.
Luhan, Mabel Dodge. *Intimate Memories*. Edited and condensed by Lois Palken Rudnick. Albuquerque: University of New Mexico Press, 1999.
Major, Mabel, and T. M. Pearce, eds. *Signature of the Sun: Southwest Verse, 1900–1950*. Albuquerque: University of New Mexico Press, 1950.
———, and ———, eds. *Southwest Heritage: A Literary History with a Biobibliography*. Albuquerque: University of New Mexico Press, 1938, 1948, 1972. (Rebecca Smith was co-author of the 1948 ed.)
Malville, J. McKim, and Claudia Putnam. *Prehistoric Astronomy in the Southwest*. Rev. ed. Boulder, CO: Johnson Books, 1989, 1993.
Mills, Enos A. *The Spell of the Rockies*. Boston: Houghton Mifflin, 1921.
Milton, John R. *The Novel of the American West*. Lincoln: University of Nebraska Press, 1980.
Montgomery, Charles. *The Spanish Redemption: Heritage, Power, and Loss on New Mexico's Upper Rio Grande*. Berkeley: University of California Press, 2002.
Mullin, Molly H. *Culture in the Marketplace: Gender, Art, and Value in the American Southwest*. Durham: Duke University Press, 2001.
Myres, Sandra. *Westering Women and the Frontier Experience, 1800–1915*. Albuquerque: University of New Mexico Press, 1982.
Norwood, Vera, and Janice Monk, eds. *The Desert Is No Lady: Southwestern Landscapes in Women's Writing and Art*. New Haven: Yale University Press, 1987.
Nusbaum, Deric. *Deric in Mesa Verde*. New York: Putnam's, 1926.
Parezo, Nancy J., ed. *Hidden Scholars: Anthropologists and the Native American Southwest*. Albuquerque: University of New Mexico Press, 1993.

Pearce, T[homas] M. *Alice Corbin Henderson*. New York: Twayne, 1969.
———. *Oliver La Farge*. New York: Twayne, 1972.
———. *Southwesterners Write*. Albuquerque: University of New Mexico Press, 1946.
Perpetual Mirage: Photographic Narratives of the Desert West. Organized by May Castleberry. New York: Whitney Museum of Art, 1996.
Poling-Kempes, Lesley. *Ladies of the Canyons*. Tucson: University of Arizona Press, 2015.
Powell, John Wesley. *Down the Colorado*. Photographs and epilogue by Eliot Porter. New York: Dutton, 1969.
Powell, Lawrence Clark. *Southwest Classics: The Creative Literature of the Arid Lands*. Los Angeles: Ward Ritchie Press, 1974.
Pratt, Mary Louise. *Imperial Eyes: Travel Writing and Transculturation*. New York: Routledge, 1992.
Reisner, Marc P. *Cadillac Desert: The American West and Its Disappearing Water*. New York: Viking, 1986.
Rosowski, Susan J. *Birthing a Nation: Gender, Creativity, and the West in American Literature*. Lincoln: University of Nebraska Press, 1999.
Rudnick, Lois Palkin. *Mabel Dodge Luhan: New Woman, New Worlds*. Albuquerque: University of New Mexico Press, 1984.
Sarton, May. *The Land of Silence and Other Poems*. New York: Rinehart, 1953.
Schaefer, Heike. *Mary Austin's Regionalism: Reflections on Gender, Genre, and Geography*. Charlottesville: University of Virginia Press, 2004.
Schlissel, Lillian, Vicki L. Ruiz, and Janice Monk, eds. *Western Women: Their Lands, Their Lives*. Albuquerque: University of New Mexico Press, 1988.
Shockley, Martin, ed. *Southwest Writers Anthology*. Austin: Steck-Vaughn, 1967.
The Sierra Club Guides to the National Parks of the Desert Southwest. New York: Stewart, Tabori & Chang, 1984, 1996.
Silko, Leslie Marmon. *Laguna Woman*. 1974. Greenfield Center, NY: Greenfield Review Press, 1974.
Smith, Sidonie, and Julie Watson. *Before They Could Vote: Women's Autobiograph-

ical Writing, 1819–1919. Madison: University of Wisconsin Press, 2006.
Stegner, Wallace. *Beyond the Hundredth Meridian: John Wesley Powell and the Second Opening of the West*. Introduction by Bernard de Voto. Boston: Houghton Mifflin, 1954.
Stouck, David. *Willa Cather's Imagination*. Lincoln: University of Nebraska Press, 1975.
Stout, Janis P. *Picturing a Different West: Vision, Illustration, and the Tradition of Austin and Cather*. Lubbock: Texas Tech Press, 2007.
_____. *South by Southwest: Katherine Anne Porter and the Burden of Texas History*. Tuscaloosa: University of Alabama Press, 2013.
_____. *Through the Window, Out the Door: Women's Narratives of Departure, from Austin and Cather to Tyler, Morrison, and Didion*. Tuscaloosa: University of Alabama Press, 1998.
Stuart, David E. *Anasazi America: Seventeen Centuries on the Road from Center Place*. 2nd ed. Albuquerque: University of New Mexico Press, 2014.
_____. *Pueblo Peoples on the Pajarito Plateau: Archaeology and Efficiency*. Albuquerque: University of New Mexico Press, 2010.
Taylor, Ronald J. *Sagebrush Country: A Wildflower Sanctuary*. Missoula, MT: Mountain Press, 1992.
Trusky, A. Thomas. *Women Poets of the West: An Anthology, 1850–1950*. Boise: Ahsahta Press, 1978, 1981.
Tucker, Anne. *The Woman's Eye*. New York: Knopf, 1973.
Udall, Sharyn R. *The Santa Fe Art Colony, 1900–1942*. Santa Fe: Gerald Peters Gallery, 1987.
Waldman, Carl. *Encyclopedia of Native American Tribes*. 3rd ed. New York: Facts on File, 2006.
Weigle, Marta, and Kyle Fiore, eds. *Santa Fe and Taos: The Writer's Era 1916–1941*. Santa Fe: Ancient City Press, 1982; Santa Fe: Sunstone Press, 2008.
Whaley, Charlotte. *Nina Otero-Warren of Santa Fe*. Albuquerque: University of New Mexico Press, 1994.
Whitt, Jan. *The Redemption of Narrative: Terry Tempest Williams and Her Vision of the West*. Macon: Mercer University Press, 2016.
Wiewandt, Thomas, and Maureen Wilks. *The Southwest Inside Out*. Photographs by Wiewandt. Tucson: Wild Horizons, 2001.
Williamson, Chilton, Jr. *The Hundredth Meridian: Seasons and Travels in the Old West*. Rockford, IL: Chronicles Press, 2005.
Witherspoon, Gary. *Language and Art in the Navajo Universe*. Ann Arbor: University of Michigan Press, 1977.
Wrigley, Richard. *Ansel Adams: Images of the American West*. New York: Smithmark, 1994.

Index

Numbers in **_bold italics_** refer to pages with photographs.

Abbey, Edward 45, 188*n*4
Abeita, Louise (E-Yeh-Shuré) 178
acequia 25, 28, 153; *see also* irrigation
Ácoma Pueblo 73, 75, 89
Adams, Ansel 29, 60, ***61***, 62, 192*n*68
Adams, Charles 94
Adams, Fred 95
Adams, Maria Henry 94
adobe houses 16, 27, 151, 153
aestheticism 14, 68
aesthetics 14, 119; *see also* beauty
Agua Caliente reservation 98
air 121; *see also* sky
Alain-Fournier 194*n*18
Albuquerque, NM 73, 90, 145, 153
Aldrich, C.R. 198–99*n*36
Alexievich, Svetlana 187*n*34
Alice Marriott Remembered 204*n*3
American Red Cross 124, 151
American Rhythm 56
Amon Carter Museum 203*n*55
Anadarko, OK 149
Analepse 59, 80
Anasazi 9, 15, 58, 90, 103, 108, 110, 112, 168, 179, 205–6*n*40; *see also* ruins
ancestors (theme) 135, 136, 138
ancestral memory 107, 129, 136, 137
androgyny, cultural 22–23
André, Carl 93
animus 125
anthropology 10, 55–57, 146, 148–49, 150, 151, 155–57, 170–71; *see also* ethnology
anthropomorphism 12, 46, 47, 51
Antiquities Act 82, 186*n*121
Apaches 16, 58
Applegate, Frank 44, 62
apricot trees 89
April Twilights 68
Arapahoes 149, 162
architecture 16, 27, 60–61, 78, 85–86, 91
Aristotle 20, 22

Arizona 1, 7, 9, 16, 32, 57, 60, 72, 77, 91, 97, 99, 115,119, 151; *see also* individual place names.
Armer, Alberta 109, 196*n*4
Armer, Austin 97, 98, 99, 107, 196*n*4
Armer, Laura Adams 1, 2, 7, 8, 9, 11, 12, 19, 21, 23, 26, 27, 28, 30, 34, 69, 85, 86, 92–119, ***96***, 142, 143, 174, 175, 186*n*18; background and career 94–95; *Cactus* 97, 98, 114; connections between art and writing 93–94, 109; copies of sand-paintings 11, 104–5; *Dark Circle of Branches* 112, 114–15; *Farthest West* 118–19; *The Forest Pool* 92, 95; *In Navajo Land* 93–94, 98, 114, 119, 146, 147, 179; marriage 95, 97, 98; mysticism 107, 109, 196*n*5; as painter 92, 93, 95, 100, 104, 109, 115; as photographer 12, 92, 95, 97–98, 102, 104, 116, 197–98*n*29; reputation 2; *Sand-Painting of the Navaho Indians* 197–98*n*29; *Southwest* 106, 107, 115–16; style 93; *The Trader's Children* 101, 114, 116–18; views on native beliefs 105, 106–8; visits to Southwest 97, 99–103; *Waterless Mountain* 3, 93, 101, 108–12, 119
Armer, Sidney 29, 95, 96–97 98–99, 106, 109, 112,116, 118
Armitage, Shelley 122, 130, 140, 200*n*6, 202*n*26, 206*n*41
Anadarko, OK 149, 161
Arnold, Matthew 12
aromas 180
The Arrow-Maker 53–54
Arroyo Hondo, NM 88, 89
Art Institute of Chicago 76
artifacts *see* Native arts
arts and crafts *see* Indian Arts and Crafts Board; Native arts
Ashi 103–4, 105, 197*n*19
Ashley Pond 132–33
Atherton, Gertrude 190*n*30
Atlantic Monthly 45, 126

215

Index

atomic research and bomb 9, 30, 122, 131, 139, 141, 175
Austen, Jane 3
Austin, Mary 1, 2, 7, 8, 9, 10, 11, 13, 18–19, 21, 22, 23, 24, 26, 28, 30, 31–64, *32*, 65, 67, 79, 85, 91, 93, 95, 97, 107, 116, 118, 121, 122, 124, 130, 133, 143–44, 147, 174, 175, 176, 178, 180, 181, 185*n*18, 187*n*35, 189*n*7, 199*n*47, 199*n*51, 200*n*5, 202*n*26, 202*n*39, 203*n*59, 205*n*26, 205*n*27, 206*n*41; achievement and legacy 32–38, 63–64; *American Rhythm* 56; *The Arrow-Maker* 53–54; *The Basket Woman* 47; *Cactus Thorn* 25, 59, 174; childhood and youth 38–40, 41; *The Children Sing in the Far West* 60; connections with Cather 73, 79, 85–86, 194*n*16; *Earth Horizon* 25, 40–41, 61–62, 135, 143, 179, 190*n*23; feminism 34–36, 44; *The Flock* 34, 41, 50–51, 53; *The Ford* 13, 34, 54–55, 119; "The Friend in the Wood" 203*n*59; genius 31, 41; and Indians 34; *Isidro* 49–50; journalism 69; *The Land of Journeys' Ending* 57–59, 62, 63, 115; *The Land of Little Rain* 33, 35, 43, 45–47, 48, 49, 51–52; *Lost Borders* 51–53; mysticism 37, 38, 39–40, 62, 189*n*13; *One-Smoke Stories* 62–63; as reformer 33, 34–36, 52; religion 36, 37, 40; reputation 2, 31; *Starry Adventure* 62; style 36–37, 40, 45–46, 51; *Taos Pueblo* 60–61; *The Trail Book* 8, 55–56; translations 34, 56–57, 191*n*59, 197*n*26; views on science 38, 190*n*15; "The Walking Woman" 42
Austin, Ruth 42, 43
Austin, Stafford Wallace 42, 43, 44
authenticity 14, 34
authorial intention 4
Awanyu *see* Plumed Serpent
Aztecs 116

Bakersfield, CA 41, 42
Bakhtin, M.M. 31
Balzac, Honoré de 71, 193*n*13
Bandelier, Adolph 11
Bandelier National Monument 142
Baptist Church 69
The Basket Woman 47
basketry 27, 28, 36, 117
Basque tales 62
Battey, Thomas 171
Baumann, Gustave 127, 195*n*44, 201*n*18
Baym, Nina 189*n*7, 190*n*28
Beale, Edward Fitzgerald 41
beauty 13, 32–33, 38, 79, 92, 116, 174
Beauty Way cycle 103
Beauvoir, Simone de 23, 24
Benét, William Rose 137
Bent, Charles 88, 195*n*43
Berkeley, CA 97, 99, 108, 117, 132

Berlin 152
Betatakin (Navajo National Monument), AZ 101, 107, 198*n*33
Bierce, Ambrose 18
Bierstadt, Albert 12
Big Bend, TX 169, 170
Big Horn Mountains 170
biology 21; *see also* botany
birds 46, 77, 108, 141
Birds of Daybreak 140–41
Black Elk 199*n*47
Black Mountain, AZ 98, 116, 199*n*42
The Black Stone Knife 171
Blackburn College 41
The Blackburnian 41
Blake, William 129
blood (theme) 136, 138
Blue Canyon, AZ 102, 110
"Blue Mesa" 146, 193*n*12, 194–95*n*27, 198*n*33, 206*n*41
Blumenschein, Ernest 73, 132
Blumenschein, Helen 132
Boaz, Franz 148, 191*n*59
Bohr, Niels 141
Bones Incandescent 122, 200*n*5
The Bookman 34
Bosque Redondo, NM 90
Boston, MA 68
botany 41; *see also* trees, plants, flowers
bowdlerizing 161
Bradford, Richard 201*n*21
Breton, Jules 76
Brett, Dorothy E. 73, 147, 198*n*33
Brooks, Van Wyck 18, 38
Bryant, William Cullen 126
Buffon, Georges-Louis Leclerc, comte de 36
Bunzel, Ruth 191*n*59
Bureau of Indian Affairs 16, 151, 186*n*18
Burke, Charles H. 16, 34, 186*n*18
Burlin, Nathalie Curtis *see* Curtis, Nathalie
Burlington and Missouri railway 66
Burne-Jones, Edward 68
Burns, Anna 40
The Burro of Angelitos 144
Bursum Bill 34, 150
Burton, Charles 186*n*18
Bynner, Witter 9, 32, 56, 69, 120, 154, 199–200*n*1, 201*n*21

Cabell, James Branch 19
Cabeza de Vaca, Álvar Núñez de 14, 58
cactus 58, 63
Cactus 97, 98, 114
Cactus Thorn 25, 59, 174
California 1, 2, 7, 9, 11, 19, 21, 31–32, 33, 40–43, 46, 49, 51, 59, 60, 62, 63, 92, 115, 123, 128, 131, 132, 137, 146, 151, 177, 179, 41; *see also* individual place names
California Historical Society 196*n*5, 196*n*7

Index

California School of Design 95
camels 41
Camus, Albert 37
Canyon de Chelly AZ 25, 58, 73, 90, 98, 117, 109, **118**, 178
Capulin Canyon, NM 135
Carlinville, IL 38
Carlisle Indian School 148, 159, 170
Carlsbad Caverns, NM 116
Carmel, CA 43, 44
Carrillo, Charles M. 145, 203n61
Carson, Kit 88, 115, 195n43
Cassidy, Gerald 57, 60
Cassidy, Ina Sizer 34, 57
Cather, Charles 65
Cather, Douglass 71, 72
Cather, G.P. 79
Cather, Mary Boak 65
Cather, Roscoe 73
Cather, Willa 1, 2, 7, 9, 13, 18, 19, 20, 21, 23, 27, 28, 29, 30, 35, 65–91, **69**, **74**, **83**, 95, 103, 114, 130, 131, 133, 147, 174, 175, 176, 179, 185n15; *April Twilights* 68; birth and childhood 66–67; "Blue Mesa" 146, 193n12, 194–95n27, 198n33, 206n41; connections with Mary Austin 73, 79, 85–86, 194n16; correspondence 2, 65–66; *Death Comes for the Archbishop* 30, 65, 71, 85–91, 112, 193n12, 195n42; "Enchanted Mesa" 75–76; feminism 67–68; fictional method 13; journalism 68–69; mysticism 193–94n13; *The Professor's House* 18, 71, 72, 78–85, 194n16; as reformer 67; reputation 2; *Sapphira and the Slave Girl* 70, 81; *The Song of the Lark* 71, 72, 76–78, 79, 84, 85, 101, 143, 194n22; style 71; visits to the Southwest 71–75
Catholicism *see* Roman Catholicism
Caves 28, 111, 112, 116, 117, 125; *see also* Anasazi, ruins
The Century (magazine) 68
Chabot, Maria 204n15
Chaco Canyon, NM 16, 25, 58, 132
Chapin, Frederick 16
Chapman, Kenneth 150
Chase, William Merritt 97
Chateaubriand, François-René de 12
Cherokees 149
Cheyennes 149, 162
Chicago 103, 147
Chicago *Sunday Tribune* 165
The Children Sing in the Far West 60
children's literature 4, 29, 47, 92, 108–15, 116–19, 144–45, 147, 161–62, 171–73
Chimayó, NM 44, 89, 155, 163
Chinle (Chin Lee) 98, 199n42
Chopin, Kate 19, 35, 193n8
Christian symbolism 50
Christianity 13, 14, 86, 107; 160; *see also* denomination names; Protestantism; Roman Catholicism
Christmas 107, 117
Church, Allen 127
Church, Fermor 126–27, 129, 131, 132, 140
Church, Hugh 127, 130
Church, Julia Hoffman 145
Church, Kathleen D. 130, 144, 145, 200n2, 203n55, 203n
Church, Peggy Pond 1, 2, 7, 9, 10, 20, 21, 23, 25, 26–27, 28, 30, 35, 36, 39, 40, 41, 44, 92, 120–45, **129**, **144**, 147, 174, 175, 176, 178, 180, 185n12, 185n12, 187n35, 198n31, 199n47; *Birds of Daybreak* 140–41; *Bones Incandescent* 122, 200n5; *The Burro of Angelitos* 144; career 130; early life 123–25; *Familiar Journey* 133, 136–37; features of her poetry 133–134; feminism 127; *Foretaste* 133–36; *The House at Otowi Bridge* 29, 121, 131, 141–43, 200n7; marriage 126–28; mysticism 120; as nature poet 120, 122; *New and Selected Poems* 139–40; pacifism 13, 131, 132; *Pancake Stories* 145; reputation 2, 120; *The Ripened Fields* 134, 140–41, 179; schooling 125, 201n14; *Shoes for the Santo Niño* 145; style 122; *This Dancing Ground of Sky* 129, 200n2; *Ultimatum for Man* 137; *Wind's Trail* 143
Church, Theodore 127
Civil War 17
class (social) 19
Claudel, Paul 134
Cleaveland, Agnes Morley 169
Clements, Forrest 148, 155
cliff dwellings *see* Canyon de Chelly; Manitou Cliff Dwellings; Mesa Verde; Walnut Canyon
Cliff Palace *see* Mesa Verde
Coles, Robert 194n17
Colet, Louise 193n8
Colette (Sidonie Gabrielle Colette) 129
collaborative books 29
collective memory *see* ancestral memory
Collier, John 150
Collier's (magazine) 78
Colorado 8, 9, 12, 15, 60, 72, 194n22; *see also* individual place names
Colorado Plateau 59
Colorado River 15, 41, 57, 59
Colorado Springs, CO 17
Columbia University 70, 148
Comanches 115, 159, 160, 162
Comer, Krista 10, 19, 45, 77
Commonweal (magazine) 87
community life 7, 8, 11, 33, 38, 55, 153, 154, 166
Connecticut 126, 128, 136
Connell, A.J. 124, 127
Connell, May 127

Conrad, Joseph 80
conservation 26, 32, 33; *see also* environmentalism
Cooper, James Fenimore 10, 54
Cooper Union 152
Corbin, Alice 9, 18, 126, 130, 184*n*3, 187*n*41, 188–89*n*5, 191*n*59, 196–97*n*11, 202*n*25
Corn Mountain, NM 27
Coronado, Francisco Vásquez de 14, 58, 99
Cortez, CO 17
Cory, Kate T. 196–97*n*11
cosmology 12, 107, 110, 119
Craig, Edward Gordon 40
The Crawler *see* Na Nai
Cripple Creek, CO 89
"Cuatro Milpas" 131
Cuernavaca *see* Mexico
Cuffari, Richard 161
cultural appropriation and plunder 102–3, 154, 155, 157
culture, definition 10, 184*n*7; and women 23, 24
Curtis, Edward S. 12, *118*
Curtis, Nathalie 9, 100, 188–89*n*5
Cushing, Frank Hamilton 62, 191*n*59, 204*n*5

Dallas, TX 169
Dallas Art Museum 161
dances 15, 16, 25, 34, 58, 61, 72, 102, 105–6, 141, 151, 153, 157, 158, 159, 163, 166, 172, 181, 185*n*18, 198*n*33, 199*n*47, 203*n*53
Dark Circle of Branches 112, 114–15
Dasburg, Andrew 132
Daw, Sarah 199–200*n*1
Dawson, Carl 50
death (theme) 138, 139–40, 145
Death Comes for the Archbishop 30, 65, 71, 85- 91, 112, 193*n*12, 195*n*42
Death Valley 99
deer *see* stag
de la Torre, Mónica 3
de Mille, Agnes 45
Denver and Rio Grande railroad 65
desert economy 47, 58
Desert Magazine 97–98
de Soto, Hernando 56
Detroit, MI 123, 124
development 10, 13, 45, 177
Dickinson, Emily 3, 69
Didion, Joan 54
Dodge, Mabel *see* Luhan, Mabel Dodge
Doré, Gustave 95
dreams 128, 203*n*59
drought 15, 41, 99; *see also* water
dry-paintings *see* sand-paintings
Dryden, John 185*n*11
Dsilyi Neyani 114
dualism 134
Duncan, Isadora 40

Dürer, Albrecht 86
Dvorak, Anton 70–71

Earth Horizon 25, 40–41, 61–62, 135, 143, 179, 190*n*23
Earth Mother (Mother Earth) 24–27, 115, 118
easel art 150–51
East Coast cultural dominance 18, 130–31, 202*n*25
Echo Cliffs 59
ecology *see* environmentalism
Edleman, Sandra 154
Egypt 132, 138
Eliot, George 68
Eliot, T.S. 133, 184*n*7
Elkins, Andrew 120
El Morro, NM 56, 58–59, 75
El Paso, TX 116
embodiment 124–25, 134, 135
Emerson, Ralph Waldo 37, 192*n*72
"Enchanted Mesa" 75–76
Enchanted Mesa, NM 73, 75, *76*, 89, 132, 193*n*9
England 132, 147; *see also* London
environmentalism 13, 32, 33, 54–55, 90, 122, 179–80; *see also* conservation
Episcopal Church 69–70, 88, 140, 155
Española, NM 65, 155
ethnology 28, 146, 155; definition 148
excavation 16, 116; *see also* Antiquities Act
exoticism 10, 13, 46, 51, 53
exploitation 1, 13, 21, 22, 32, 35, 54–55, 59, 121
explorations 14–15, 58
Exposition of Indian Tribal Arts 34, 198*n*29

Familiar Journey 133, 136–37
Fanon, Frantz 177
Farthest West 118–19
Father Sky 93, 115
Faulkner, William 18
Faye, Paul Louis 99, 100
Fechin, Nicolai 152
feminine condition *see* women's situation
feminine vision 13, 21, 22, 24, 147, 169, 181
feminism 19, 127; definition 19; *see also* individual authors' names
feminist criticism and interpretation 2, 19, 33
Fergusson, Erna 27
Fetterly, Judith 19
Fewkes, Jesse Walter 72 194–95*n*27, 198*n*33
Field Columbian Museum, Chicago 147
film *see The Mountain Chant*
"Finished in beauty" 13, 92, 103, 150,119, 185*n*14
Fink, Augusta 203*n*59
Firestone, Shulamith 185*n*12, 189*n*8

Fitzgerald, F. Scott 70
Five Southern ("Civilized") Tribes 148
Flagstaff, AZ 77, 151
Flaubert, Gustave 68, 193n8
Fletcher, John Gould 9, 32
The Flock 34, 41, 50–51, 53
floods 110, 117, 201n8
The Ford 13, 34, 54–55, 119
The Forest Pool 92, 95
Foretaste 133–36
Fort Sill, OK 160, 172
Fort Smith, AR 41
Fort Sumner, NM 112
Fort Wingate, AZ 103
fossils 19, 116–17, 199n37
Foster, Betsy 153
Foucault, Michel 19
Four Corners 9
France, Anatole 84, 195n34
Franciscans 14
Frazier, James G. 129, 198n36
Freud, Sigmund 4
Freudian criticism and interpretation 169
Frijoles Canyon 142
Frost, Robert 130
Fuller, Margaret 1

Gadsden Purchase 15
Gallup, NM 118; *see also* Harvey House
Ganado, AZ 110
Ganado Reservoir 116
Ganado Trading Post 101.
Garland, Hamlin 19, 198n33
gender 20–21, 67, 202n26; *see also* sexuality
Genette, Gérard 80
Geneviève, Saint 87
Georgi-Findlay, Brigitte 22
Ghost Ranch 132
Gide, André 8, 79–80, 195n28, 203n43
Gilpin, Laura 23, 26, 60, 85, 153, 180, 192n69, 197–98n29, 203n55
Gioia, Dana 38
Glen Canyon Dam 102
Gold King Mine 180
Goodman, Susan 50
Goombi, Millie Durgan 171–72
Gospels 129
Gosse, Edmund 53
Grand Canyon 59, 60, 110
grandmother bundles *see* medicine bundles
Grau, Shirley Ann 3
Graulich, Melody 45, 54, 55
Great Chain of Being 116
Great Plains 2, 8, 65; *see also* Nebraska, Oklahoma
Great War *see* World War I
Greeks 32
Greeley, Andrew 38

Green River 15
Greener Fields 164, 170–71, 179, 197–98n29

Haines, John 121
hair 34, 186n18
Haltermann, Father 73, 87
Halverson, Cathryn 206n41
Hamburg, Jan 67, 193n5
Hardy, Thomas 52
Harper's (magazine) 75, 108
Harte, Bret 43
Harvard University 126, 201n21
Harvey House 197–98n29
Harwood Foundation 132
Hawthorne, Nathaniel 19
healing ceremonies *see* Medicine Men; sand-paintings
heathenism *see* paganism
Heilbrun, Carolyn 186–87n31
Heinemann (publisher) 76
Hell on Horses and Women 4, 23–24, 168–70
Hemingway, Ernest 70, 101
Hemlock Society 132
Henderson, Alice Corbin *see* Corbin, Alice
Henderson, William Penhallow 9, 126, 130, 196–97n11
Hewett, Edgar Lee 9, 17, 150
Hill, Thomas 12
Hillerman, Tony 9
Hispanics 16, 25, 44, 62, 70, 89, 90, 175, 180; *see also* Mexicans; New Spain
history and historical writing 3, 19–20, 49, 55
Hoffman, Malvina 197n20
hogans 27, 98, 115, 179
Holbein, Hans 86
Hollywood 106
homesteading 2, 32
Hopis 15, 58, 89, 92, 105, 107, 147, 149, 177, 186n18
Horgan, Paul 205n23
horses 125
Hotevilla, AZ 105
Houghton Mifflin (publisher) 59, 65
The House at Otowi Bridge 29, 121, 131, 141–43, 200n7
houses and dwellings 27, 33, 47, 80, 84, 90, 127–28, 167, 169; *see also* adobe houses; architecture; cliff dwellings; hogans; ruins; tepees; wikiup
Howells, William Dean 73, 206n2
Howlett, William Joseph 87, 88
Hubbell, Adele 101
Hubbell, Barbara 101
Hubbell, Charlie 102
Hubbell, George 101, 116
Hubbell, John (Juan) Lorenzo ("Father") 100–1, 116, 197n21

Index

Hubbell, Lorenzo 100–1, 102, 105, 106, 108, 109, 115
Hubbell, Roman 101, 106
Hubbell Trading Posts 101, 110, 197*n*21, 199*n*52
Hugo, Richard 120
Hugo, Victor 50
humor 18, 63
Humphreys Peak 194*n*22
Hunt, George 157, 160, 172
Hunter, George (brother) 39, 45
Hunter, George (father) 38, 39, 40
Hunter, James 35, 39, 40, 41, 44
Hunter, Jennie 39, 40
Hunter, Mary *see* Austin, Mary
Hunter, Mary (niece) 44–45
Hunter, Susanna Savilla Graham 35, 38–39, 40, 41, 42
Huntington Library 143

ideal 7, 11, 12
Illinois 1, 32, 40
illustrations 14, 185*n*15, 196*n*2, 199*n*45
image, definition 133
Imagism 189*n*10
imago 7
In Navajo Land 93–94, 98, 114, 119, 146, 147, 179
Indian Annie: Kiowa Captive 71
Indian Arts and Crafts Board 17, 150–51
Indian Arts Fund 44
Indian Market, Santa Fe 150
Indian School, PA *see* Carlisle Indian School
Indian School (Sherman Institute), Riverside, CA 151, 161
Indian School, Santa Fe 117, 205*n*35
Indians, as term 3
Indians, as topic 16, 33, 34, 47–49, 53–54, 55, 56, 58, 60–61, 70, 75, 78, 123, 149, 175, 177; status in 1900 16; *see also* individual tribe names
Indians of the Four Corners 168
Indians on Horseback 163
industrialization 10, 13, 33
Interstate 40 41
interviewing 114, 148, 155, 157, 158, 164–65, 171, 205*n*21
Inyo County, CA 54
irrigation 33, 61, 135; *see also* water
Isidro 49–50
Isleta Pueblo 73

Jackson, Helen Hunt 176, 206*n*3
James, William 38
Jauss, Hans Robert 4
Jeffers, Robinson 120
Jemez Mountains 123
jewelry 27, 99–100, 102–3, 115

Jewett, Sarah Orne 19, 28, 69, 71
Jews 67, 193*n*5
Johnson, Samuel 181
Johnson, Willard "Spud" 9
Jones, Theodore Elden 95
Jornada del Muerto, NM 57
Jung, Carl 4, 44, 98, 128, 129, 130, 193*n*6, 198–99*n*36
Jungian criticism and interpretation 107, 128–29, 136, 140; *see also* ancestral memory
juvenile literature *see* children's literature

Kaibab Plateau, AZ 110, 199*n*42
Käsebier, Gertrude 22
Kayenta, AZ 198*n*33
Keam, Thomas V. 197*n*21
Keams Canyon 101
Kern County, CA 41, 54
Kierkegaard, Søren 37
Kiet Seel (Navajo National Monument), AZ 15, 112, 198*n*33
King, Grace 19, 23
Kino, Eusebio 58
Kiowa language 149
Kiowas 2, 8, 30, 146, 149, 155–60, 160–63, 166, 171–73, 174, 175, 177, 204*n*5
Kipling, Rudyard 126
kiva, definition 12
Klah, Hostiin 147, 197–98*n*29 [spelling sic]
Kloss, Phillips 9
Knopf (publisher) 78, 86
Korean War 170
Kristeva, Julia 23
Kroeber, A.L. 199*n*40
Krutch, Joseph Wood 7, 188*n*4
Kunstschule des Westens 152
Kupper, Winifred 50

Laboratory of Anthropology, Santa Fe 195*n*32, 204*n*8
Lacan, Jacques 4
La Farge, Oliver 9, 105, 107, 108, 110, 111, 147, 197–98*n*29, 199*n*42, 205*n*26
Laguna Pueblo 89
Laguna Pueblo Church 90
Laid, W. David 120
Lamy, Jean-Baptiste 30, 86–87, 88, 195*n*43, 205*n*35
The Land of Journeys' Ending 57–59, 62, 63, 115
The Land of Little Rain 33, 35, 43, 45–47, 48, 49, 51–52
landscape 15, 21, 25–26, 35–36, 61, 77–78, 135, 179, 187*n*34, 194*n*22; definition 7
Lang, Andrew 125
Lao-Tzu 107
Las Vegas, NM 123
Laughing Boy 105, 107

Index

Lawrence, D.H. (David Herbert) 9, 73, 93, 106, 154, 176, 198n33, 202n33
Lawrence, Ernest 131
Lawrence, Frieda 9, 73, 106, 152, 154, 202n33
Lear, Edward 126
Lee's Ferry 102
Lefranc, Margaret 23, 29, 148, 151–54, 163, 168, 171, 179, 204n15, 205n40
Lehmer, Derrick 99
Leopold, Aldo 188n4
lesbianism 23, 67, 77, 152, 193n5
Lessing, Doris 129
Levertov, Denise 129
Lewis, Edith 65, 72–73, 79, 87, 192n2, 194n23
Lhôte, André 152
Liberty, Margot 168
light 73, 75, 93, 194n17
Lincoln, Abraham 172
Lincoln, Kenneth 11
Lincoln *Courier* 68
Lindbergh, Anne Morrow 93
Lindsay, Vachel 189n10
literary innovation 184n8
Little Colorado River 15, 59, 89, 102, 178
Lockwood, Ward 202–3n39
London 43
London, Jack 35, 43, 97
Lone Pine, CA 42, 60
Long, Alice 139–40, 201n21
Long, Haniel 121, 128, 137, 139–40, 200n5, 201n21, 202n25
Long Walk 112
Longfellow, Henry Wadsworth 54, 94
Longmans Green (publisher) 109
Loretto, Sisters of 89
Los Alamos, NM 9, 130, 142, 153, 202n25
Los Alamos Ranch School 124, 131
Los Angeles, CA 33, 41, 43, 103, 123
Lost Borders 51–53
Louÿs, Pierre 79
Lubbock, Percy 108
Luhan, Mabel Dodge 9, 23, 43, 62, 73, 106, 121, 132, 154, 147, 184n3, 190n32
Lujan, Tony 73, 106, 184n5, 196n47
Lukács, Gyorgy 29
Lukacs, John 20
Lummis, Charles 43, 57, 186n18

MacDougal, Daniel T. 44, 57, 190n32
Machebeuf, Joseph P. 86, 87
Machu Picchu 129
Mackenzie, Sandra 154
MacKinnon, Catharine 21
Magoffin, Susan Shelby 206n3
male characters 28, 71
male myth 22
Malinowski, Branislaw 198–99n36

Malraux, André 4
Mancos, CO 82
Mancos River 185n17
Manifest Destiny 21
Manitou Cliff Dwellings 17
Many Feathers, Mary 148
Marble Canyon, AZ 59
Marfa, TX 170
María: The Potter of San Ildefonso 146, 155, 163–68
marriage and conjugal relationships 128, 130, 175
Marriott, Alice Lee 1, 2, 3, 7, 8, 9, 10, 11, 12–13, 14, 17, 19, 21, 23, 25, 27, 30, 58, 124, 146–73, **152**, **156**, **164**, 174, 175, 176, 184n7, 190n32, 199n48; *Alice Marriott Remembered* 204n3; *The Black Stone Knife* 171; education and early work 148–49; as ethnologist 2, 146–47, 154; friendship with Lefranc 151–54; *Greener Fields* 164, 170–71, 179, 197–98n29; *Hell on Horses and Women* 4, 23–24, 168–70; *Indian Annie: Kiowa Captive* 71; *Indians of the Four Corners* 168; *Indians on Horseback* 163; *María: The Potter of San Ildefonso* 146, 155, 163–68; mysticism 13; *Plains Indian Mythology* 162–63; reputation 2; style 165, 171; *The Ten Grandmothers* 30, 146, 155–60, 162, 165, 167, 172; *The Valley Below* 153; *Winter-Telling Stories* 160–62
Marriott, Richard Goulding 147
Marriott, Sydney Cunningham 147
Martin du Gard, Roger 24
Martínez, José 89, 90, 195n43
Martínez, Julián 151, 163, 164, 166, 167, 168
Martínez, María 131, 146, 151, 154, 163–68, **164**, 186n21
masks 111–12, **113**
Mason, Charles 15
Mathews, Arthur 95
Matisse, Henri 95, 147
matriarchal or matrilineal organization 25, 61, 167
Matthews, Washington 17, 103, 106, 186n20, 191n58
Mauldin, Michael 203n55, 203n61
Maupassant, Guy de 68
Mayas 116
McCaleb, Walter F. 186n31
McClung, Isabelle 67, 192n2
McClure, Samuel 67
McClure's Magazine 69, 71
McElhaney, Ioleta Hunt 157
medicine bundles 157, 162
Medicine Men 27, 103, 105, 106, 112, 114, 116, 117, 162, 197–98n29; *see also* dances; sandpaintings
medicine woman 53
Menuhin, Yehudi 67

Meredith, George 140, 203*n*51
Merriam, C. Hart 15
Merry del Val, Cardinal Rafael 43
Merton, Thomas 129
Mesa Encantada *see* Enchanted Mesa
Mesa Verde, CO 15, 65, 72, 79, 82, 115, 185*n*17, 192*n*1, 194*n*22, 194–95*n*27, 195*n*32
Mesoamericans 108
mestizos 15, 50
Methodist Church 36, 38
Mexican-American War 15, 87
Mexicans 71, 72, 90, 114, 115
Mexico 9, 15, 49, 108, 115, 116, 151, 171
Miller, Stephen 65
Millet, Jean-François 76
Mimbres pottery 140
miners 43, 47, 49, 52, 100
miscegenation 50
Modernism 30, 34, 70, 133–34, 184*n*8, 189*n*10, 193*n*11
Modoc Indians 171
Moers, Ellen 35
Mojave Desert 9, 97, 107
Momaday, N. Scott 185*n*14
Monroe, Harriett 126, 201*n*16
Montaigne, Michel de 185*n*11
Montana 168
Montezuma 100
Montoya, Atilano **142**, 180, 203*n*55
Montoya, Fray Baltazar 87
Mooney, James 17, 157–58, 171, 205*n*22
Mora, Joseph J. 100
Mora, NM 89
Mora County 123
Mora River 123
morada 136, 202*n*39
moral vision 11, 14, 31, 93–94, 115
Morgan, Barbara 8, 12
Morrison, Toni 3
Mountain Chant 105, 112, 114
The Mountain Chant 9, 106, 198*n*34
Muir, John 13, 26, 37, 118, 188*n*4, 191*n*47
mules 87, 168
murder 88, 89, 195*n*43
Museum of Indian Arts and Culture 204*n*8
Museum of Modern Art, New York 146
Museum of Natural History, New York 55, 106
Museum of Navajo Ceremonial Art 196–97*n*11
Museum of New Mexico 150, 204*n*8
Muskogee, OK 148
mysticism 12–13, 37, 38, 39–40; definition 13; *see also* individual author's names; spirituality
myth and mythology 7, 12, 37, 47, 48, 55, 102, 103, 107, 108, 114, 115, 117, 125, 129, 138, 141, 155–57, 160–63, 181

Na Nai (The Crawler) 27, 106, 112–15
Na Tsai *see* Hubbell, John Lorenzo
Naef, Weston J. 60
Nambé Pueblo 135, 153
Nape, Noreen Groover 56
narrative as desire 184*n*8, 194*n*23
narrative ethnology 146
narrative technique 40, 43, 51–53, 59, 62, 79–81, 86, 114, 141–42, 155, 157–58, 163–65
narratological analysis 80–81
Native Americans *see* Indians; individual tribe names
Native arts and crafts 17, 27–28, **104**, **113**, 117, 150–51; *see also* basketry; jewelry; masks; Native music; Native poetry; pottery; sand-paintings; silversmithing; weaving and textiles
Native lore *see* cosmology; mythology
Native music 99, 188–89*n*5
Native poetry 34, 56–57, 188–89*n*5
Naturalism (literary) 29, 46, 50, 68
Naturalism in photography *see* pictorialism
nature 12, 24, 35, 37, 189*n*8 passim
Navajo National Monument *see* Betatakin; Kiet Seel
Navajos 11, 12, 25, 26, 27, 30, 89, 90, 92, 98, 99–100, 103–18, **118**, 119,142, 177, 180
Nebraska 66, 67, 70, 75, 77, 168
Nelson, Barney 33
Nelson, Rodney 131
Neruda, Pablo 129
Nevada 9, 168
New and Selected Poems 139–40
New England 12, 18, 69, 131, 136, 152; *see also* Connecticut; East Coast cultural dominance; Vermont
New Haven, CT *see* Connecticut
New Mexico 1, 2, 7, 9, 16, 26, 32, 50, 57, 62, 63, 72, 73, 79, 84, 88, 89, 120–45 passim, 147, 149, 151, 174; *see also* individual place names
New Mexico Governor's Award for Excellence in the Arts 132, 152
New Oraibi, AZ *see* Oraibi, AZ
"New Southwest" 10, 184*n*6
New Spain 14–15
New York, NY 43, 44, 59, 63, 65, 73, 91, 103, 131, 152
New York *Herald Tribune* 165
New York literary establishment *see* East Coast cultural dominance
New York *Times* 53, 62, 108, 141, 146
New York Times Book Review 121
New York *World* 18, 85
New Yorker 147, 170
Newcomb, Frances (F.J.) 197–98*n*29
nezhoni see beauty; "Finished in beauty"

Niagara Falls 12
Nietzsche, Friedrich 37
Night Chant 103, 105, 112, 197n26; see also Medicine Men
noble savage 185n11
Nordenskiöld, Gustaf E.A. 16
Norris, Frank 54
Norris, Nell 44, 190n34, 204n3
North Dakota 168
Northeast (U.S.) see East Coast cultural dominance
novel 29–30; see also narrative technique; thesis novel
Noyes, Stanley 120
Nusbaum, Deric 195n32

Occidental traditions 185n12
oil 54–55
O'Keeffe, Georgia 23, 60, 95, 132, 153, 154, 194n23
Oklahoma 2, 7, 9,146–49, 171, 174; see also individual place names
Oklahoma City 147, 149, 155
Oklahoma City University 148
Old Age River 119, 199n56
Oñate, Juan de 14, 58, 203n60
One-Smoke Stories 62–63
Oppenheimer, J. Robert 131, 141
Oraibi, AZ 89, 100, 102, 103, 105, 112, 186n18, 196n47
Oregon 99, 148, 171
Orozco, José Clemente 95
Osages 149–50, 162, 204n6
Otero-Warren, Nina 16, 150
"The Other" 11, 177
Otowi, NM 142
Out West 43
Overland Monthly 42, 95, 97
Owens Valley, CA 33, 42, 45, 50, 57

pacifism 13, 132
paganism 86, 90
Paglia, Camille 24
Painted Desert 72, 99
Paiutes 8, 37, 38, 47, 48, 61, 177, 186n18, 188–89n5
Pajarito Canyon and Plateau, NM 89, 123, 127, 131, 143, 146, 147, 151, 166, 200n7
Palmquist, Peter 109
Pampa, TX 168
Pancake Stories 145
pantheism 13, 47, 50, 134
Papagos 58
Paris 152
Parker, Quanah 160
Pasadena, CA 98
pastoralism 13; see also sheep; sheepherding
The Path on the Rainbow 34, 56, 188–89n5

pathetic fallacy 12
patriarchy 4, 24, 35
Paulus, Stephen 145
Pawnee Indians 162
peach trees 115, 135, 179
Pearce, T.M. 53, 135
Pecos River 112, 115
pedagogy 29, 47, 56 60
Pelicanos 112, 114, 115
Penitentes 136, 155, 202–3n39
petroglyphs 7, 20, 46, 143
peyote religion 160
photography 12, 26, 60, 185n11, 196n8, 196–97n11, 197n24, 197n25, 197–98n29
pictograph see petroglyph
pictorialism 95, 196n8
Pike, Zebulon 58
Pittsburgh, PA 65, 67, 68
Pittsburgh Press 67–68
Pizer, Donald 185n13
Plains Indian Mythology 162–63
Plains Indians 61, 146, 159, 162, 163; see also individual tribe names
Platonism 13, 116
Platte River 75
Plumed Serpent 108, 116, 143
Poetry (magazine) 18, 126, 130, 188–89n5, 202n25
Poets' Roundups 10, 130, 202n25
Pojoaque Pueblo 135
polygamy 159, 160, 205n27
Pond, Ashley, Jr. 123–24, 128
Pond, Ashley, III 124, 132
Pond, Hazel Hallett 123
Pond, Margaret Hallett see Peggy Pond Church
Poolaw, George 158
Porter, Katherine Anne 4
Posada, Alonso de 15, 34
pottery 8, 19, 27, 78, 97, 143, 150, 163, 164, 167; see also Mimbres pottery
Pound, Ezra 133
Powder River 170
Powell, John Wesley 15
Powell, Lawrence 57, 120, 130, 140
prayer 40, 43, 93
pre-Columbians 7, 15, 28, 55–56, 57–58, 60, 71, 72, 78, 82, 85, 111, 143, 194–95n27; see also Anasazi; ruins
primitive (term) 11
primitivism see romanticism
Princeton University 70
prizes and awards 69, 92, 95, 105, 109, 121, 126, 144, 146
The Professor's House 18, 71, 72, 78–85, 194n16
prolepse 59, 80
Protestantism 13, 37; see also names of denominations

Proust, Marcel 94
Pryce, Marjorie 19
Pueblo Indians 11, 25, 58, 61, 62, 89, 90, 122, 146, 171, 177; *see also* individual pueblo names
Pueblo Revolt 15
Pulitzer Prize 69
Puvis de Chavannes, Pierre 87
Puyé Canyon and ruins 151, 166

Quail 46
Questa, NM 89
Quetzalcoatl *see* Plumed Serpent
quilt 94, 117

race 19, 149, 204n6
Rachlin, Carol 29, 148, 154
racial memory *see* ancestral memory
rain 26, 53, 55, 116, 137, 143, 199n48; *see also* water
Raine, Kathleen 129
Ranchos de Taos, NM 89, 132
Ranchos de Taos Church 60
Ransom, John Crowe 21, 202n36
reader-reception theory 4, 31
Red Cloud, NE 66, 69, 77
Red Cross *see* American Red Cross
Red-Eagle 53
Red Earth 120
Redondo Peak, NM 135
Redwood National Park 99
regionalism 17–19, 202n36
religion 12; *see also* Christianity; cosmology; mysticism; spirituality
Rilke, Rainer Maria 129
Rio Grande Pueblos *see* Pueblo Indians
Rio Grande River 9, 57, 73, 142, 151
Rio Grande Valley 25
The Ripened Fields 134, 140–41; 179
Rivera, Diego 95
Rockefeller Foundation 151
Rodin, Auguste 22
Roethke, Theodore 120
Roman Catholicism 16, 37–38, 88, 166
romance (genre) 87
romanticism 10, 12, 34, 37, 49–50, 71, 101
Romanticism (European) 11, 29, 49–50
Rome 43
Romero, José de la Cruz de 155
Roosevelt, Theodore 26, 118, 123, 195n32
Rossetti, Dante Gabriel 68
Roswell, NM 123
Rousseau, Jean-Jacques 33
Route 66 41
rugs *see* weaving and textiles
ruins 12, 20, 77, 143, 179; *see also* Anasazi; Chaco Canyon; Mesa Verde; pre-Columbians; Puyé Canyon
Ruskin, John 39, 68

Said, Edward 177
Saint Catherine's Indian School 165, 205n35
Saint John's College 132
Saint Louis, MO 123
Saint Nicolas (magazine) 126
Saint Vrain, Céran 195n43
Sale, Kirkpatrick 22, 26
San Antonio, TX 88
San Francisco, CA 41, 42, 54, 94, 95, 103
San Francisco Cathedral, Santa Fe 85–86, 88, 89
San Francisco earthquake 38
San Francisco Golden Gate Exposition (Indian Exhibition) 146, 171, 197–98n29
San Francisco Mountain *see* Humphreys Peak
San Francisco Mountains, AZ 77, 194n22
San Ildefonso Pueblo 142, 149, 151, 165–66, 167, 180
San Joaquin Valley, CA 41, 50
San Juan River 199n56
San Miguel Church, Santa Fe 88, 89
San Xavier del Bac Church, AZ 89
Sand, George 1, 68
Sand-Painting of the Navaho Indians 197–98n29
sand-paintings 11, 27, 102, 103–5, **104**, 106, 117, 181, 197–98n29
Sandburg, Carl 189n10
Sandhills 77, 206n42
sandstorm 51, 52, 63
Sangre de Cristo Mountains, NM 62, 123, 187n39
Santa Clara Pueblo 151
Santa Cruz Pueblo 73
Santa Fe, NM 9–10, 15, 44, 45, 63, 71, 73, 89, 124, 129, 130, 132, 133, 151,153, 154, 167, 203n54
Santa Fe Opera 145
Santa Fe railroad 41, 71, 123, 192n1, 202n25
Santistevan, Corina A. 127, 129, 132, 201n18
Santo Domingo Pueblo, NM 89, 135, 151
santos 44, 73, 127, 148
Sapphira and the Slave Girl 70, 81
Sarton, May 24, 121, 129, 140, 201n24
Sartre, Jean-Paul 55
Saturday Review of Literature 34, 57, 62, 130, 137
Schoolcraft, Henry Rowe 17, 148
Schoonover, Margaret *see* Lefranc, Margaret
Scott, Walter, Sir 50
The Secret of the Golden Flower 201n22
Sergeant, Elizabeth Shipley 34, 67, 69, 137, 189n13, 192n72, 193n6
Seton, Ernest Thompson 26, 118
Seven Cities of Cíbola 14
sexual essentialism 3, 20
sexual identity *see* gender

sexuality 19, 125, 194n23; *see also* lesbianism
Shakespeare, William 20
Shaw, George Bernard 43
sheep 24, 49, 60, 66, 191n42, 192n67
sheepherding 33, 49, 50–51, 135
shells 19–20, 110, 117, 199n4
Shiprock, NM 132
Shockley, Martin 146
Shoes for the Santo Niño 145
Shonto Plateau, AZ 198n33
Shoshones 42, 46, 47, **48**, 186n18
Silko, Leslie Marmon 177
silversmithing 150, 205n40; *see also* jewelry
Simms, William Gilmore 17
Sinclair, Upton 54
sky 26, 62, 73, 75, 77, 119, 139, 143, 161, 194n17 passim
Slavitt, David R. 14
Sloan, Lenore 151, 168, 204n10
Smith College 126
Smithsonian Institution 72, 82, 84, 158, 197–98n29
Snake Dance *see* dances
Snyder, Sharon 125, 128, 145, 200n3
sociobiology 166, 205n38
Socorro, NM 57
The Song of the Lark 71, 72, 76–78, 79, 84, 85, 101, 143, 194n22
Sonoran Desert 108
sounds 180
South Dakota 170
Southwest (term) 9, 43
Southwest 106, 107, 115–16
Southwest Review 147
Spain 132
Spanish Americans *see* Hispanics
Spanish Colonial Arts Society 44
Spinden, Herbert 56
spirituality 12–13, 37; *see also* mysticism
Stafford, William 120
stag 50, 191n45
Stanford University 128
Starry Adventure 62
Steffens, Lincoln 43, 44
Stegner, Wallace 7, 18, 200n7
stereotypes 16, 186n18
Stevens, Wallace 133
Stevenson, James 17, 103
Stevenson, Matilda Coxe 17
Stevenson, Robert Louis 126, 194n18
Stineman, Esther Lanigan 56–57
Stone Age 56
stone imagery 27, 139, 187n41
Stout, Janis P. 21, 22, 23, 35, 67, 184n3, 194n16
Stovall Museum 154
Sunset 97
sustainability *see* environmentalism

swastika 199n53
Sweet Briar College 170
Swift, Jonathan 14–15
Swinburne, Algernon 133
Swinnerton, James 95

taboos 199n54
Tahiti 95
Taos, NM (town and pueblo) 9, 44, 60–61, **61**, 73, 87, 88, 89, 132, 137, 152, 176
Taos Pueblo 60–61
Taos rebellion 88
taste (sense) 181
Taylor, Cynthia 45
Tejon Ranch 41, 42
The Ten Grandmothers 30, 146, 155–60, 162, 165, 167, 172
Tennyson, Alfred Lord 121, 133
tepees 167
Terrero, NM 131
Tesuque Pueblo 89
Tewa pueblos 185n16; *see also* San Ildefonso Pueblo; Taos Pueblo
Texas 9, 50, 63, 88, 151, 172
textiles *see* weaving and textiles
textual immanence 4
textures 180
Theatre Arts Monthly 34
thesis novel 54
Third Mesa 100
This Dancing Ground of Sky 129, 200n2
Thoreau, Henry David 10, 37, 191n49
Tilano *see* Montoya, Atilano
Tiresias 204n16
Tiwa pueblos 14, 185n16
tourism and tourists 51, 141
The Trader's Children 101, 114, 116–18
The Trail Book 8, 55–56
trees, plants, flowers 27, 46, 47, 49, 58, 97, 125, 136, 138, 145 passim; *see also* apricot trees; peach trees
Triumphalism 21, 22
Truchas Mountains, NM 89, 178
Tsiegi Canyon, AZ 112, 115, 198n33
Tucson, AZ 89, 97, 128
Turner, Frederick Jackson 21, 176, 177
turquoise 99–100, 110, 116
Turquoise Mountains 99
The Turquoise Trail 191n59
Twain, Mark 19, 43

Ultimatum for Man 137
Underhill, Ruth 165
UNESCO World Heritage Site 16
University of Central Oklahoma 147
University of Nebraska 68
University of Oklahoma 148, 151, 54
Utah 9
Utes 63, 114

Valéry, Paul 193*n*8
Valles Caldera National Preserve 127
The Valley Below 153
Valmora, NM 123
Vermilion Cliffs, AZ 102
Vermont 125, 126, 136
Veronica, Mother 43
Vibert, Jehan Georges 86
Villagrá, Gaspar Pérez de 14
Virgin Mary 25
Virgin River 59
Virginia 66, 70, 88
vision 14, 22, 45 passim; *see also* feminine vision; moral vision; mysticism
Voltaire 185*n*11

Walnut Canyon 72, 77, 82
Walters, Andrea Fellows 145
Ward, Elizabeth 169
Warner, Edith 26, 29, 30, 121, 122, 131, 141–43, 187*n*39, 200*n*7
Warren, Robert Penn 18
Washington, D.C. 82, 85
water 10, 15, 33, 41, 42, 46, 55, 58, 88, 110, 116, 124, 153
water rights 54, 55
water wars 180
Waterless Mountain 3, 93, 101, 108–12, 119
Waterless Mountain, AZ 109–10, 116, 199*n*42
Watrous, NM 123
weaving and textiles 27–28, 36, 97, 104–5, 150, 168, 197–98*n*29
Wells, H.G. 43
Welty, Eudora 18, 54, 66, 129
Wetherill, Clayton 72, 185*n*17
Wetherill, John 106, 198*n*33
Wetherill, Louisa 106
Wetherill, Richard 15, 72, 82, 185*n*17, 195*n*32
Wharton, Edith 114
Wheelwright, Mary 147, 197–98*n*29, 204*n*15
Wheelwright Museum 147, 196*n*8, 196*n*11, 197–98*n*29, 198*n*34
Whirling Logs 112, *113*, 197–98*n*29
White, Hayden 3, 20
White House Cliff Dwellings *see* Canyon de Chelly

Whitehorse, Roland 161
Whitman, Walt 133, 189*n*10
Whitney Museum of American Art 109
wikiup 43
Wilder, Laura Ingalls 109
Williams, William Carlos 17, 133, 136
Wilmette, IL 147
Wilson, Edward O. 205*n*38
Wilson, Lanford 121
Wind's Trail 143
Winnemucca, Sarah 176; *Life Among the Paiutes* 206*n*3
Winslow, AZ 71, 72, 112
Winter-Telling Stories 160–62
Winters, Yvor 120
Wittick, Ben 197*n*25, 198*n*33
Wittig, Monique 185*n*12
women and authorship 20–21
women and earth *see* Earth Mother
Women's Christian Temperance Union 39
women's nature 24, 25–26
women's situation 1, 3–4, 20–21, 23–25, 28, 35–36, 53, 59, 124–25, 127–28, 130, 136, 166–67, 168–69
Woodress, James 67
Woolf, Viginia 127
Woolson, Constance Fenimore 23
Wordsworth, William 37
World War I 63, 69, 79, 131, 132, 142
World War II 151, 160, 165
World's Fair 147
Writers' Editions 130, 202*n*25
Wyatt-Brown, Bert 66
Wyoming 170, 194*n*22

Yale School of Drama 34
Yale University 70, 123, 201*n*8
Yeats, William Butler 43
Yeibichai *see* dances; sand-paintings; Whirling Logs
Yosemite National Park 12, 34, 50–51
Young, R.V. 2

Zuni pueblo and Zunis 14, 15, 27, 58, 60, 62, 73, 89, 90

www.ingramcontent.com/pod-product-compliance
Lightning Source LLC
Chambersburg PA
CBHW032051300426
44116CB00007B/691